RULING COMMUNIST
PARTIES
AND DÉTENTE

RULING COMMUNIST PARTIES AND DÉTENTE

A Documentary History

Jeffrey Simon

American Enterprise Institute for Public Policy Research
Washington, D. C.

Jeffrey Simon is assistant professor of government at Georgetown University.

ISBN 0-8447-3181-1 (paper)
ISBN 0-8447-3182-X (cloth)

Foreign Affairs Study No. 25, September 1975

Library of Congress Catalog Card No. 75-21854

Printed in the United States of America

Names are much more persistent than the functions upon which they were originally bestowed . . . institutions constantly undergo essential alterations of character, whilst retaining the names conferred upon them in their first estate.

Woodrow Wilson
Congressional Government, 1885

. . . a continuous misinterpretation of basic concepts is visible and extremely dangerous within the fast-moving social and political sciences which are especially affected by the time lag between ideological perception and historical reality. A heritage of a quarter of a century's standing is often used. In a time of transition such a situation may be deadly.

Sigmund Neumann
Permanent Revolution, 1942

CONTENTS

3 GROUP TWO   186

PREFACE

This book is meant for two kinds of readers, college students who will read it in conjunction with their work in the general field of comparative politics or the relatively new field of comparative communism, and general readers who are concerned about the course of the American policy of détente with the leading powers of the Communist world.

In comparison to things as they were during the cold war period, recent events on the international stage seem to be at times confusing, if not contradictory. This book presents, in documentary form, the responses of the ruling Communist parties (CPs) to the changing international climate so that the reader can compare the world views of the ruling CPs with those of the West, determine whether détente has the same meaning for the ruling CPs as it does for the United States, and evaluate the future prospects for détente.

My approach to the study of comparative Communist foreign policy focuses on a special practice among the ruling CPs. In Communist countries, top political leaders make periodic reports to the highest party and state bodies. In the case of the party, the report is generally presented to the party congress on behalf of the central committee (CC). It usually reviews developments since the previous report, assesses the current situation, and identifies new problems and policies. Usually the report is presented in two parts, with a discussion of the international situation followed by plans for internal development.

The documents in this book, in the main, are taken from the most recent key reports of the top party leaders of thirteen of the fourteen ruling Communist parties, the exception being North Vietnam. (It is still too early to make an accurate evaluation of the likely foreign policy positions of the new ruling Communist parties in Southeast Asia.) The documents are grouped according to the substantive world views and/or sets of procedures for coordinating group policy of the ruling CPs. There are three such groups, and I have included a chronological series of documents for the leading CP of each of them. For the Soviet Union, which dominates in what I have labeled Group I, I have included documents from 1966 to 1973; for Yugoslavia, the leader of Group II, I have included documents from 1964 to 1974; and for the People's Republic of China, pre-eminent in Group III, there are documents from the period 1969–1973. For reasons which will become clear at a later point, I have also included multiple documents for Romania in Group II. Cuba has not developed any clear commitment to the policies of any one group, but for the sake of convenience, the sole Cuban document included here appears with the Group III papers. Only the foreign policy sections of the reports are presented here.

Reports to party congresses are highly authoritative statements of party position. Very often, the party leader himself has a hand in authoring these reports, and they may be compared with the inaugural address or state of the union message of an American President. Generally, a report is approved or its main points are incorporated in a resolution adopted by the party congress to which it is delivered. The report is not intended for the general public, although many of its pronouncements subsequently become the basis of material for mass consumption. The main purpose of the report is to inform middle-level leaders about the position of the nation in the world. It is also often used as a device for communicating with foreign leaders through open channels.

The chief advantages in approaching the study of ruling-CP policy through these reports are that (1) the reports are authoritative, (2) they demonstrate the entire range of differing views found among the ruling CPs, and (3) they are readily adaptable to comparative analysis. Nevertheless, there are some disadvantages, and a few caveats are in order. First, although these reports are authoritative, they are not necessarily comprehensive. They do not discuss all of the international problems faced by the respective party leaderships, and for a more complete picture, it is often necessary to resort to supplementary sources. Second, as political statements, the contents of these reports cannot always be accepted at face value. Often the true implication of the evolving policy statements must be searched out behind an outer shell of party rhetoric.

A further word of caution is necessary regarding the unevenness in the quality of the translations of the various reports. Many language groups are represented among the fourteen ruling CPs. While the Slavic predominates, there are also Romance (Romania and Cuba), Teutonic (East Germany), and Finno-Ugric (Hungary and Mongolia) languages, as well as the Asiatic tongues of Chinese, Korean, and Vietnamese. The ability to translate, let alone to develop a sensitivity to nuance in these various languages, is far beyond the capacity of any one scholar. In light of this, wherever possible, translations in this collection have been taken from official CP sources, though these vary considerably in quality. The Soviet Union, Yugoslavia, Romania, and China generally provide translations of reliable quality. On the other hand, official translations produced by such states as Albania, Mongolia, North Korea, and Hungary are of extremely poor quality or are not made available at all.

In cases where it was not possible to acquire translations from official CP sources, I have used the *Foreign Broadcast Information Service Supplements*. These are generally translations from original sources, but they also vary in quality. Thus to a degree, which differs from document to document, much subtlety of nuance has been lost in the translations, which often read with a certain misleading awkwardness. This is an unavoidable drawback in a cross-polity analysis of such wide breadth.

Although my guiding purpose has been to leave intact the stylistic and substantive identity of each piece, some editorial modifications have been necessary. Many of the redundant and superfluous passages which frequently overburden many of the documents have been excised. In addition, obvious errors of diction and usage have been corrected, and spelling and punctuation have been regularized. (All italics in the documentary texts are from the original.) In part because of these adjustments, and primarily because of the widely varying quality of the available translations, perfect comparison of the documents cannot be achieved.

I have written an introductory essay which hopefully will assist the reader in probing the documentary texts. The first part of this essay is an attempt to put the policy of détente into a global and historical perspective, while the second half is an examination of the recent history of the Communist parties and their response to détente through a survey of the documents which appear in Part II of this volume. In light of the European Security Conference which is being held in Helsinki as this book goes to press, this examination appears even more relevant to the future course of U.S. policy and to academic discourse.

July 1975   Jeffrey Simon
                                                              Washington, D. C.

PART ONE
THE DOCUMENTS IN CONTEXT

1
ANALYSIS OF SELECTED DOCUMENTS OF RULING COMMUNIST PARTIES

Bipolarity in Decline

World Order and Paradigmatic Shifts. The 1970s have seen presidential visits to Peking and Moscow and the entrance of the People's Republic of China (P.R.C.) to the United Nations. Negotiations have opened between such formerly bitter international enemies as Japan and the P.R.C., and West Germany and the ruling Communist parties of Eastern Europe. Such developments would seem to confirm that détente is a real force in the world. However, over the same period, the United States has gone on military alert in response to Soviet activities in the Middle East and has mined Haiphong harbor in order to block military assistance to North Vietnam. There does not seem to be a pattern behind such events, and formulation of a coherent world view has become exceedingly difficult. To many the world has become ambiguous, if not incomprehensible.

One explanation of these contradictory phenomena, and the premise of this essay, is that we are witnessing today a fundamental shift in the nature of world order. This is the source of the uncertainty we experience as we try to organize and come to terms with recent world events. For one of the first effects of this kind of shift is to call into question that knowledge about the world which we have acquired through practice, but which we have never articulated or questioned explicitly. This may be described as tacit knowledge consisting of paradigms—the sets of shared assumptions and patterns through which we as a community perceive the world.[1]

---

[1] Michael Polanyi has brilliantly developed this notion of "tacit knowledge." See Michael Polanyi, *Personal Knowledge* (Chicago: University of Chicago Press, 1958), particularly Chapters 5 and 6.

Thomas Kuhn has applied the paradigm concept to the sciences and written about the problems which result from the transformation of those paradigms which have had an impact on man's view of the natural world, and indirectly, on his own self-perception and sense of identity.[2] For example, when the concept of an infinite universe replaced the earth-centered view of natural order, or when science moved from the security of a mechanics-oriented physics to the uncertainty of relativistic physics, man's sense of order was transformed and his sense of identity challenged. Technological developments allied with science have produced a similar kind of change. For example, the telescope and the electron microscope, which have widened our perceptual horizons by many orders of magnitude, as well as the development of weapons employing the primal energy of the atom, have also affected man's sense of order and self.[3]

In the field of international relations, a paradigm is an approximation of reality which becomes a device for approaching world order in the formulation of policy.[4] In the history of world politics, paradigmatic shifts have consistently followed in the wake of great wars. The Treaty of Westphalia, which in 1648 concluded the Thirty Years' War, signified a normative change in the nature of European state relationships, as religion ceased to be a basis for war in Europe. Similarly the Treaty of Utrecht, concluding in 1713 the War of Spanish Succession, legitimized the principle of dynastic succession as the basis for authority in European politics. In turn, the French Revolution challenged this norm, as the French deposed and executed Louis XVI and established a republic. Napoleon's campaign to conquer all of Europe extended this challenge, but the principle of dynastic succession was reestablished, at least temporarily, by his defeat and the subsequent formulation of the Treaty of Vienna in 1815.

Before 1900, world order transformations occurred no more than once in a century. The twentieth century, however, has already witnessed two complete transformations. The first of these followed

---

[2] Thomas Kuhn, *The Structure of Scientific Revolutions* (Chicago: University of Chicago Press, 1962).

[3] Karl Jaspers, *The Future of Mankind* (Chicago: University of Chicago Press, 1961). Also see Hannah Arendt, *The Human Condition* (Chicago: University of Chicago Press, 1958).

[4] I am indebted to Robert J. Pranger for his idea of applying paradigms to international politics and his introduction of the notion of indeterminacy in political action. For a more detailed view see Robert J. Pranger, *Defense Implications of International Indeterminacy* (Washington, D. C.: American Enterprise Institute, 1972).

4

in the wake of World War I. Here the new guiding principle for European statecraft became the concept of national self-determination, which stipulated that every European nation or nationality was entitled to expression of its collective identity through statehood. This was expounded by Woodrow Wilson in his Fourteen Points, and in 1918 was established as a basis for world order by the Treaty of Versailles. The application of Woodrow Wilson's principles led to the creation of such new states as Czechoslovakia, Poland, and Yugoslavia.[5]

The norms which guided state action in recent decades have their roots in the World War I period; the basic difference of the post-World War II period is that, while the nation-state norm had first been intended for application only within the geographical confines of Europe, since 1945 this norm has been applied worldwide. The United Nations Charter has enshrined national self-determination as a universal principle for state action. To this extent, the post-World War II era witnessed the creation of a new world order for the second time in this century.[6]

Although World War I was responsible for promoting the identification of nationality with statehood as a principle for world order, it also marked the appearance of what can best be described as a "counter-norm." The revolutionaries who established the Soviet Union and posited social class as the eventual basis for world order rejected the norm of nation and state. In parallel fashion, when the originally Euro-centric principle of national self-determination was expanded and applied worldwide at the end of World War II, the counter-norm also gained broader adherence, as a group of states that shared the Communist framework of the Russians emerged. This worldwide proliferation of opposing norms led to the over-arching paradigm of bipolarity that characterized the cold war era.

---

[5] Wilson also had impact on Lenin's thought. See Louis Fischer, *The Life of Lenin* (New York: Harper and Row, 1964), pp. 159-180.

[6] A paradigmatic shift of this kind will entail a corresponding shift in values throughout the affected culture. There is a great difference between the values which legitimized imperialism as an official governmental policy in the nineteenth century British empire as expressed in the literature of Rudyard Kipling and others, and the values of writers like Jean-Paul Sartre and Maurice Merleau-Ponty, who in the twentieth century were arguing against their own state's presence in "alien" territory (that is, Indo-China and Algeria), using the values of "national self-determination" of the first and second world-order reorganization as a normative guide for state action. For an excellent study which illustrates how norms shift in relationship to transformations in world order, see Morton A. Kaplan and Nicholas deB. Katzenbach, *The Political Foundations of International Law* (New York: John Wiley & Sons, 1961).

For the West, Winston Churchill's "Iron Curtain" speech [7] marked the origins of this sensibility. As American opinion, both public and official, became alerted to the bipolar nature of the new post-World War II world, it was necessary to develop an adequate American response. As a result, the United States emerged into this bipolar era with a new sense of world responsibility.

This began to show its effect on policy in March 1947, when President Harry S. Truman asked for $400 million to send military, economic, and technical aid to Turkey and Greece. He took this action explicitly to fill the vacuum created by the withdrawal of British support, and implicitly to prevent these countries from falling under Communist rule. His explanation for these actions became known as the Truman Doctrine.

This pattern of support was expanded in size and scope with the Marshall Plan, announced in June 1947, which set the course for a massive transfer of U.S. resources abroad and the general reconstruction of Europe. As a result, in the late 1940s and early 1950s the United States became a towering force on the European continent and exercised an impressive degree of influence on European events and decisions. In reviewing the American contribution towards European recovery, one analyst has written, "It is important to note . . . that while the actions taken by the United States were in accord with what it conceived to be its own long-range historical interests, it defined these interests in such farsighted terms that they coincided to a great extent with the interests of the European nations." [8] In other words, in the case of European recovery there was a symmetrical relationship between the American national interest and the various European national interests. [9] Not until the decade of the 1960s would strains between American and European national interests begin to develop.

At his 1949 inauguration Truman addressed the problem of the world's emerging nations, announcing the Point IV Program. He described this as "a bold new program for making the benefits of our

---

[7] Reprinted in Hans J. Morgenthau and Kenneth W. Thompson, eds., *Principles and Problems of International Politics* (New York: Alfred A. Knopf, 1950), pp. 408-417.

[8] Andrew M. Scott, *The Revolution in Statecraft: Informal Penetration* (New York: Random House, 1965), p. 77.

[9] It is the author's view that this could be cited as the primary explanation for the Marshall Plan's early success. There are, of course, those who disagree with this interpretation. See for example Barton J. Bernstein, ed., *Politics and Policies of the Truman Administration* (Chicago: Quadrangle Books, 1970), especially pp. 78-114.

scientific advances and industrial progress available for the improvement and growth of underdeveloped areas." [10] Like the Marshall Plan, the program utilized technical assistance as an instrument for aiding developing nations. The policy was symbolic of the process whereby Americans, both official and public, began to perceive American national security not only in European terms, but in worldwide terms.

Thus Churchill's Iron Curtain address and a further elaboration of the bipolar world view by George F. Kennan provided the paradigmatic basis for a new sense of world order which gained expression through the policies of Harry Truman. We have been living not only with the rhetoric, but also with a reality shaped by policies exercised under this paradigm for the past thirty years.

The first official American intimation of a new paradigm was the formulation of the Nixon Doctrine during 1969 and early 1970. President Nixon felt that his doctrine reflected certain new realities, perceived generally as follows: although America must maintain a major role in world affairs, other nations ought to assume greater responsibilities. The President also noted that emerging polycentrism in the Communist world presents new challenges and opportunities, and he claimed that new approaches were required to replace the strategy based on massive retaliation with one of realistic deterrence.[11]

Any fundamental shift of this kind is difficult for the individuals who must experience it, for it forces them to question their own sense of identity.[12] Because the present transformation is ambiguous, reflecting only tentative responses to gradual shifts in world order, it will be harder to come to terms with than those of the past, which followed the drastic and unmistakable trauma of great wars.

The essential concepts stressed by the Nixon Doctrine, negotiation, partnership, and strength, added up to a distinct shift in the official confrontation rhetoric common to the period of the previous paradigm (1945–1969). However, unlike the Truman Doctrine, the Nixon approach did not present a clear and distinct guide for future

---

[10] Harry S. Truman, *Years of Trial and Hope, 1946-1952* (New York: Doubleday & Co., 1956), p. 230.

[11] Richard M. Nixon, *U.S. Foreign Policy for the 1970s* (Washington, D. C.: U.S. Government Printing Office, February 1971), p. 11.

[12] Harold Lasswell, *World Politics and Personal Insecurity* (New York: The Free Press, 1965), especially Chapters 1 and 10. Also see Karen Horney, *Neurosis and Human Growth* (New York: Norton, 1959), *passim.*

policy.[13] While it did mark a move away from the previous paradigm, it did not conceptually organize contemporary world reality into a fully formed new paradigm.[14]

Another unique characteristic of the present situation is that, because of the comparatively gradual nature of the current shift in the world order, it is not likely that either of the two camps that emerged after World War II will either prevail or capitulate totally. There will be no political vacuum of the kind created by the collapse or withdrawal of defeated powers during a major war. Whatever synthesis arises will have to reflect in part that which is permanent and essential to each of the two camps. Therefore, détente can only proceed from the formulation of a new paradigm that will allow this synthesis to take place.

A paradigm has two components, objective facts and subjective assumptions. There is an interaction or a dynamic relationship between these two components, for a nation's assumptions actually shape reality itself. This is especially so for the great powers. Obviously, however, the extent to which these assumptions can change reality is limited, for some things are fixed and immutable. The problem for the policy maker is to separate the immutable from the mutable in formulating his options. Therefore the policy maker must make a continual effort to test his assumptions against reality, always improving the accuracy of his paradigm.

In a world characterized by two counter-norms, one way to accomplish this is to seek a better understanding of the opposing perspective. This has been our purpose in collecting the documents presented in this volume. In the past, source materials have not been widely available and early efforts at Communist studies were marred by the inability of many scholars to transcend assumptions underlying the cold war. Therefore there are two reasons for looking briefly at the history of Communist studies. First, this will show how paradigms and their inherent assumptions can affect the conclusions drawn by those who apply them. Second, as background for an examination of the documents, it will illustrate the evolution of American percep-

---

[13] One of the complicating factors, the difficulty a President may face in attempting to transform American public opinion, has already been demonstrated many times during this century. There are the examples of Woodrow Wilson after the Treaty of Versailles, the role of Franklin D. Roosevelt during the decade of the 1930s, and of Harry Truman during the 1945-1947 period. An excellent study in the difficulty of coordinating the "moods" of American public opinion can be found in Gabriel A. Almond, *The American People and Foreign Policy* (New York: Frederick A. Praeger, 1964).

[14] A thorough consideration of this problem can be found in Pranger, *Defense Implications of International Indeterminacy.*

tions of communism, the other component norm of the emerging world order.

The Soviet Union: From the Sole Communist State to a Plural System.

The majority of academic research in the field of Communist studies has been done on the Soviet Union. This has been in part because the U.S.S.R. was the first Communist state, but also because since its beginnings, the U.S.S.R has been a Communist state with "great power" potential, and hence could come to threaten the security of the United States.[15]

Most of the research done in the immediate aftermath of World War I took the form of ideographic studies. Research of this kind begins with the assumption that the object of investigation is unique, *sui generis*. One of the inherent weaknesses of applying this ideographic approach to the U.S.S.R. was the fact that during this period there was only *one* U.S.S.R. and only *one* Communist state, and they were one and the same. Therefore there was bound to be much confusion among theorists as to which aspects of Soviet behavior derived from the Russian culture and which aspects were attributable to the new Communist ideological overlay.

The third-world movements of national liberation (that is, decolonialization) that have emerged with great regularity in the wake of World War II have led to a great deal of research focusing on the common problems faced by these new nations. Much of the academic work over the past two decades that has been helpful in this regard has come from nomothetic research. This approach substitutes the assumption that there are phenomena which are common across polities for the ideographic assumption of uniqueness.[16]

This research has come from several social-science disciplines, especially the fields of economics,[17] sociology,[18] and political science.[19]

---

[15] During the interwar period both the U.S.S.R. and the United States experienced a period of isolation. The success of the Red Army at Stalingrad in February 1943 can be viewed as the approximate date of Soviet accession to great-power status. See Alexander Werth, *Russia at War 1941-45* (New York: E. P. Dutton & Co., 1964), pp. 493-563. Of course, it should be recognized that Imperial Russia had earlier been a great power.

[16] Just as the ideographic sciences are limited by the assumption of the uniqueness of the object of their investigation, the nomothetic sciences are likewise limited by their assumption of common characteristics. This is not to suggest that either one or the other is the correct assumption, but rather, that each approach has an underlying assumption that is bound to influence its findings. Each is useful for different heuristic purposes.

[17] W. W. Rostow, *The Stages of Economic Growth: A Non-Communist Manifesto* (London: Cambridge University Press, 1960), especially pp. 145-167.

[18] Seymour Martin Lipset, *Political Man: The Social Bases of Politics* (New York: Anchor Books, 1963), especially Chapters 1 and 13. Barrington Moore, Jr., *Social*

All this work has assumed commonality between developing nations either in the economic developmental process, the degree of social stratification and/or social mobilization, and in political patterns (which are more often than not, authoritarian in nature).

As to the application of the nomothetic approach to Communist studies, only with the appearance of a plural Communist system following the end of World War II did it become possible for scholars to compare different Communist systems and determine the relative influence of shared Communist assumptions and individual national cultures upon their policies and behavior, to differentiate between the *uniquely* national and the *universally* Communist.[20] However, for several reasons, the nomothetic approach was rarely applied to the field of Communist studies, where ideographic research prevailed through the mid-1960s.[21]

An interaction of the cold war bipolar paradigm with the ideographic approach to Communist studies led to a heavy emphasis on the elements of ideology and terror within the Communist system. This perhaps exaggerated the totalitarian aspects of the system and

---

Origins of Dictatorship and Democracy: Lord and Peasant in the Making of the Modern World (Boston: Beacon Press, 1967), especially pp. 484-508. Alex Inkeles, Social Change in Soviet Russia (Cambridge: Harvard University Press, 1968), especially pp. 381-433.

[19] Gabriel A. Almond and G. Bingham Powell, *Comparative Politics: A Developmental Approach* (Boston: Little, Brown & Co., 1966). David E. Apter, *The Politics of Modernization* (Chicago: University of Chicago Press, 1965). Samuel P. Huntington, *Political Order in Changing Societies* (New Haven: Yale University Press, 1968), especially pp. 265-278. John H. Kautsky, *Communism and the Politics of Development: Persistent Myths and Changing Behavior* (New York: John Wiley & Sons, 1968).

[20] The distinction between nationalist and Communist movements is still often difficult to make when trying to determine the nature of any particular movement. Yet we can make ideal-type generalizations about the differences and similarities between the two kinds of movements. See John H. Kautsky, ed., *Political Change in Underdeveloped Countries: Nationalism and Communism* (New York: John Wiley & Sons, 1962), particularly Kautsky's chapter, "An Essay in the Politics of Development." See also John H. Kautsky, *The Political Consequences of Modernization* (New York: John Wiley & Sons, 1972), pp. 237-251.

[21] Ideographic research generally concluded that the Soviets' intentions were predictably expansionist and followed certain despotic patterns, either based upon some salient characteristic of their Russian culture (see for example, the writings of Nicholas P. Vakar, Dinko Tomasic, Karl Wittfogel and Geoffrey Gorer) or based upon some aspect of Communist ideology (for example, the writings of Nathan Leites, Gerhardt Niemeyer, and Zbigniew K. Brzezinski in *Ideology & Power in Soviet Politics* (New York: Praeger, 1964). The most commonly accepted ideal-type representation of the U.S.S.R. has been totalitarianism. See Carl J. Friedrich and Zbigniew K. Brzezinski, *Totalitarian Dictatorship and Autocracy* (New York: Praeger, 1965). Totalitarianism is an ideographic ideal-type which entails the assumption that the sociopolitical system under consideration is unique.

distorted the American perception of it. When the nomothetic assumption of commonality was finally applied to the U.S.S.R., it led to a perception of the Soviet experience more as a model of *development* than a model of *politics*—the emphasis of the totalitarian approach.

Many third-world leaders who were not directly affected by the cold war, viewed the Soviet experience in this way. In a world increasingly populated by developing nations seeking rapid industrialization and growth, the perception of Soviet experience and the Communist system as models of development may in fact be more prevalent than the American view.

This question of interpretation between politics and development will not be solved here, nor does this writer believe that a solution is near at hand. Historical and data limitations prevent us from making a final judgment. Because the U.S.S.R. has existed only since 1917, and because the Communist system has only been a plural system since 1945, no clear answer has yet emerged.[22]

Nonetheless, as a result of the recent application of nomothetic research to Communist studies, there has arisen a renewed discussion in the United States regarding the problems of interpretation of Communist systems in general, and the Soviet system in particular.[23] For example, one controversial interpretation has been posited by Alfred Meyer, who portrayed the Soviet Union as a large corporation, with the Politburo membership as a board of directors and the Communist party (CPSU) membership as corporate stockholders. This approach perceived Soviet politics as essentially a bureaucratic politics, rather than as a politics of ideology and terror, as emphasized by the totalitarian model.[24]

From these differing perceptions there arose different conclusions regarding the future of the Soviet system. One scenario speculates

---

[22] The historical limitation is cited as a weakness of the developmental approach by Alex Inkeles, "Models and Issues in the Analysis of Soviet Society," *Survey*, July 1966, pp. 3-17. It must also be said that this is one of the major weaknesses of the totalitarian model, which is a static representation that accounts for only a very short period of Soviet experience.

[23] Roger E. Kanet, ed., *The Behavioral Revolution and Communist Studies* (New York: The Free Press, 1971); Frederic J. Fleron, Jr., ed., *Communist Studies and the Social Sciences* (Chicago: Rand McNally & Co., 1971); Chalmers Johnson, ed., *Change in Communist Systems* (Stanford: Stanford University Press, 1970); and Lenard J. Cohen and Jane P. Shapiro, *Communist Systems in Comparative Perspective* (New York: Anchor Books, 1974).

[24] Alfred G. Meyer first incorporated this view in his article "USSR Incorporated," *Slavic Review*, October 1961, pp. 369-376. It was further developed in his book, *The Soviet Political System: An Interpretation* (New York: Random House, 1966).

that the system will become immobile and stagnant, subsequently petrifying or decaying.[25] Another variant explores the possibility of the Soviet system becoming more pluralistic.[26] This is usually posited as the result of large-scale bureaucratic organization which emphasizes the values of rationality and efficiency and requires a delimitation of decision making based upon specialist expertise within the various bureaucracies. Because in the Soviet context it is often institutional interests that articulate demands, the Soviet Union demonstrates a "limited pluralism," in contrast to the associational and nonassociational interest group pluralism common to Western political experience.

Before considering the evolution of American policy towards the Communist world, it must be reemphasized that only since World War II have we been confronted with a plural Communist system. Before the late 1940s, the problem of resolving the culture-ideology enigma was very difficult since there was only one Communist state in the world. Under such circumstances, Soviet intentions and behavior were commonly described in terms of Russian cultural precedents, Communist ideology or great-power geopolitical ambitions. With the emergence of a plural Communist system it has been possible to make distinctions between what is uniquely national and what is universally Communist by examining similarities and differences between Communist political systems.

Concomitant with this change in world order has been a paradigmatic shift exemplified by the application of social-science methods. This renewed discussion of the problems of interpreting Communist systems, particularly that of the Soviet Union, initially focused upon domestic systemic features. It has recently led to a reexamination of foreign policies, and it is to this area that we shall now turn.

Past Policies and Assumptions. Both the scholars and the policy makers of the cold war period saw the Soviet Union as an expansionist totalitarian state. This led to three general approaches for

---

[25] This is one possibility considered by Zbigniew Brzezinski, a previous advocate of the totalitarian ideal-type, in his recent book *Between Two Ages* (New York: The Viking Press, 1971).

[26] The scholars who are associated with this interpretation are Philip Stewart, *Political Power in the Soviet Union* (New York: Bobbs-Merrill, 1968); Jerry Hough, "The Soviet System: Petrification or Pluralism?", *Problems of Communism*, March-April 1972, pp. 25-45; and Gordon Skilling and Franklyn Griffiths, eds., *Interest Groups in Soviet Politics* (Princeton, N. J.: Princeton University Press, 1971).

dealing with the Soviet Union and the Communist world: containment, liberalization, and counterforce strategy. We shall now examine some of the assumptions underlying these general policies.

The concept of containment, frequently associated with George F. Kennan, is one of the most well-known strategies for dealing with the Communist world, and lay at the basis of postwar American policy.[27] The key assumption behind this policy is that the Soviet regime cannot be radically weakened or made more moderate in its policies by any external action short of war. While Kennan did allow that indigenous forces in Soviet society might in time weaken the regime or transform it, he argued that it was necessary for the United States to construct a policy that would resist Soviet aggression while allowing time and internal forces to do their work.[28]

Since its first formulation, the concept of containment has been adapted to deal with the post-Stalin Soviet Union. Contemporary containment theorists, including Kennan himself, argue that we in the United States cannot expect any internal moderation to lessen the Soviet threat.[29] The development of new weapons technologies has increased the capacity of the Soviet Union to endanger the United States, so that if anything, the U.S.S.R. has become more dangerous since Stalin's death. Hence, these advocates urge a U.S. policy that will concentrate on containing a Soviet outward movement which is becoming an increasingly powerful challenge to our world position.

Advocates of containment policy generally argue against direct action that is aimed at either weakening or destroying the U.S.S.R., believing that such a strategy (counterforce strategy) increases the danger of war; at the same time, they are generally against any action that will help to moderate Soviet policy, for fear that this approach (liberalization strategy) would lead to one-sided and often fruitless concessions.

Kennan's original, but secondary, assumption that time would moderate the Soviet regime became the dominant idea behind the strategy of liberalization. Proponents of this view argue that time will lessen the Soviet commitment to world revolution as well as the

---

[27] Containment was first advocated by George F. Kennan in his famous "Mr. X" article, "The Sources of Soviet Conduct," *Foreign Affairs*, July 1947, pp. 566-582.

[28] George F. Kennan, *American Diplomacy, 1900-1950* (Chicago: University of Chicago Press, 1951), pp. 136-137.

[29] George F. Kennan, *Memoirs 1925-1950* (Boston: Little Brown & Co., 1967), pp. 357-363, and more recently, George F. Kennan, "The Realities of Détente," *Washington Post*, December 18, 1974, p. 14.

hostility that results from this commitment. This has been the position of Frederick Schuman and Edward Crankshaw.[30]

Those who aim at moderating the Soviet regime as an end, criticize containment policy as passive, with the United States only reacting to events rather than effectively shaping them. Likewise, they regard a strategy of counterpressure aimed at total victory as dangerously bellicose. Both containment and counterpressure strategies are rejected as likely to injure the chances of reform inside the Soviet Union, the desired ends of the liberalization advocate. Thus, these theorists would inhibit the American response to particular Soviet pressures, if this seemed necessary in order to achieve their objective.

John Foster Dulles was the major advocate of the third policy approach, counterforce strategy.[31] He posited that the Soviet regime was a fundamentally immoral totalitarian dictatorship, and was therefore not susceptible to reform or gradual moderation of its policy. His second key assumption was that the Soviet Union's coercive control over its diverse nationalities internally and its satellites externally is its major vulnerability.

Advocates of a total-victory policy argue that the United States and its allies should exploit these vulnerable points through counterpressure aimed at weakening the Soviet regime and, if possible, defeating it in the cold war. They criticize the strategy of containment as defeatist and the strategy of liberalization as capitulation.

These three policy approaches have been treated here as discrete and separate primarily for heuristic purposes. In practice they overlap and blend into each other. Nonetheless, all three share one general problem: each is rooted in a particular assumption about the future. To this extent they may be described as deterministic. Containment advocates assume a continual strengthening of Soviet power; liberalization advocates expect a continued moderation of Soviet policy; counterpressure theorists feel that the essentially evil nature of the Soviet regime is predetermined and unalterable over time. In each case, an unprovable assumption about the future shapes the form of policy.

---

[30] Frederick L. Schuman, *Government in the Soviet Union* (New York: Thomas Y. Crowell Co., 1961), pp. 162-168. Also see Edward Crankshaw, *Khrushchev: A Career* (New York: The Viking Press, 1966), *passim*.

[31] Townsend Hoopes, "God and John Foster Dulles," *Foreign Policy*, no. 13 (Winter 1973-74), pp. 154-177. For a slightly different interpretation, see Michael A. Guhin, "Dulles' Thoughts on International Politics: Myth and Reality," *Orbis*, vol. 13, no. 3 (Fall 1969), pp. 865-889.

Because of the dynamic relationship between the objective and subjective components of a policy paradigm, American postwar policy influenced the nature of reality itself, and not necessarily to America's advantage. This is the basis of an argument made in the above-mentioned AEI study by Robert J. Pranger. Though speaking directly to the policy of containment, his analysis would apply equally to the other two deterministic strategies. In summarizing the period 1947–1969 in American policy, he argued the following:

> In a word, creative containment proved a dynamic model that shaped the world as it saw the world. By the time national power passed from one party to the other in the 1960 presidential election, it had become increasingly difficult for American policy to distinguish what was really happening in the world from what was idealized as purely a model of that reality: where did the facts working in the world, beyond control by the United States, break off, and where did American imagination of that world begin? Surely some facts are always conditioned by what one imagines to be facts—particularly in policy where the object is to create certain sets of conditions but not everything is malleable or possible.[32]

In other words, determinism may provide a kind of comfort by giving the world a comprehensible order, but it inherently contains a potential danger: by acting on the world with certain deterministic assumptions, our policy makers may become blinded to important areas of flexibility in the changing world order. The numerous areas characterized by such flexibility tend to undermine any strictly deterministic policy approach, and indicate that world order is moving towards a state of indeterminacy. Factors contributing to this trend will be our next subject for consideration.

The Advent of Indeterminacy

The Soviet State: Internal Factors. Myron Rush has posited a theory of Soviet politics which emphasizes the susceptibility of the Soviet regime to succession crises.[33] This could be applied equally to other Communist states. Because the potential for such crises is always present, the future course of behavior for these countries is highly indeterminate.

---

[32] Pranger, *Defense Implications of International Indeterminacy*, p. 9.

[33] Myron Rush, *Political Succession in the USSR*, 2nd ed. (New York: Columbia University Press, 1968).

Rush examined the different methods by which political succession and the transfer of political power can take place. In constitutional political systems tenure in power is limited and/or requires renewal at certain intervals. The transfer of power usually occurs through elections. Even if such a polity were to unexpectedly lose its leader through death, assassination, or incapacity, the manner in which power is transferred is clearly prescribed and is often firmly rooted in custom and tradition.

On the other hand, according to Rush, in the U.S.S.R. and the other Communist countries, the problem of succession can be expected to produce a crisis. Rush offers two reasons for this. First, there is no established decision-making center whose authority is recognized at all times; second, for the foregoing and other reasons, no orderly method of succession has been or is likely to be devised.[34] The stability of the system depends upon dictatorship, yet dictatorial authority adheres in no specified office or title. The designation of an heir has not been a successful device for transferring power in the Soviet system. Neither Lenin nor Stalin, nor for that matter Khrushchev, was able to determine his successor. There is in fact no rule for establishing the legitimacy of the dictator. In general, power in the Soviet Union comes to the ruler not by an orderly transfer of authority, but by the leader arrogating power to himself. This tends to be disruptive to the entire political process and represents a structural weakness in the Soviet political system.

Rush continues his argument by stating that the chief function performed by the political leader in the Soviet Union is to provide authoritative decisions. Therefore, although the prolonged absence of an entrenched dictator need not necessarily bring on the collapse of the Soviet system, it might cause the state to lose some of its great powers through its inability to exercise them effectively.

Thus, the susceptibility of the Soviet system to succession crises is one factor that contributes to the likelihood of an indeterminate future. Although Rush's theory indicates no particular strategy for the United States, it does point toward the necessity of adopting a flexible stance, which would not only permit us to face contingencies as they arise, but which also would provide a greater potential for affecting Soviet policy, particularly during the time of a succession crisis.

The structural weakness of the Soviet political system described by Rush is equally a factor in other Communist states, although sometimes for different reasons. We should keep this in

---

[34] Ibid., pp. 72ff.

mind particularly when we examine the leading parties of the other two groups, led by the People's Republic of China and Yugoslavia.

An examination of the process of succession as it has occurred in the Soviet Union over the past fifty years will illuminate the indeterminate aspects of this structural weakness in the Soviet system. According to the political process in the Soviet Union, a new CPSU general-secretary must increase his sources of support in the Politburo and the Central Committee (CC) of the CPSU in order to retain and solidify his position of power. This challenge has confronted Stalin, Khrushchev, and Brezhnev. Thus after Brezhnev's succession in October 1964, his efforts to accomplish consolidation could be seen in the gradual leadership changes that began immediately after Khrushchev's ouster. Brezhnev influence was apparently behind the slow but deliberate process of increasing the number of candidates to the Politburo, which, by mid-1967, resulted in there being eleven members and nine candidates on this body.[35] This was a comparatively high proportion of candidates to members,[36] and one could assume that these new candidates would be available to serve if any full time members of the Politburo were to fall. Under Stalin, a high proportion of candidate members had been a sign of impending purge. But in order for Brezhnev to initiate a purge and install his men in the Politburo, he would have needed the support of the CC CPSU, and as of mid-1966 (after the Twenty-third CPSU Congress) this did not seem likely.[37]

Under Brezhnev's rule, there has been remarkable continuity in the All-Union Central Committee membership, despite the organizational and political changes which have occurred since 1961. Jerry Hough has demonstrated that of the surviving 166 full members of the 1961 CC elected by the Twenty-second CPSU Congress, 83 percent were reelected to the 1966 CC by the Twenty-third CPSU Congress.[38] This pattern of continuity was also carried over to the Twenty-fourth CPSU Congress, held in 1971. More recently Hough has argued that "all of the members or candidate members of the Politburo elected in 1966 were renamed to this body in 1971, while

---

[35] Ibid., p. 268.

[36] At the end of the Twenty-second CPSU Congress, 31 October 1961—the last party congress held under Khrushchev's tenure—the ratio of members to candidates on the Politburo was eleven to five.

[37] The size of the CC was fairly stable between the Twenty-second and Twenty-third CPSU congresses. In October 1961 there were 175 members and 155 candidates on the CC. By the Twenty-third CPSU Congress in 1966, the body had only grown to 195 members and 165 candidates.

[38] Jerry Hough, "In Whose Hands the Future?" *Problems of Communism*, March-April 1967, p. 19.

81 percent of the living full members of the 1966 Central Committee retained their membership in 1971." [39]

In contrast, Khrushchev's consolidation was relatively swift, with a considerable degree of turnover in CC membership. For example, less than 50 percent of the members of the 1956 CC were reelected to the 1961 CC. It could be argued that it took Khrushchev only about four years initially to consolidate his rule, from March 1953, when he became de facto first secretary [40] of the party, to the June 1957 CC plenum and the expulsion of the "Anti-Party Group." It also took Stalin about the same length of time to consolidate his rule, from December 1922, when Lenin tried to impose his will upon the succession, to early 1926.[41] All of this would seem to indicate that Brezhnev's consolidation of political power has been rather slow in comparison with previous periods of succession.

Brezhnev did in 1971 finally complete his consolidation of power. For despite stability with respect to holdovers on the CC from previous congresses, changes of another kind did occur. There were dramatic changes in the size of the All-Union CC: Brezhnev expanded it from 195 to 241 full members, and thereby gained the opportunity for promoting his supporters to this body. It was only after this congress that the Politburo, formally elected by this new and enlarged CC, came to have fifteen full members and six candidates. This represented a significant change in the top echelons of Soviet political leadership and was most likely related to the consolidation process reaching the end of the succession period.[42]

Nevertheless, there had been a period of close to seven years in which there was fluidity in the Soviet political process due to the

---

[39] Jerry Hough, "The Soviet System: Petrification or Pluralism?" *Problems of Communism*, March-April 1972, p. 32.

[40] Khrushchev became de jure first secretary at the September 1953 CC plenum. The formal title of the head of the CPSU was changed to first secretary at the Nineteenth CPSU Congress in October 1952. This remained in force until the Twenty-third CPSU Congress of March-April 1966, when Brezhnev changed it to its former designation, general secretary.

[41] Early 1926 witnessed a significant change in the balance of Soviet political leadership. The Politburo elected after the Fourteenth Party Congress of December 1925 was expanded from the seven members and four candidates of the Thirteenth Congress of March 1924 to nine members and five candidates. Those newly elected were largely Stalin men, as Stalin had been general secretary of the party since 1922. Also, the three key challengers to Stalin—Trotsky, Zinoviev, and Kamenev—had suffered reverses in their political fortunes by this time. See Leonard Schapiro, *The Communist Party of the Soviet Union* (New York: Random House, 1970), pp. 297-300.

[42] The *coup de grace* seemed to have been the April 1973 change in the Politburo. The size of the Politburo was expanded to sixteen, with major changes occurring in the membership. For details, see footnote 136, below.

crisis of succession. Rush speaks of these fluid periods as being situations of prolonged oligarchic rule where power, while presumably still centered in the Politburo, may become in reality limited—if not controlled—by the CC. If the latter condition ever did occur, we would see a situation where institutional interests, through their representatives on the Politburo and CC, would have a direct influence not only on the choice of political leaders, but also on policy. This would represent a basic change in the very character of the Soviet regime.[43]

Thus, the crisis of succession is a period in which the state might suffer a loss of power during circumstances in which no one individual is able to exercise the complete control the system requires. Therefore the inevitability of some form of succession crisis injects an element of indeterminacy into the course of future policy for states subject to this phenomenon.

A second internal factor operating simultaneously with the succession crisis factor is the phenomenon of the generational factions present in contemporary Communist state leadership. Borys Lewytzkyj sees a conflict of generations arising within the top Soviet political leadership, and concludes that the younger generation does not play a major role in Soviet policy formulation.[44] Instead the generation of "apparatchiki" who joined the party during World War II still dominates at top levels of political leadership.

The "Great Patriotic War" was the decisive experience in the lives of these men. The impact of the Nazi invasion and occupation of large parts of the Soviet Union during World War II upon the collective psyche of this generation of Soviet leaders will be seen in the documents included here, which consistently contain fears of German revanchism and neo-nazism. It is safe to assume that these statements are more than simple propaganda, and reflect deep-seated fears prevalent among this generation of leaders.

Despite the dominance of these men, a sizable younger generation has arisen in the party. As of January 1966 more than 50 percent

---

[43] Rush sees this possibility for change. See Rush, *Political Succession in the USSR*, pp. 266-271. Henry Roberts, on the other hand, disagrees with this interpretation. He sees the dictator–succession crisis–dictator sequence as inevitable but superficial, and sees no room for change within the system. See Henry L. Roberts, *Eastern Europe: Politics, Revolution and Diplomacy* (New York: Alfred A. Knopf, 1970), pp. 278-292.

[44] Lewytzkyj's sizable data pool included 200 full and candidate members of the Politburo and the bureaus of fourteen Soviet republics, and 139 party first secretaries of oblasts, krais, autonomous republics, and autonomous oblasts. See Borys Lewytzkyj, "Generations in Conflict," *Problems of Communism*, January-February 1967) pp. 36-40.

of the CPSU membership was not yet forty years of age, and about half had joined the party since Stalin's death. Lewytzkyj argues that since these younger cadres were politically formed during the years of de-Stalinization, they have different views than the elite of the World War II era. The problem for the party, Lewytzkyj argues, is that the older leaders have not yet made accommodations to this generation.

For example, although the party statutes [45] at one time called for the rotation of cadres, which could have facilitated the rise of younger party members into the CC, the top bodies of the party apparatus resisted these reforms. After the removal of Khrushchev, who first suggested the policy of cadre rotation, arguments were made against the policy at the CC plenum of March 1965, and the rules were finally repealed at the Twenty-third Party Congress. Thus the significance of the Twenty-third Congress, for Lewytzkyj, was the determination of the war generation to keep the younger element out of power.

The conflict-of-generations argument may be overstated, for Lewytzkyj assumes that the younger cadres have a group self-consciousness which they may or may not in fact have.[46] Nonetheless, the data does portray a pattern of generational development that is likely to have some ramifications for the future. The above mentioned membership continuity in the Soviet All-Union CC from 1961 to 1971 has further compounded the increasingly gerontocratic character of the Soviet administrative system. The average age of the membership of the CC has been on a constant increase since the October Revolution. In 1917, the average age of CC members was thirty-six

---

[45] These new statutes were adopted by the Twenty-second CPSU Congress in October 1961. In the cases of the CC and Politburo, at least 25 percent of the memberships were to be replaced at each regular party congress, and a limit of three consecutive terms was adopted. However, an exception was provided for party workers who demonstrated exceptional authority or other qualities. Such members could be elected for more than three terms if they received three-quarters of the votes cast by the CC.

[46] For the conflict of generations to have the significance that Lewytzkyj attaches to it, this younger group must perceive itself as a group; it must be perceived by the older political leadership as a group; and it must feel alienated in the way that Lewytzkyj portrays. Unfortunately, we have no empirical data to either support or refute this hypothesis of group self-consciousness. Survey research would help, but it is not available.

Milton Lodge has posited three operational conditions which would have to be present if the younger elites are to satisfy the sociological definition of a group: (1) group self-consciousness; (2) ascribed group status—they must be perceived as a group by other elites; and (3) the group must possess a set of shared values. See Milton Lodge, "Groupism in the post-Stalinist Period," *Midwest Journal of Political Science*, vol. 12, no. 3 (August 1968), pp. 330-351.

years; by 1934, the year of the Seventeenth CPSU Congress and Kirov's assassination, it was still less than forty-five years. By the end of Stalin's rule in 1952, the average age of CC members was forty-nine years, and the trend continued during the Khrushchev era. In 1956, the year of the Twentieth CPSU Congress and the beginning of de-Stalinization, the average age of CC members was fifty-one years, and by the Twenty-second CPSU Congress in 1961 it was fifty-two years.

During the Brezhnev era the average age of top political leadership continued to increase. By the Twenty-third Congress in 1966, the average age was fifty-six years, and by 1971, the year of the Twenty-fourth Congress, it was fifty-eight years.[47]

There are two possible implications of this trend towards gerontocracy. First, some analysts predict that the aging process may result in conservatism and inflexibility among entrenched leaders. On the other hand, when the inevitable turnover among top Soviet administrators does occur, particularly in the military and industrial institutions, the resulting changes in the All-Union CC may affect the base of the present collective leadership. Since the attempted 1957 succession and the successful 1964 succession required at least the semblance of support of the CC, the presence of younger representatives of key institutions on that body are likely to affect the course of Soviet succession in the near future.

In 1971 General Secretary Brezhnev may have used the increasing age of the party leadership to his advantage in consolidating his rule. At the Twenty-third CPSU Congress in 1966, over 85 percent of the delegates were over fifty years of age and over 33 percent were over sixty years of age. In light of this, the expansion of the CC which took place at the Twenty-fourth CPSU Congress could have been justified as an effort to rejuvenate party leadership. If this is the case, the gerontocratic trend could level off, further increasing the chances for shifts in Soviet policy.

As with the systemic weakness of succession crises, this potential for generational conflict is not unique to the Soviet political system. It has similar implications for the rest of the Communist world. In these countries, the revolutionary leaderships which have exercised power since World War II are exhibiting similar gerontocratic tendencies. For them, World War II was also the formative experience of their lives. This not only affected their perception of the world (for example, it ingrained the deeply held fears of German and Japanese

---

[47] These figures can be found in Jerry Hough, "In Whose Hands the Future?", p. 20. Also Jerry Hough, "The Soviet System: Petrification or Pluralism?", p. 37.

revanchism among the East European and Asian Communist political leaderships, respectively) [48] but it also means that the political leaderships in these countries will soon be due for replenishment.

No doubt we can expect in the not-too-distant future the succession of Mao Tse-tung and Josip Broz Tito in the People's Republic of China (P.R.C.) and Yugoslavia. Changes in the highest party positions occurred in Romania in 1965 (Gheorghe Gheorghiu-Dej succeeded by Nicolae Ceausescu), in Czechoslovakia in 1968 (Antonin Novotny succeeded by Alexander Dubcek then Gustav Husak), in Poland in 1970 (Wladyslaw Gomulka by Edward Gierek), and in East Germany in 1971 (Walter Ulbricht by Erich Honecker). The full impact on policy of these changes in top political leadership has not yet become apparent.

In spite of these recent successions of new party chiefs, the older World War II cadres have not yet suffered a loss of influence to the newer apparatchiki.[49] The eventual replenishment of aging leadership by men not sharing the formative World War II experience could have an impact on the foreign policies of these states and could shape the future of détente.

The documents in Part II of this volume contain examples of policy shifts which have already occurred, such as recent agreements the U.S.S.R., Poland, and Czechoslovakia made with the Federal Republic of Germany (F.R.G.); East German discussions with the West Germans; and Chinese negotiations with the Japanese. Whether or not generational factors are at work here, these policy shifts reflect a significant change in the perception of ruling CP leaderships away from the World War II outlook. Possibilities for future developments

---

[48] For more on the issue of how collective crises can affect perception and identity, see Robert Jay Lifton, *Boundaries: Psychological Man In Revolution* (New York: Random House, 1969). Also by the same author, see *History and Human Survival* (New York: Random House, 1970).

[49] This was the conclusion of Derek Waller's analysis of the CCs elected by the Eighth Party Congress in 1956 and 1958 in the P.R.C. See "The Chinese Communist Political Elite: Continuity and Innovation," in Beck, Fleron et al., *Comparative Communist Political Leadership* (New York: David McKay Co., 1973), pp. 154-201. In a recent follow-up study by Donald Klein and Lois Hager, this continuity was also seen to have been maintained in the CC elected by the Ninth Party Congress in 1969. See "The Ninth Central Committee," in L. J. Cohen & J. P. Shapiro, eds., *Communist Systems in Comparative Perspective* (New York: Anchor Books, 1974), pp. 222-243.

This was also the conclusion of Carl Beck concerning the CC and Politburo memberships in Bulgaria, Czechoslovakia, Hungary, Poland and Romania. See "Career Characteristics of East European Leadership," in R. Barry Farrell, ed., *Political Leadership in Eastern Europe and the Soviet Union*, (Chicago: Aldine, 1970), pp. 157-194.

with regard to mutual and balanced force reductions (MBFR) between NATO and the Warsaw Treaty Organization (WTO), and progress towards Strategic Arms Limitations (SALT) also remain open in light of the unresolved tension in perceptions between World War II leaders and subsequent generations.

Indeterminacy: An External Factor. Over time, the once unified Communist system has become divided into three separate, and increasingly independent groups. This phenomenon of intra-bloc fluidity—the degree of freedom the various Communist states have to formulate their own policies—also contributes to the indeterminate nature of world order.

Because the movement of the ruling Communist parties is relatively young and most of the fourteen nations under Communist rule are in close geographic proximity to the Soviet Union,[50] the basic problem that most ruling-CP leaderships must face is that the power of their own countries is very small vis-à-vis the power of the Soviet Union.

What this has meant for policy formulation in these countries is that policy has been shaped not just by indigenous interests, but also by Soviet interests and control. (Its size and population make the P.R.C. an exceptional case among the Communist powers, and it has always been treated as such by the Soviets.) Thus any discussion of ruling CP leadership and policy must deal with the shifting division of authority between Soviet interests on the one hand, and the domestic interests of the specific state concerned on the other.

For the purposes of this analysis, the relationship between the Soviet Union and the other ruling CPs may be divided into four time periods. The first three periods, each of which was characterized by qualitatively different kinds of relations among the ruling CPs, are now recent history; the fourth and last period, from 1969 to the present, is still open to interpretation and is the period represented by the documents in this collection. We shall first briefly examine the three prior periods, the first of which extends from after the Communist takeovers in Europe in 1945–1948 until approximately the time of Stalin's death in March 1953. This has often been referred to as

---

[50] Bulgaria, Romania, Yugoslavia, Albania, Hungary, Czechoslovakia, Poland, and East Germany. The Asian ruling CPs are those in the P.R.C., North Korea, North Vietnam, and Mongolia. The remaining ruling CP is Cuba's, and is outside both regions.

the satellite period.[51] In general this era was characterized by the Soviet transfer of their own economic, political, and cultural models to the states of East Europe, without regard to the applicability of these models.

In every field the relationship between the U.S.S.R. and Eastern Europe was one of command rather than consultation, and terror was the instrument used to effect obedience. For many idealistic East European Communists this was a period of great disillusionment and widespread defection from ruling circles. The type of political leadership which subsequently arose in East Europe was comprised of people whom the Soviets believed to be dependable. As a result, the policy choices for the East European political leaderships were greatly constricted, and the major policy decisions remained in the hands of Soviet planners. After the June 1948 Tito-Cominform rift, Yugoslavia became the only exception. This marked the beginning of the emergence of Yugoslavia as the leader of a second group within the ruling Communist parties and the first sign of fluidity within the Communist bloc.[52]

The second period, often referred to as the period of the "New Course," began with a greatly expanded allocation of authority to the East European Communist parties. This period of "thaw" began with the rule of Malenkov in March 1953, and was further refined and developed by Khrushchev up to the Twentieth CPSU Congress in February 1956. It closed with attempts at compromise and retrenchment from November 1957 through the end of 1960.

The first move of this period was the recall of many Soviet advisors and the removal of some of the administrative-control agencies from the East European states. Several Khrushchev initiatives

---

[51] Hugh Seton-Watson refers to this as the period of Sovietization. See Hugh Seton-Watson, *The East European Revolution* (New York: Frederick A. Praeger, 1964), pp. 167 ff. Brzezinski breaks this period into two phases: Phase One (1945-1947)—The People's Democracy—and Phase Two (1947-53)—Stalinism. See Zbigniew K. Brzezinski, *The Soviet Bloc: Unity and Conflict*, rev. ed. (New York: Frederick A. Praeger, 1965).

[52] Among the materials on Yugoslavia's independent road to socialism are Hamilton Fish Armstrong, *Tito and Goliath* (New York: Macmillan, 1951); Adam B. Ulam, *Titoism and the Cominform* (Cambridge: Harvard University Press, 1952); Vladimir Dedijer, *Tito Speaks* (London: Widenfeld and Nicolson, 1953); F. W. Neal, *Titoism in Action* (Berkeley: University of California Press, 1958). The documents regarding the Tito-Cominform rift have been published in: *White Book on Aggressive Activities by the Governments of the U.S.S.R., Poland, Czechoslovakia, Hungary, Romania, Bulgaria and Albania Towards Yugoslavia* (Belgrade: Ministry of Foreign Affairs of the Federal People's Republic of Yugoslavia, 1951). Excerpts of these documents can be found in Arthur E. Adams, *Readings in Soviet Foreign Policy: Theory and Practice* (Boston: D. C. Heath & Company, 1961), pp. 256-267.

followed. First there was the famous May 1955 Belgrade reconciliation between Tito and Khrushchev. A few months later the doctrine of "separate roads to socialism" and the condemnation of Stalin in the so-called "cult of personality" statement were adopted by the Twentieth CPSU Congress.[53]

After the uprisings in Poland and Hungary in October and November of 1956, there came a renewed Soviet insistence on control. Soviet concern over growing ethnocentric tendencies revealed by disturbances in many of the East European states led to a conference of twelve ruling Communist parties in November of 1957. A struggle for consensus can be seen in the conference declaration, an ambiguous document reflecting the tension between the smaller states' desire for limited independence in policy, as exemplified by such slogans as "separate roads to socialism," and the Soviet desire for control, as exemplified by the intervention in Hungary.[54]

The declaration was an apparent attempt at compromise, dividing responsibilities between the Soviets and the East European CPs. The Soviets would control foreign policy, bloc economic policy, defense policy, and basic ideological lines, while in domestic areas the other ruling CPs would have authority and independence. Thus Poland was permitted great deviations in the areas of religion and private ownership in agriculture.[55] In methods of administrative control, great diversity developed among the East European countries. East Germany and Bulgaria followed the Soviet model very closely, while Poland and Hungary turned sharply from it.

In each ruling CP, factions began to develop between conservatives, who closely followed the Soviet line, and revisionists, who were advocating wider definitions of national self-determination. The strength of the revisionist wing varied from one CP to another and, over time, within each party.[56] In spite of these allowed deviations from the Soviet model, definite limits as to how "separate" the roads were to be persisted. Thus, this second period offered new possibilities and greater, but still restricted, powers to the East European leaders. The contradictory character of Soviet policy gave these states a limited freedom for maneuver.

---

[53] Documents of the Twentieth Congress can be found in Leo Gruliow, ed., *Current Soviet Policies, II* (New York: Columbia University Press, 1957).

[54] The Declaration of the Twelve Communist Parties can be found in: Dan N. Jacobs, ed., *The New Communist Manifesto and Related Documents*, 3rd rev. ed. (New York: Harper & Row, 1965), pp. 169-182.

[55] For statistical evidence of this deviation, see Brzezinski, *The Soviet Bloc*, p. 412.

[56] The change in characteristics of political leaders in Eastern Europe and the U.S.S.R. has been noted by R. Barry Farrell. See Farrell, *Political Leadership*, pp. 88-107.

The tension between increasing Soviet desire for control and the increasing independence of other CPs which arose at the close of the second period became the dominant characteristic of the third period, which extends roughly from 1961 up to the August 1968 invasion of Czechoslovakia. This period was characterized by a structural transformation in the nature of the relationships between the ruling CPs, which resulted in part from the breakdown in Soviet relations with the People's Republic of China and Albania.

The Sino-Soviet rift was dramatically aired in public at the Twenty-second CPSU Congress, which was held in Moscow in October 1961.[57] At this Congress, de-Stalinization was reemphasized by Khrushchev and Albania was specifically denounced for maintaining a Stalinist stance. Subsequently, Chou En-lai stalked out of the congress, placed a wreath on Stalin's grave in protest,[58] and returned to Peking. The rift was to have a profound impact on ruling CP relationships, and it established the Chinese as the leaders of a third distinct group of Communist states.

What is interesting about this Twenty-second Congress is the fact that Khrushchev apparently had not anticipated the consequences of his Albania policy for Sino-Soviet relations. In his address to the congress on 17 October, he even singled out the Chinese and expressed sympathy for their cause. He noted, "Our people regard with deep sympathy the successes of the Chinese people and the other fraternal peoples in socialist countries and wish them further glorious victories." [59] Ironically, just two paragraphs later in the same speech Khrushchev noted that: "With the appearance of a large group of sovereign socialist states in the world arena, life presented the problem of organizing mutual relations and cooperation among them on fundamentally new principles." [60] Here Khrushchev probably had in mind Yugoslavia, which recently had begun to exercise increased independence under the policy of nonalignment. His statement does seem to indicate a general recognition of the phenomenon of intra-bloc fluidity.

In 1961 Yugoslavia began to sponsor what was to become a series of international conferences of nonaligned nations, and confirmed its

---

[57] The documentary record of this congress can be found in: Charlotte Saikowski and Leo Gruliow, eds., *Current Soviet Policies, IV: The Documentary Record of the 22nd Congress of the Communist Party of the Soviet Union* (New York: Columbia University Press, 1962).

[58] Stalin's corpse had been removed from Lenin's mausoleum to symbolize the break with the Stalinist period.

[59] Gruliow, *Current Soviet Policies, IV*, p. 43.

[60] Ibid., p. 43.

fundamental divergence from those Communist states dominated by the U.S.S.R., Group I. The first conference met in Belgrade, 1-6 September 1961. It was attended by participants from twenty-five nations and dealt with the business of organizing a nonaligned bloc.[61] The fact that the Soviets were displeased with this action was demonstrated by Khrushchev's address to the Twenty-second CPSU Congress cited above. Khrushchev singled out Yugoslavia for explicit rebuke when he charged that

> Only the leaders of the League of Communists [of] Yugoslavia, who plainly suffer from national narrowmindedness, have turned from the straight Marxist-Leninist road on to a winding path that has landed them in the bog of revisionism. . . . Revisionist ideas pervade not only the theory but also the practice of the leadership of the Yugoslav League of Communists. The line they have adopted . . . is harmful and dangerous. It plays into the hands of imperialist reaction, foments nationalist tendencies, and may in the long-run lead to the loss of socialist gains in the country.[62]

This independent policy of nonalignment has been continued by the Yugoslav League of Communists (LCY) up to the present period. There was a second conference of nonaligned nations held in Cairo in October 1964, attended by representatives of forty-seven countries,[63] and the general policy of nonalignment was then outlined and formally adopted at the Eighth LCY Congress, which met in December 1964.[64] This was followed in September 1970 by a third nonaligned conference, held in Lusaka, Zambia, and attended by fifty-four participants.[65] In September 1973 a fourth conference was held in Algiers.[66]

The structural transformation in the system—with the failure of the Tito-Khrushchev rapprochement on the one hand, and the development of the Sino-Soviet rift on the other—gave the smaller ruling Communist parties greater freedom of maneuver. Yugoslavia began

---

[61] See *Documents of the Gatherings of Non-Aligned Countries, 1961-1973* (Belgrade: Secretariat for Information of the Federal Executive Council, 1973), pp. 3-19.

[62] Gruliow, *Current Soviet Policies, IV*, p. 48.

[63] See *Documents of the Gatherings of Non-Aligned Countries, 1961-1973*, pp. 35-49.

[64] The speech of Josip Broz Tito concerning the "General Characteristics of the International Situation—," appears in this collection as Document No. 11, pp. 186ff.

[65] See *Documents of the Gatherings of Non-Aligned Countries*, pp. 61-80.

[66] Since the Cubans have never held a party congress, Castro's speech made at the Algiers conference is included for the Cuban foreign policy viewpoint. Document No. 20, pp. 308ff.

to exhibit greater flexibility in her foreign policy, establishing a basis for a small but distinct second group (Group II) of ruling CPs, and Albania was by the end of 1961 closely allied with the People's Republic of China, forming the basis for a third group (Group III) among the ruling CPs. Even the ruling CPs remaining in Group I (Hungary, Poland, and Czechoslovakia) exhibited policies increasingly independent of the U.S.S.R. Of all of these developments, the rift with the P.R.C. was the most serious for the Soviets, because the P.R.C. was not just another small Communist country maneuvering with some independence; it was a state with great-power aspirations.

Besides these challenges that had arisen from the political leaderships in Albania, the P.R.C., and Yugoslavia, a major new challenge arose in Romania. In April of 1964 a plenum of the CC of the Romanian CP defined courses of action involving not only substantial deviation from the Soviet thinking guiding the Council for Mutual Economic Aid, but also significant de-Russification measures.[67] Later, in 1967, Romania would continue her challenge to Soviet policy, and the policy in East Germany and Poland as well, by establishing diplomatic relations with West Germany. Romania began to coordinate its policy with that of Yugoslavia, with which it came to comprise Group II. From an orthodox Soviet perspective, such developments could only suggest a great need for reordering. Khrushchev's failure to control this highly fluid situation within the ruling Communist party camp may have contributed to his downfall. Moreover this disorder was growing at a time when Khrushchev's policy toward the United States, particularly with regard to the Cuban missile crisis of 1962, must have been causing great concern for some of the top Soviet political leadership.[68] Although they were obviously not completely responsible for his demise, Khrushchev's problems with foreign policy, specifically his inability to control the tendency toward intra-bloc fluidity, probably did play a significant role.

The installation of Brezhnev may well have reflected the desire for a new leader who could rectify these foreign policy problems. Although, as mentioned above, Brezhnev was very slow to consolidate his rule, his efforts to reassert Soviet control over the ruling CPs

[67] See *Statement on the Stand of the Romanian Workers' Party Concerning Problems of the World Communist and Working Class Movement, Endorsed by the Enlarged Plenum of the Central Committee of the Romanian Workers' Party held in April 1964* (Bucharest: Ager Press, 1964), especially pp. 5-51.

[68] This must have been one of the "hair-brained schemes" that the new leadership referred to in their general statement regarding the reasons for Khrushchev's retirement. The statement was published in *Pravda* (17 October 1964) and can be found in Michel Tatu, *Power In the Kremlin: From Khrushchev to Kosygin* (New York: The Viking Press, 1969), p. 422.

began immediately. As Table 1 indicates, the maintenance of order among the ruling Communist parties has been a major concern during the third period. Beginning in 1961, the relationship among ruling CPs has been consistently the first order of business dealt with by the general secretary in his report to CPSU congresses, and the issue was perhaps the major concern of the Soviet political leadership after Khrushchev's fall from grace. Brezhnev's address to the Twenty-third CPSU Congress dealt with this general concern:

> The CC CPSU puts forward for the future as *one of the main orientations of the Party and the Soviet state in the sphere of foreign policy the development and consolidation of ideological, political, and organizational bonds with the Communist Parties of all the socialist countries based on the principles of Marxism-Leninism; the development and consolidation of political, economic and other bonds between the USSR and the socialist states; the promotion in every possible way of the cohesion of the socialist community and the strengthening of its might and influence. The CPSU will do everything in its power to ensure that the world socialist system becomes still more powerful and advances from victory to victory.*[69]

The tension between some of the smaller ruling CPs and the continuing Soviet efforts to dominate them climaxed with the series of events that occurred in Czechoslovakia between January and August of 1968. In January, Antonin Novotny was removed as first secretary of the Czechoslovak Communist party (CzCP), and was succeeded by Alexander Dubcek. One of the major programs advanced by the new leadership was the so-called Action Program, adopted by the CC CzCP on 5 April 1968.[70] This initiative called for major internal structural changes in both the nature of the party and the government, as well as new foreign policy positions deviating sharply from the Soviet line.

This reform effort ended with the 20 August military intervention of Warsaw Treaty Organization (WTO) forces in Czechoslovakia. Soviet demands upon the Czechs since this period give some indication of their thinking on the proper balance between independence and coordination between the East European political leaders and the Soviet leadership. The so-called Brezhnev Doctrine of 1968

---

[69] Report of the CC of the Communist Party of the Soviet Union to the Twenty-third CPSU Congress delivered by Leonid Brezhnev, first secretary of the CC CPSU, 29 March 1966. Document No. 1, p. 72.

[70] This document can be found in Paul Ello, ed., *Czechoslovakia's Blueprint for "Freedom"* (Washington, D. C.: Acropolis Books, 1968), pp. 89-178.

Table 1

GENERAL TOPIC HEADINGS OF FOREIGN POLICY REPORTS OF GENERAL SECRETARY TO CPSU, 1961, 1966, 1971

22nd Congress, 1961 [a]	23rd Congress, 1966 [b]	24th Congress, 1971 [c]
"Further Growth of Might and Brotherhood of Socialist Nations"	"The World Socialist System, the Efforts to Strengthen Unity and Might"	"For the Further Development of the Friendship and Cooperation of the Socialist Countries"
"Sharpening Contradictions in Capitalism and Upsurge in National Liberation"	"Exacerbation of the Contradictions of the Capitalist System . . . ,"	"The Peoples Against Imperialism. Imperialism, Enemy of the Peoples and Social Progress"
"Peaceful Coexistence, General Course of Soviet Foreign Policy"	"The CPSU Works for the Unity of the World Communist Movement"	"Rebuff to the Imperialist Policy of Aggression, Peace and the Security of Peoples"
"Seek Solution of World Problems by Peaceful Means, Improve Relations"	"Development of the National Liberation Movement . . . ,"	
	"Struggle of the Soviet Union against the Aggressive Policy of Imperialism for Peace and World Security"	

Sources:

[a] Charlotte Saikowski and Leo Grullow, eds., *Current Soviet Policies, IV* (New York: Columbia University Press, 1962), pp. 42-53.
[b] Document No. 1, pp. 69-87.
[c] Document No. 3, pp. 110-128.

asserted the right of the Soviet Union to intervene militarily in a "fraternal" country which displays either a deviation from the "common laws governing socialist construction" or a "threat to the cause of socialism." [71]

Such statements seem to reflect the desire of the Soviet political leadership that the ruling CPs of Eastern Europe follow their initiative in the areas of foreign policy, defense policy, and in certain aspects of ideology, culture, and economic organization. Brezhnev may also have opposed changes in Eastern Europe because of the possible appeal of such developments to revisionists within the Soviet leadership itself. Because the period of succession had still not ended,[72] these changes could have had a potentially divisive effect upon the Soviet leadership.[73] Under these circumstances, the Czech developments would have been particularly threatening.

Their actions made clear that the Soviet leaders who supported the intervention in Czechoslovakia were still insisting that for certain areas of policy Eastern Europe must continue to follow the Soviet lead, retaining a subordinate role. In its demands upon Czechoslovakia the Soviet Union was seeking at least as large a role as had been implied in the November 1957 Declaration of the Twelve Communist Parties. This concern for coordination of the ruling CPs would again be in evidence at the June 1969 Conference of Communist and Workers' Parties (Moscow) and in subsequent conferences.[74] However, by this point, divergences among the ruling CPs (as evidenced by Yugoslavia and Romania, and the P.R.C. and Albania)

---

[71] See S. Kovalev, "Sooverenitet i internatiosionalniye obyazannosti sotsialisticheskikh stran," Pravda, 26 September 1968, p. 4. The views expressed in the Pravda article were later reiterated by Brezhnev at the Fifth Congress of the Polish United Workers' Party in November 1968, and have since been referred to as the Brezhnev Doctrine. See also the remarks of Andrei Gromyko before the United Nations General Assembly on 3 October 1968 on the rights of states to intervene.

[72] As mentioned above, Brezhnev was moving very slowly in the consolidation of his political leadership. By late 1968 his position was still tenuous; he made real progress in his consolidation only after the Twenty-fourth CPSU Congress, which finally met 30 March-9 April 1971.

[73] Morton Kaplan made a similar observation in a recent study on NATO: "The case of Czechoslovakia is very interesting for two important reasons. In the first place, there is reason to believe that the surprise for the Czechoslovaks resulted less from the deliberate employment of a ruse by the Russians than from the inability of the Soviet Union to achieve agreement within its Politburo over this issue." See Morton Kaplan, The Rationale for NATO (Washington, D. C.: American Enterprise Institute, 1973), p. 58.

[74] "Tasks at the Present Stage of the Struggle Against Imperialism and United Action of the Communist and Workers' Parties and All Anti-Imperialist Forces." Document No. 2, pp. 88-109.

had reached such an extent that, despite the show of strength in Czechoslovakia, it would be increasingly difficult for the U.S.S.R. to enforce its will. The growing intra-bloc fluidity during the three periods reflects structural changes within the ruling CPs which are beyond the control of the Soviet political leadership.

We have discussed two internal factors which will work to insure an indeterminate future in international affairs. The first is the basic problem of succession in Communist countries due to the lack of orderly procedures for the transfer of power. The second is the generational leadership-shift that these systems are presently encountering. Since most of the ruling CPs came to power at roughly the same period of time, they are simultaneously facing the common problem of elite replenishment. We have also outlined one external factor which further contributes to an indeterminate future as far as the policy of these ruling CPs is concerned—the phenomenon of greater intra-bloc fluidity since 1961. Thus it is clear that there are structural factors at work which make the future behavior and policy of the Soviet Union and the other Communist states unpredictable, and the future course of world order indeterminate.

One more factor contributing to international indeterminacy which is particularly reflected in the documents in this collection is the realization on the part of the ruling CPs that the behavior of the United States is equally uncertain, that the West seems to be making a fundamental shift in its view of world order, a shift articulated by the Nixon Doctrine. The move toward détente and the ruling-CP perception of this shift is likely to affect the operation of the structural factors we have already encountered.[75]

Although the ultimate impact of the Nixon Doctrine upon the leaders of the ruling CPs cannot be foreseen, it is significant for them that America's official reexamination of its world role took place. In this respect, the period of the Nixon Doctrine (1969–1971) was similar to

---

[75] That their perception of Nixon's intimations is important cannot be overstated. Along this line, Erving Goffman has described two kinds of communication: the expression that an individual *gives*, and the expression that he *gives off*. The first involves verbal symbols or their substitutes, which he uses solely to communicate the information that he and others are known to attach to these symbols (traditional communication). The second involves a wide range of action that others can treat as symptomatic of the actor, the expectation being that the action was performed for reasons other than the information conveyed in this way (theatrical communication). See Erving Goffman, *The Presentation of Self in Everyday Life* (New York: Doubleday Anchor Books, 1959), pp. 2-4. See also Robert Jervis, *The Logic of Image in International Relations* (Princeton, N.J.: Princeton University Press, 1970). The recognition of the complexities of communication and the dangers of the misperception of intention are implicitly recognized by the existence of the "hot line."

the periods of 1945–1947 and 1918–1920 in that it was characterized by fundamental questions about the role of the United States in world affairs.[76] Even though there has been no world war to serve as a catalyst for this change, the shifts implicit in the Nixon Doctrine do constitute a third paradigmatic shift in the twentieth century.

The Nixon Doctrine has brought with its rhetoric a series of policy initiatives and explorations in the sphere of strategic arms limitation and mutual and balanced force reductions with the Soviet Union, as well as the beginning of a new era of dialogue with the People's Republic of China. However, these initiatives have in most areas led not to concrete results, but only to further tentativeness. There have been no solid developments to indicate a greater definition of a coming world order or to confirm the achievement of a "generation of peace." The rhetoric of the Nixon Doctrine is ambiguous and leaves the structure of world order unclear.

A Survey of the Documents

American national security will be affected by the manner in which the leaders of the ruling Communist parties and our European allies—as well as the rest of the world—react to these changes in U.S. policy. The documents in this collection illustrate how the ruling CPs in different—and in some cases limited—ways, see these changes and are responding to them.

The Ruling Communist Parties: 1969—A Critical Year. As the Nixon presidency began, Soviet foreign policy continued to emphasize the goal of reasserting control over the ruling CP camp. Although the Soviets attempted to pursue this problem at the Conference of Communist and Workers' Parties in Moscow, 5–17 June 1969,[77] the proceedings of this conference, as well as contemporary statements of several ruling CPs, show the extent of resistance to Soviet authority. The conference was attended by seventy-five party delegations, but five of the ruling CPs were conspicuous by their absence. These were the parties of the People's Republic of China, North Korea, North Vietnam, Albania, and Yugoslavia. Moreover, two of the ruling CPs which did send representatives to the conference, the Romanian and

---

[76] The significance of the 1945-1947 period is expressed in the title of Dean Acheson's memoirs. See Dean Acheson, *Present at the Creation* (New York: W. W. Norton, 1969). Pranger refers to these periods as "seedtimes" for new policies. See Pranger, *Defense Implications of International Indeterminacy*, p. 14.

[77] Document No. 2.

Cuban Communist parties, directly expressed their dissenting views over the Czechoslovakian intervention and other aspects of Soviet policy.

The Romanian Communist party (RCP) took issue with the Soviets first over the invasion of Czechoslovakia, and second, over the situation with the P.R.C. Before the conference the Romanians had expressed concern about rumors that the Soviets were intending to "excommunicate" the Chinese from the Communist movement, as Stalin had done to Tito in June 1948. Although this did not occur, the Romanians continued to have points of difference with the Soviets, which they expressed at their Tenth Party Congress in August 1969. In his report to that congress, Nicolae Ceausescu outlined the general position of the RCP as follows:

> We start from the fact that Communist and workers' parties carry on their activities in different historical, social and national conditions, that the different levels of development of the productive forces and of social relations themselves lead to the approach to certain problems of contemporary development and to the tasks of the immediate struggle being different from one country to another. To understand this reality means to consider as absolutely natural that the Communist and workers' parties, guided by the universal truths of Marxism-Leninism, should independently work out their policy, strategy and tactics.[78]

After stating the general position of the RCP, Ceausescu criticized the Soviets in an oblique fashion for their recent behavior. He noted that:

> Unfortunately, when differences of opinion crop up in one problem or another, the labelling of certain parties is resorted to. . . . [The] taking [of] a different stand by one party can by no means be interpreted as an attitude against another party. The existence of sharp divergencies, as well as criticism levelled against other Communist parties have, in our opinion, diminished the efficiency of the [Moscow conference].[79]

The Cuban delegation, led by Carlos Rafael Rodriguez, was also critical of some of the points made in the main report of the conference. In particular Rodriguez noted: "an inadequate denunciation of bourgeois reformism as a tool of imperialism for maintaining its

[78] Report of the CC of the Romanian Communist Party to the Tenth Party Congress by Nicolae Ceausescu. Document No. 14, p. 235.
[79] Ibid., pp. 235-236.

domination over the Third World."[80] He also took issue with the heavy stress placed on unity as a way to achieve peace rather than as a way of eliminating "imperialism." In spite of these areas of disagreement, Rodriguez did conclude that much of the main report was quite acceptable to the Cuban CP.[81]

Two of the five ruling Communist parties not present at the June 1969 Moscow conference—Yugoslavia and the P.R.C.—had held party congresses earlier in the same year (March and April, respectively). This in itself is an important indication of their independent stances, for the more cooperative CPs tend to schedule their party congresses after the CPSU congress so that they can reflect Soviet positions in their own subsequent statements. The serious substantive areas of Yugoslavian and Chinese disagreement with Soviet policy become clear in the CC reports on foreign policy made to their congresses.

The Yugoslav Congress. It must be said that the relationship between Yugoslavia and the Soviet Union has always been a stormy one. The expulsion of the LCY from the Cominform in June 1948 was followed by a period of hostility which lasted until 1955–1956, when Khrushchev attempted to patch the rift. Since that time Yugoslav-Soviet relations have moved back and forth between periods of cordiality and hostility, with the Yugoslav policy of nonalignment a source of constant irritation to the Soviets since 1961.

The invasion of Czechoslovakia brought the Soviet-Yugoslav relationship to a new low, and by 1969 there had arisen genuine Yugoslav fears that the Soviets might encroach upon Yugoslav territory.[82] This tension became even more apparent in March 1969, with the Soviet and East European boycott of the Ninth LCY Congress.[83] This congress, which met 11–15 March 1969, took issue with the Soviets on a number of points. On the domestic front, the Yugoslav model of socialism differed markedly from the Soviet model, and there were also significant differences in the area of foreign

---

[80] *Yearbook on International Communist Affairs, 1970.* (Stanford: Hoover Institution Press, 1971), p. 392.

[81] It should be noted that ever since this period, Soviet-Cuban relations have been improving. This can be illustrated by Castro's statements made at the Algiers Conference of Non-Aligned Nations in September of 1973. Document No. 20.

[82] After the Czech invasion, Yugoslav civil defense units were formed and in 1969 these were organized down to the factory level. Also on 17 February 1969 the Federal Assembly passed a law on national defense which gave the process legality.

[83] Romania was a notable exception to this boycott, further aligning itself with Yugoslovia by its attendance.

policy. Tito voiced strong and explicit objection to the invasion of Czechoslovakia and the Brezhnev Doctrine:

> Yugoslavia, as a socialist country, has always attached great importance to cooperation with other socialist countries, regarding this as being in the common interest in terms of the consolidation of peace, international cooperation and development of socialism in the world. . . .
> The military intervention by five socialist countries in Czechoslovakia had, however, a negative influence on the development of cooperation. . . .
> This action, which violated the independence of a sovereign state and which is completely at odds with the generally accepted principles of international law and the UN Charter, dealt a grave blow to the interests of progress, peace and freedom—all the more so as it was undertaken by socialist countries in the name of protecting socialism.[84]

The P.R.C. Congress. The second ruling Communist party to express its dissent by holding a party congress before the Moscow conference and by boycotting that conference was the CP of the People's Republic of China, which held its Ninth Congress in Peking 1–24 April 1969. After Mao's address opening the congress, Lin Piao delivered the political report of the CC. This report was a Maoist apology for the excesses of the recent cultural revolution, as well as an outline of the general direction of future party policy.

Section seven of the eight-part report dealt with China's foreign affairs. Particular attention was given to the poor state of relations with the U.S.S.R. During the preceding month, there had been two major clashes (on 2 and 15 March) with Soviet troops at Chenpao (Damansky) Island in the Ussuri River, on the Heilungkiang-Siberian border. Lin claimed that: "The Soviet revisionist clique is a paper tiger. . . . Since Brezhnev came to power . . . the Soviet renegade clique has been practicing social-imperialism and social fascism more frantically than ever." [85] Significantly, before this, the epithet "paper tiger" had been the usual Chinese characterization of the United States.

In further implicit criticism of the U.S.S.R., Lin claimed that Chinese foreign policy would be based upon principles of mutual respect for territorial integrity and sovereignty, mutual nonaggression,

---

[84] Report of the CC of the Yugoslav League of Communists to the Ninth Party Congress by Josip Broz Tito. Document No. 12, pp. 211-212.

[85] Report of the CC to the Ninth Party Congress of the People's Republic of China by Lin Piao. Document No. 16, pp. 260-261.

noninterference in the internal affairs of other nations, equality and mutual benefit, and peaceful coexistence. These principles had originally been enunciated as the "Five Principles" of foreign policy in 1954. They were now to be implemented within the overall context of opposition to the "imperialist policies of aggression and war" [86] waged by both the United States and the Soviet Union.

The Soviet Position. Thus, the Soviets faced serious dissension at the time of the 1969 Moscow conference. Five ruling CPs did not attend, and there was dissent from two ruling CPs which did attend. In spite of these differences, the participants at the Moscow conference did reach some common conclusions regarding the world situation. There was ideological agreement on the forces which should come together in the common struggle against imperialism. These were commonly perceived to be the world socialist system, the international working class, and the national liberation movement. The conference deemed unity through common struggle as essential, because according to the main report, the last third of the twentieth century is to be marked by the sharpening of the struggle between the forces of socialism and imperialism.

The report singles out the United States as the main imperialist power in the world and condemns its participation in the Vietnam War as well as its actions in the Mediterranean, Cuba, and the Far East. Despite these American efforts, general optimism was expressed regarding the irreversibility of recent socialist developments: "Imperialism can neither regain its lost historical initiative nor reverse world development. The main direction of mankind's development is determined by the world socialist system, the international working class, [and] all revolutionary forces." [87]

The conference document also contains some elements of compromise. It makes no reference to either the special role of the CPSU or the theory that the experience of the CPSU should have special value for other CPs. Instead, the report states that: "All parties have equal rights. As there is no leading center of the international Communist movement, voluntary coordination of the actions of parties in order effectively to carry out the tasks before them acquires increased importance." [88] This is in direct contrast to both the conference of 1957, which acknowledged the Soviet Union as head of the Communist movement and leader of the socialist camp, and the

---

[86] Ibid., p. 264.
[87] Document No. 2, p. 90.
[88] Ibid., p. 107.

conference of 1960, which described the CPSU as "the universally recognized vanguard of the world Communist movement." [89]

In apparent further compromise, the document makes no direct reference either to Czechoslovakia or to China, apart from calling for China's admission to the UN and the "return" of Taiwan to the P.R.C. Thus the main report glossed over the major issues that divided the ruling CPs and barely touched upon the subject of the five absent CPs. After stating that *"the cohesion of the Communist and workers' parties is the most important factor in rallying together all the anti-imperialist forces,"* [90] the report concludes that the participants "consider that the absence of certain Communist parties should not hinder fraternal ties and cooperation between all Communist parties without exception." [91]

The report of the 1969 conference, as well as the documents of the dissenting parties, illustrate that the year 1969 was a transition year, which seems to mark the beginning of a new seedtime—a period of ferment and problems for the CPSU leadership, as well as for many of the rest of the ruling CPs. In spite of a near decade-long effort to preserve control, the position of the Soviet leaders had become worse rather than better.

This was the situation at the beginning of the year and a half of negotiations which were to culminate in the formulation of the Nixon Doctrine. The responses to these American initiatives become apparent in the documents of the ruling CPs over subsequent years. As Table 2 indicates, by 1969 the division of the CP camp into three groups led by the U.S.S.R., Yugoslavia, and the P.R.C. had already become a clear trend. During the ensuing period, these divisions have been reinforced, in part because of the continuing operation of the internal and external factors of indeterminacy, but also because of the three groups' differing perceptions of the Nixon Doctrine and its impact on world order.

1970: A Continuing Period of Seedtime. The year 1970 saw little innovation in either doctrine or policy among the ruling CPs. Within the group of ruling CPs which were closely aligned with the Soviet Union (Group I), only Hungary held a party congress, its tenth. The other significant event within this group was the unrest in Poland, which culminated in a change of leadership in December.

---

[89] *Yearbook on International Communist Affairs, 1970,* p. 794.

[90] Document No. 2, pp. 106-107.

[91] Ibid., p. 109.

The CPs of Groups II and III continued to move along established courses during 1970, with increasing competition among Yugoslavia, the P.R.C., and the U.S.S.R. for influence in the developing nations. For its part, Yugoslavia sponsored the third conference of nonaligned nations in Lusaka. Meanwhile, the P.R.C. responded to continued tension with the U.S.S.R. over territorial boundaries with harsh anti-Soviet rhetoric, denouncing the CPSU leadership as "neo-tsarist imperialists." Such rhetoric reflected the Chinese desire to discredit the U.S.S.R. and place themselves at the vanguard of the struggle for "national liberation."

Over this period, the Soviet Union itself attempted to assert its leadership over the ruling CP camp through the promotion of political, military, and economic integration. Among the CPs of Group I it achieved substantial success in the economic sector—chiefly through the Council for Mutual Economic Aid (CMEA), which greatly expanded its operations.[92] In January 1970 a CMEA office was established in Moscow for the exchange of scientific and technological information. At the CMEA session in May it was announced that long-term economic integration would be advanced by coordinating with Moscow the 1971–1975 five-year plans of the CMEA countries. In July a joint CMEA investment bank began operation.[93]

The decision to coordinate CMEA five-year plans led to changes in the regulations regarding the periodicity of party congresses for these CPs, since the coordinated plans must be ratified at the respective party congresses. This is reflected in Table 2 by the timing of the ruling-CP congresses of Group I since 1971. In this way the Soviet plan of economic integration led to increased political coordination, at least within Group I.

The Hungarian Congress. The only party congress of Group I to occur before the Twenty-fourth CPSU Congress of March–April 1971 was the Hungarian Tenth Party Congress, held 23–27 November 1970. Aside from the independence in timing, this congress took a substantive divergence from the Soviet line. In the area of domestic policy, the congress emphasized Hungary's so-called New Economic Mechanism (NEM), which had been inaugurated in 1968.

---

[92] Essentially, this organization is comprised of the CPs of Group I. In early 1949, when CMEA was founded, there were six charter members—the U.S.S.R., Bulgaria, Czechoslovakia, Hungary, Poland, and Romania. Subsequently, three other countries were added—Albania in February 1949, East Germany in September 1950, and Mongolia in June 1962. Albania withdrew in December of 1961, while Romania has exhibited considerable independence in her economic policies since 1963.

[93] *Yearbook on International Communist Affairs, 1971* (Stanford, California: Hoover Institution Press, 1972), p. 92.

Table 2
RULING COMMUNIST PARTY CONGRESSES, 1951–1974

Group/CP	Year/Month(s) of Congress									
	'51	'52	'53	'54	'55	'56	'57	'58	'59	'60
Group I										
U.S.S.R.		Oct.				Feb.			Jan.	
Bulgaria				Feb.-Mar.				June		
Czechoslovakia				June				June		
Mongolia				Nov.				Mar.		
East Germany				Mar.-Apr.				July		
Poland				Mar.					Mar.	
Hungary	Feb.-Mar.			May					Nov.	
Group II										
Yugoslavia		Nov.						Apr.		
Romania					Dec.					June
Group III										
P.R.C.						Sep.		May		
Albania		Mar.-Apr.			May-June					
North Korea						Apr.				
Miscellaneous [a]										
Cuba					.					
North Vietnam										Sep.

[a] Cuba and North Vietnam are classified as "miscellaneous" because their party congresses have not developed any periodic pattern over the past fifteen years.

Note: Two patterns emerge in this table: (1) coalescence of Groups I and II, and (2) within these two groups, in each periodic cycle the leading CP holds its congress first. There is no pattern in Group III.

Source: Author.

Year/Month(s) of Congress

'61	'62	'63	'64	'65	'66	'67	'68	'69	'70	'71	'72	'73	'74
Oct.					Mar.					Mar.			
	Nov.				Nov.					Apr.			
	Dec.				June					May			
July					June					June			
		Jan.				Apr.				June			
			June				Nov.			Dec.			
	Nov.				Nov.				Nov.				
			Dec.					Mar.					May
				July				Aug.					Nov.
								Apr.				Aug.	
Feb.					Nov.					Nov.			
Sep.									Nov.				

41

This policy differed from the Soviet model in that under it individual enterprises respond to market demand, and prices, rather than being fixed by central planners, tend to reflect the market value of the article produced.

In spite of these domestic differences, Hungarian foreign policy continued to follow the line of the Soviet Union. In general, First Secretary Janos Kadar gave unequivocal support to the U.S.S.R. and to the WTO. Kadar claimed that Hungary had acted according to the principle of "internationalism" when it participated in the 1968 invasion of Czechoslovakia. The subordination of Hungarian national interests to "internationalism" (essentially, the interests of the Soviet Union) was emphasized by Zoltan Komocsin, the party secretary in charge of international affairs. In his speech to the congress, Komocsin said:

> If life produces situations in which our specific interests clash with joint interests, we subordinate them to joint interests in the conviction that this can only lead to success in the long run. Our national interests and the common objectives of our world system cannot be lastingly antithetical.[94]

It will be interesting to follow Hungarian developments along two fronts, as the apparent harmony with the Soviet Union in the area of foreign policy could be threatened by continued domestic divergence and the pursuit of the NEM, a policy which may or may not run counter to CMEA "joint" economic interests. One clue to the resolution of this question was in the timing of the March 1975 Hungarian party congress, which continued the deviation from the periodic pattern of the congresses of the ruling CPs of Group I. Another clue can be seen in Kadar's speech to the Eleventh Congress which illustrated that the "joint interests" were beginning to clash with specific Hungarian interests. In his foreign policy address, Kadar noted that

> in 1973 and 1974 considerable changes occurred in capitalist markets. Along with the acceleration in the inflation rate, the world market price of fuel and power sources and raw and basic materials rose by leaps and bounds. This was only slightly balanced by an increase in the price of finished goods. Consequently our foreign trade balance worsened and our national economy had to face significant losses. These changes are not temporary.[95]

---

[94] Speech to the Hungarian Tenth Party Congress by Zoltan Komocsin. Document No. 10, pp. 182-183.

[95] *Foreign Broadcast Information Service, Eastern Europe, Daily Report*, vol. 2, no. 53 (18 March 1975), p. F16.

While the speech explicitly blamed "capitalist markets" for Hungary's economic setbacks, Kadar was implicitly criticizing the U.S.S.R., which, being Hungary's main supplier of fuel and power, had been hiking its prices along with OPEC since October 1973.

Developments in Poland. The other significant event of 1970 in Group I occurred in Poland. During this year Poland's foreign policy centered principally on negotiations with the Federal Republic of Germany (F.R.G.).[96] Far more important for Poland were developments in the domestic sphere. The announcement of a policy of general price increases met with strong public protest. In addition to several strikes, riots broke out in Gdansk, Gdynia, and Szczecin. The effect of this was to undermine the position of First Secretary Wladyslaw Gomulka, who had held his post since October 1956. At a CC meeting on 20 December, Gomulka was replaced by Edward Gierek. Despite this change, Polish adherence to the general Soviet foreign policy line showed little deviation.

A continued trend toward consolidation among all of the ruling CPs of Group I, achieved in part through the economic consolidation of the CMEA and evidenced in the timing of the 1971 party congresses, is clearly reflected in the content of the foreign policy reports to those congresses by the party secretaries. These documents will be found in Chapter 2.

Developments in Group II. At the same time that the solidarity of Group I was increasing, the ruling CPs of Groups II and III maintained their independent tendencies. The Yugoslav stance of nonalignment continued to evoke a negative Soviet response. The Soviet leadership expressed fears that the world would become divided into a northern and southern sphere and that the policy of nonalignment would lead to the creation of a third force, undermining socialism as well as capitalism.

Romania, the other member of Group II, also continued to pursue its independent line. General Secretary Ceausescu continued to oppose the Brezhnev Doctrine, and by refusing to join the CMEA investment bank, frustrated continued Soviet attempts to integrate Romania into Soviet-sponsored economic structures. Ceausescu also consistently drew attention to Romania's good relations with the P.R.C., which, of course, was a further source of irritation for the Soviets. In fact, the interest of Romania, and Yugoslavia as well,

---

[96] These were carried on in close consultation with the Soviet Union, and only after the Soviet-F.R.G. accord of August 1972 was a Polish-F.R.G. agreement finally completed. The agreement normalized relations between the F.R.G. and Poland and recognized the Oder-Neisse line, which had been established by the Potsdam Conference as the western boundary of Poland.

in maintaining independence in relation to the U.S.S.R. continued to provide the stimulus for a limited rapprochement of both states with Albania and China. The pursuit of independence also resulted in a new friendliness of Group II nations toward the West. By and large, the highlight of 1970 for Romania was the fifteen-day trip of Ceausescu to the United States in October. This is one indication of the movement of Yugoslavia and Romania towards improved relations with the United States—complementing the openings toward China and the developing nations—seemingly as a buffer against the powerful interests and influence of the U.S.S.R.

Continued Divergence of Group III. Group III, led by the P.R.C., maintained a stance of hostility to the U.S.S.R. during 1970. Although Kosygin and Chou En-lai had tried to resolve differences in a September 1969 meeting, any softening in the tone of the confrontation brought little real modification of the political and ideological conflicts which still divided the two powers. Thus by the end of the year the positions of the two powers seemed to be frozen, with no chance of thaw in sight.

As reported in the Albanian press, Albania continued to support China's position, endorsing both the domestic and foreign policies of the P.R.C. In particular, party General Secretary Enver Hoxha echoed the strong Chinese support of Romanian and Yugoslavian policies. Improved relations between the ruling CPs of Groups II and III were apparently sought by both parties as a counter to the influence of the Soviet Union.

The North Korean Congress. The second party congress of 1970 was the North Korean. Held 2–12 November 1970, it was that country's first congress in almost a decade. In his report to the congress, Kim Il-sung presented an extremely parochial and heavily ideological world view. He spoke of a world filled with hostility, in which North Korea faced the aggressive challenge of imperialism, dominated by the United States and its "surrogate militarist agent, Japan." According to Kim, threats to North Korean autonomy were evident in the *Pueblo* incident, frequent reconnaissance overflights, and the continual "imperialist" efforts to frustrate the "true" Korean interests embodied in the North Korean concept of *chuche*, which calls for unification of North and South as a prelude to a Korean "cultural revolution."

In his report, Kim devoted the greatest amount of attention to the United States and the threat of imperialism:

> The aggressive ambition of U.S. imperialism knows no bounds. . . . While overtly pursuing the "policy of strength,"

the U.S. imperialists are putting up ostentatious signboards of "peace," "negotiation," "intercourse," and what-not, and ballyhooing about what they call "peace strategy." [97]

Kim then referred specifically to the new policy intimations embedded in the Nixon Doctrine, discrediting them entirely:

In an endeavor to cover up their policy of Asian aggression, the present U.S. rulers are clamoring about a sort of change in their policy. But there has not been, nor can there be, any change in the aggressive policy pursued by the U.S. imperialists in Asia. The only change, if any, is that their aggressiveness and craftiness have further increased. While stepping up aggression by mobilizing their armed forces directly, the U.S. imperialists are seeking a more sinister means to easily realize their aggressive designs on Asia, mainly by "making Asians fight Asians," raking up Japanese militarism and other satellite countries and puppets in Asia in accordance with the notorious "new Asia policy." [98]

As a result of this intensely defensive perception of a pervasively hostile world, most of the speech deals with national defense. The party leadership calls insistently for all-out preparation against the threat of potential—even immediate—invasion. The report proudly stresses the fact that every man, woman, and child is trained in the use of weapons and is always ready to maintain vigilance and protect the homeland. Such a world view leaves little room for consideration of détente. Similar hostility on the part of the other CPs of Group III has made this group the least responsive to the Nixon initiatives. Further, all the CPs of Group III were in 1970 still heavily involved with the most basic of national concerns, the protection of territorial integrity and national survival. As witnessed by the speeches of Lin Piao and Kim Il-sung to their respective congresses, the world was perceived as being highly dangerous and hostile, and the resulting policy statements were heavily ideological, with the division of good and evil pushed to the extreme.

1971: Soviet Consolidation Comes to Fruition. The year 1971 was a busy one for the ruling CPs of Group I. It opened with the Twenty-fourth CPSU Congress, which met 30 March to 9 April in Moscow. All the ruling CPs, with the exception of the Chinese and Albanian,

---

[97] Report of CC to Fifth Korean Workers' Party Congress, delivered by Kim Il-sung. Document No. 19, pp. 300-301.

[98] Ibid., pp. 301-302.

sent delegations to this congress. The congress proceedings reveal a dual and often contradictory approach in Soviet foreign policy, which aims, first, to provide a firm rebuff against imperialism and to support national liberation movements, and second, to simultaneously strive for peaceful coexistence with states of differing social systems. This second emphasis has been consistently criticized by the Chinese and other ruling CPs of Group III as "revisionist."

Some underlying tensions rose to the surface during the congress over certain specific issues. The Romanian and Yugoslavian delegations again condemned the Czechoslovakian invasion, stressing the principles of "sovereignty, independence, noninterference, and self-determination." This naturally led to the issue of whether or not the Soviet Union was to play the role of "leading center" of the ruling CPs. This was firmly rejected by the Yugoslavs, who continued to stress the "separate roads" approach.

Despite such strains, strong support for the U.S.S.R. by the ruling CPs in Group I was quite evident. Criticism of the Chinese political leadership was expressed by Bulgaria, Czechoslovakia, Hungary, Mongolia, and Poland, all of which gave outright support to the Soviet position. This Soviet stance was stated most clearly in Brezhnev's foreign policy report:

> . . . the Chinese leaders have put forward an ideological-political platform of their own which is incompatible with Leninism on the key questions of international life and the world Communist movement. . . . They unfolded an intensive and hostile propaganda campaign against our party and country, made territorial claims on the Soviet Union, and in the spring and summer of 1969 brought things to the point of armed incidents along the border. . . .[99]

Brezhnev then considered the relationship between the Soviet Union and the United States. He claimed that when it comes to the problem of imperialism:

> One must deal above all with U.S. imperialism, which . . . seeks to dominate everywhere, interferes in the affairs of other peoples, high-handedly tramples on their legitimate rights and sovereignty, and seeks by force, bribery and economic penetration to impose its will on states and whole areas of the world.[100]

---

[99] Report of the CC CPSU to the Twenty-fourth Party Congress, by Leonid Brezhnev. Document No. 3, p. 114.
[100] Ibid., p. 118.

In spite of this analysis, toward the end of his speech he made a case for improving relations with the United States and posed the question of whether the Nixon Doctrine's emphasis on negotiation was credible:

> We proceed from the assumption that it is possible to improve relations between the U.S.S.R. and the U.S.A. Our principled line with respect to the capitalist countries, including the U.S., is consistently and fully to practice the principles of peaceful coexistence, to develop mutually advantageous ties, and to cooperate, with states prepared to do so, in strengthening peace, making our relations with them as stable as possible. But we have to consider whether we are dealing with a real desire to settle outstanding issues at the negotiation table or attempts to conduct a "positions of strength" policy.[101]

This could be viewed as a Soviet response to the intimations of the Nixon administration, which was stressing negotiation, partnership, and strength, and simultaneously attempting to wind down the war in Vietnam. When the Vietnam War was at its peak, the policy of the Soviets towards the U.S. reflected a hard-line allegiance to the bipolar paradigm of the cold war. To them, American involvement in Vietnam represented a policy of continuing and outright imperialist aggression. Recognition of the American effort to wind down this confrontation was evident in Brezhnev's own statement, which showed what seemed to be an opening towards potential diplomatic exploration and negotiation.

The Soviet responsiveness may also have been due to the increased stature of Leonid Brezhnev within the CPSU. Several factors point toward this conclusion: (1) the changes in the membership of the Politburo and CC which occurred at this congress, (2) Brezhnev's marked success in coordinating the ruling CPs of Group I, and (3) a certain degree of success with the ruling CPs of the other groups, as evidenced by the attendance at the congress of Yugoslavia, North Korea, and North Vietnam—all of which had been absent from the 1969 Moscow conference—and (4) a warming of Soviet-Cuban relations. Thus by 1971 Brezhnev had apparently made important strides towards consolidating not only his position within the CPSU, but also the position of the Soviet Union within the Communist camp. Though his gains with the ruling CPs outside of Group I were limited, it seemed that his position had improved to such an extent that it became possible to take initiatives which

---

101 Ibid., p. 126.

might have previously raised a challenge to his personal position of leadership. In short, Brezhnev's increased stature probably brought him greater decision-making flexibility.

The Bulgarian Congress. As is shown in Table 2, all the ruling CPs of Group I, except that of Hungary, held their party congresses in the eight months immediately following the Twenty-fourth CPSU Congress. The first was the Bulgarian Tenth Party Congress, which met from 20–25 April 1971 in Sofia. From the Soviet point of view, the Bulgarian Communist party (BCP) congress was "correct," both procedurally and substantively. The Bulgarians changed their party rules to assure coordination with future CPSU congresses, extending the length of time between congresses from four to five years. Moreover the Bulgarian leadership adopted a world outlook identical to that of the CPSU. In references to imperialism in general, to the United States specifically, to the P.R.C., and to Czechoslovakia, General Secretary Zhivkov's statements were in perfect harmony with those of Brezhnev. The capstone to this exercise in orthodoxy came at the end of the foreign policy report to the party congress. Here Zhivkov rather rapturously concluded that:

> *The Bulgarian Communist party and the Bulgarian people need Bulgarian-Soviet friendship the way all living things need the sun and air; it is a centuries-old friendship and a friendship to last centuries; it is one of the main motive forces of our development; it is a prerequisite and guarantee for the future upsurge of our socialist country and of its morrow.*[102]

The Czechoslovakian Congress. The next party congress among the ruling CPs of Group I occurred 24–29 May in Czechoslovakia. Because problems in this country had recently been the cause of so much Soviet concern, the Czechs attempted at their congress to prove to the Soviets and the rest of the world that "normalization" had finally been achieved. Several procedural changes adopted at this Congress mirrored recent CPSU adjustments. The title of the Czech party chief, Gustav Husak, was changed from first secretary to general secretary, following the similar change in terminology made by the Soviets at the Twenty-third CPSU Congress. Like the Bulgarian CP, the Czech CP altered its rules so that party congresses would meet every five years instead of every four years. As with the Bulgarian CP, this facilitated increased coordination with Soviet policy lines. The Czechs were also in substantive accord with the

---

[102] Report of the CC to the Tenth BCP Party Congress, delivered by Todor Zhivkov. Document No. 5, p. 144.

platform adopted by the Soviets at the Twenty-fourth CPSU Congress, and Husak apologized at some length for the 1968 "deviation."[103]

The Mongolian Congress. The next Group I party congress was the Sixteenth Mongolian Workers' Party (MWP) Congress in June. Mongolia had coordinated her party congresses with the CPSU since 1966. Only one deviation from the Soviet example was in evidence at the 1971 congress: Yumzhagiin Tsedenbal continued to hold not only the post of general secretary, but also the Mongolian premiership, even though the division of top party and state posts had been maintained in the Soviet Union since the removal of Khrushchev in October 1964. Aside from this idiosyncrasy, the Mongolian congress was in procedural and substantive accord with the Twenty-fourth CPSU Congress. Tsedenbal stated that: "Mongolian-Soviet relations can be characterized as follows—our friendship with the Soviet Union is socialist internationalism in action."[104] He added that: "It was with profound satisfaction that the MPR Communists and working people received the magnificent program for building Communism in the Soviet Union outlined by the Twenty-fourth CPSU Congress."[105] In further parallel to the Soviet outlook, Tsedenbal had nothing but criticism to offer on the subject of the P.R.C.:

> Our party is waging a principled struggle against the Chinese leaders' anti-Marxist political line. The Chinese leaders are attempting by their divisive actions to disunite the socialist countries, undermine and split the ranks of the Communist movement. . . . The course pursued by the Chinese leaders, who have taken belligerent nationalism and anti-Sovietism into their armory, has led to China's isolation from the socialist countries and to armed provocations against Lenin's motherland—the U.S.S.R.[106]

The East German Congress. The party congress held in the German Democratic Republic (G.D.R.), 15–19 June 1971, followed on the heels of the leadership change of May, in which Walter Ulbricht resigned his top party post and was succeeded by Erich Honecker. One of the immediate consequences of this change was

---

[103] Report of the CC CzCP to the Fourteenth Party Congress, delivered by Gustav Husak. Document No. 6, pp. 146ff. A longer evaluation of the causes of the 1968 crisis had been released by the CC CzCP in January 1971, and Husak's CC report to the Fourteenth CzCP Congress referred extensively to this document.

[104] Report of the CC MWP to the Sixteenth MWP Congress, delivered by Yumzhagiin Tsedenbal. Document No. 7, p. 153.

[105] Ibid., p. 154.

[106] Ibid., p. 158.

the development of even closer G.D.R. cooperation with the Soviet Union. There was also a marked tendency toward the closer integration of the G.D.R. with the other members of the WTO and CMEA.

At the congress, Honecker generally echoed the Soviet world view, while placing great stress on European peace and security in a "Five-Point Program for Peace," which he submitted to the congress. Under this program, the G.D.R.:

(1) [calls for] the convocation of a European security conference . . . ,

(2) [is] willing to become a member of the UN . . . ,

(3) [is] willing to establish normal diplomatic relations with all states . . . ,

(4) advocates establishment of normal relations, with the FRG, and

(5) [is] willing to contribute to the normalization of relations with West Berlin. . . .[107]

This report made little reference to Asian affairs and, significantly, contained not a single reference to the P.R.C., though Honecker went quite far in expressing praise for the Soviet Union:

The CPSU has proved to be the most experienced and most battle-tested party—the vanguard of the international Communist and workers' movement . . . in all questions . . . there is perfect unanimity between our parties and states. In this spirit, our Eighth Party Congress sends fraternal greetings to the CPSU Central Committee . . . we will never forget what the Soviet people and their glorious army did to free us from Hitlerite fascism.[108]

Honecker's view of peaceful coexistence derived from the Soviet interpretation. In his speech he noted that "imperialism . . . is the main obstacle on the road to secure peace and social progress. If we make every effort to enforce the policy of peaceful coexistence between states with different social systems, then we do so in full awareness that imperialism has not changed its character." [109]

The East German response to the Nixon Doctrine and détente with China ran in a similar vein: "Nixon has grandiloquently described his forthcoming visit to Peking as a 'journey for peace.' Public opinion rightly wonders whether the aim is to pursue the old

[107] Report of the CC of the SED to the Eighth Party Congress delivered by Erich Honecker. Document No. 8, pp. 169-170.
[108] Ibid., p. 163.
[109] Ibid., p. 165.

aggressive policy of imperialism with new, more flexible methods." [110]
Later in the year, when it was announced that Nixon would visit
Moscow, the East German CP saw in this the failure of the plans
of Peking's leaders to use their flirtation with Washington for the
establishment of an anti-Soviet bloc. [111]

The Polish Congress. The last 1971 party congress in Group I
was that of Poland, the Sixth Polish United Workers' Party (PUWP)
Congress, which met in Warsaw 6–12 December. One of the basic
tasks of the Polish political leadership was to convince the Soviet
Union and the rest of the world that the internal crisis of 1970 was
solved and that warm Polish-Soviet relations would continue. After
outlining reasons for the conflict in 1970, General Secretary Edward
Gierek went on to praise the role of the CPSU and the closeness of
Polish-Soviet relations. He particularly emphasized the economic
sphere:

> In our international policy the key role is played by the
> fraternal relations with the Soviet Union. They provided
> . . . guarantees of independence and security for the Polish
> nation. . . .
> The prospects of Poland's further development . . . can
> be fully implemented only within a framework of coopera-
> tion with the Soviet Union. . . .
> The Communist Party of the Soviet Union . . . [is] the
> most experienced party within the Communist move-
> ment. . . . [112]

Gierek's references to the Chinese CP were similarly in line with
the Soviet position. He stated that:

> . . . our party is opposed to all divisive tendencies, and
> especially to the particularly dangerous fomenting of anti-
> Soviet nationalism and chauvinism. . . . Anti-Sovietism . . .
> cannot be reconciled with the genuine struggle against im-
> perialism. . . . The Chinese leadership which is basically
> contrary to Marxism-Leninism and proletarian international-
> ism, is bringing harm to the cause of socialism. [113]

By the time of this meeting, there had been much publicity and
discussion about the Nixon initiatives and the forthcoming summits.

---

[110] *Neues Deutschland* (29 July 1971) as reported in: *Yearbook on International
Communist Affairs, 1972,* (Stanford: Hoover Institution Press, 1973), p. 35.
ND is the official party organ of the G.D.R.

[111] Ibid., p. 35.

[112] Program Report of Political Bureau for the 6th PUWP Congress, delivered by
Edward Gierek. Document No. 9, p. 174.

[113] Ibid., p. 176.

In this regard the general secretary's interpretations of peaceful coexistence are particularly revealing:

> It does not mean class peace; it is a form of ideological struggle and manifold confrontation between socialism and imperialism on a global scale. It is also, however, a form of struggle which makes it possible to settle the contradictions between socialism and capitalism without general armed conflict, and at the same time creates broad opportunities for peaceful cooperation between nations.[114]

This shows an apparent effort to tailor the concept of peaceful coexistence (a phrase coined by Khrushchev at the Twentieth CPSU Congress in 1956) to the Nixon initiatives and an awareness of the potential for shifts in the world order.

As we have attempted to illustrate, during 1971 the Soviet Union made major advances in the coordination and political integration of the ruling Communist parties of Group I. Not only were there important shifts in the procedures facilitating coordination, but also, as demonstrated by the foreign policy reports of the party chiefs at their respective party congresses, there seemed to be general substantive agreement among the ruling CPs of Group I with the Soviet world view as expressed by Brezhnev at the Twenty-fourth CPSU Congress. Brezhnev also made marginal gains in his relations with the Cuban, Yugoslav, and Romanian CP political leaderships, though intra-bloc fluidity continued to be an important factor in relations between the ruling CPs.

In the face of the new initiatives being pursued by President Nixon in 1971, Brezhnev was operating more than ever from a position of consolidated rule. The office of CPSU general secretary was in all probability more formidable than it had been at any time since the demise of Khrushchev. Brezhnev was certainly well prepared for the Soviet-American summit planned for 1972.

Intra-bloc Fluidity and Détente: The Response of Group III and Group II in the 1970s. The ruling CPs of Group III have taken the hardest line in their attitudes toward the "imperialist United States," as well as toward the "revisionist, social-imperialist Soviet Union." These views had been enunciated at the Chinese Ninth Party Congress of April 1969 and taken up at the North Korean Fifth Party Congress in November 1970.[115]

---

[114] Ibid., p. 177.
[115] See pp. 36-37 and 44-45 above.

The Albanian Congress. The Group III perception of détente gained clearer resolution at the Albanian Sixth Party Congress, held in Tirana, 1–7 November 1971. By and large, the views of the Albanian Workers' party (AWP), presented by Enver Hoxha in his foreign policy report to the congress, were quite similar to those expressed one year earlier by Kim Il-sung of North Korea. For example, when referring to the P.R.C., Hoxha said, "The triumph of the great proletarian revolution, begun and guided by the great Marxist-Leninist, Comrade Mao Tse-tung, constitutes a victory and a source of inspiration for the entire world revolutionary movement. . . ." [116] Hoxha's perception of the Nixon Doctrine was also strikingly similar to the perception of Kim Il-sung:

> Nixon's new doctrine on the alleged "Vietnamization of the war" and his maneuvers to start "peace negotiations" cannot be met with success. Vietnamization means extension and continuation of the imperialist aggression; it means pitting Vietnamese against Vietnamese, Asians against Asians in order that the American imperialists can dominate, oppress, exploit, and use them as cannonfodder in the interest of their own policy of aggression and hegemony.[117]

The Albanian world view did differ from that of Korea on two very significant points: (1) in its attitude toward the U.S.S.R., and (2) in its attitude toward European security. On the first point, while Kim Il-sung had maintained neutrality toward the Soviets, apparently trying not to antagonize them,[118] Hoxha expressed a vehement disparagement:

> Today we are witnessing the transformation of the revisionist Soviet Union into a chauvinistic and neocolonialist state. . . . The transition of Soviet revisionism to social imperialism, the intensification of its expansionist policy and activity

---

[116] Main report to Sixth Albanian Workers' Party Congress, delivered by Enver Hoxha. Document No. 18, p. 281.

[117] Ibid., p. 286.

[118] This was true to such an extent that a fair case can be made for categorizing North Korea with North Vietnam and Cuba and not including the North Korean CP in Group III. We have chosen to include it in Group III because of the warm professions of friendship for the P.R.C. and its revolution, as well as the apparent similarity in the degree of social mobilization found in North Korea and the other states of Group III. This view is shared by at least one student of North Korea, who noted in a recent article that "North Korea, while carefully refraining from taking sides in the Sino-Soviet dispute, has nevertheless made it plain that, in its eyes, Peking is 'more equal' than Moscow." See B. C. Koh, "The Korean Workers' Party and Détente," *Journal of International Affairs*, vol. 28, no. 2 (1974), pp. 180-181.

gave new tasks to the revolutionary and anti-imperialist forces. . . . The Soviet-American alliance is the biggest counter-revolutionary force opposed to the peoples' struggle for freedom and socialism.[119]

Nearly two-thirds of Hoxha's speech was devoted to such attacks on the policies of U.S. "imperialism" and Soviet "revisionism," referring to them collectively as the greatest enemy of "the true revolution and socialism" represented by the Albanian and Chinese parties.

As for European security, Hoxha claimed that "the conclusion of the Soviet-German treaty has created fresh tension in Europe, provoked by the serious threats of the Soviet revisionists and the German revanchists made against the interests, sovereignty and rights of European countries, by their wish to insure hegemony and domination over our continent." [120] This emphasis stems from concern over the recent changes which had occurred in close geographic proximity to Albania rather than from any ideological divergence from the Korean and Chinese perception.

Perhaps a common concern about potential Soviet encroachment was behind improved Albanian relations with Romania and Yugoslavia. In this regard, the Albanians emphasized that the three nations shared an interest in maintaining the security of the Balkan Peninsula. Thus this point of difference between North Korea and Albania reflected only the individual geographic and political conditions bearing upon each country. Though the two take different positions towards the U.S.S.R., they remain united in their professions of friendship and alliance with the leader of their group, the People's Republic of China.

Developments for the P.R.C. For the P.R.C. itself, the gradual shifts in world order over the seedtime period of the previous two years came to fruition in several significant developments. The Nixon openings to China and the presidential visit of 1972 may have been a significant departure in American policy, but this was even more so the case for China. As might have been expected, the Chinese were criticized by the ruling CPs of Group I, who charged them with collusion with imperialism.[121]

Another event boding a new role for China in the newly emerging world order came in October 1971 when the P.R.C. re-

---

119 Document No. 18, pp. 284-285.

120 Ibid., p. 287.

121 See for example the *Neues Deutschland* editorial cited above, in footnote 110. It also created a trauma for some Maoists outside China. See, for example, H. Bruce Franklin, *The Essential Stalin* (New York: Doubleday & Co., 1972), pp. 1-38. Franklin left the Maoist fold and returned to Stalinism.

placed the Nationalist government on Taiwan as China's representative in the United Nations. With her admission to the UN, the P.R.C. immediately became eligible for admission to a number of international organizations, making her a more active participant in the shifting and indeterminate global structure.

In spite of these developments in late 1971 and the summit meeting of 21–26 February 1972, in their rhetoric the Chinese maintained a firm and "principled" political line. At the Tenth Party Congress, which met in Peking, 24–28 August 1973, Chou En-lai's report deliberately conveyed a strong sense of continuity with the previous Chinese world view as presented by Lin Piao at the Ninth Party Congress in 1969. Although Lin Piao himself was now in disgrace and his name was subjected to the same kind of abuse Lin had heaped on Liu Shao-chi in 1969, the line toward the United States and the Soviet Union remained consistent. After linking the U.S. and the U.S.S.R. together as ambitious hegemonic superpowers, Chou further attacked the U.S.S.R. specifically by linking the "counter-revolutionary conspiratorial clique" of the alleged traitor Lin Piao with Brezhnev, "the chief of the Soviet revisionist renegade clique." To this point Chou argued:

> The essence of the counterrevolutionary revisionist line they pursued and the criminal aim of the counterrevolutionary armed coup d'etat they launched was to usurp the supreme power of the party and the state . . . radically change the party's basic line and policies for the entire historical period of socialism, turn the Marxist-Leninist Chinese Communist party into a revisionist, fascist party, subvert the dictatorship of the proletariat, and restore capitalism. . . . Internationally, they want to capitulate to Soviet revisionist social-imperialism and ally themselves with imperialism, revisionism and reaction to oppose China, communism and revolution.[122]

In response to Soviet-led attacks against China's foreign policy, Chou stressed the general importance of maintaining a correct ideological line: "Chairman Mao teaches us that THE CORRECTNESS OR INCORRECTNESS OF THE IDEOLOGICAL AND POLITICAL LINES DECIDES EVERYTHING. If one's line is incorrect, one's downfall is inevitable. . . . If one's line is correct . . . political power will be gained. . . ."[123] He then explained why the Chinese line

---

[122] Report of the CC CCP to the Tenth Party Congress, delivered by Chou En-lai. Document No. 17, pp. 269-270.
[123] Ibid., pp. 270-271.

was correct with regard to the events of the previous two years: "We should point out here that necessary compromises between revolutionary countries and imperialist countries must be distinguished from collusion and compromise between Soviet revisionism and U.S. imperialism." [124]

Thus in their rhetoric, the Chinese were able to draw distinctions which permitted them to respond to the détente initiatives under the Nixon Doctrine without acknowledging any discontinuity with their established perception of the world. Under the Chinese conception of the infallibility of the party line, once this dual course of action had been rationalized, any seeming contradiction could not be questioned. This dual stance on the part of the leading country of Group III would seem to explain the complete rejection of détente by the two secondary CPs of that group whose support of the Chinese line was unflagging despite the warming of Sino-American relations.

Apparently the P.R.C. has not attempted to coordinate the party congresses of the other ruling CPs of Group III. This probably reflects the lack of the kind of economic integration which helped the U.S.S.R. gain increased control over the ruling CPs of Group I. In spite of this absence of progress towards procedural coordination among the Group III CPs there is a common persistence in maintaining an unswerving foreign policy line.

The recent changes in Sino-American relations and the greater participation of the P.R.C. in world affairs have been looked upon favorably by the ruling CPs of Group II. There are, however, other significant areas in which Yugoslavia and Romania have continued to show those characteristics which differentiate them from Groups I and III.

The 1972 Romanian National Conference. The address to this conference [125] by Secretary General Ceausescu maintained general substantive continuity with the positions of the Tenth Party Congress of August 1969, though in some respects his tone had softened

[124] Ibid., p. 274. The Chinese have always been careful to make it clear that any shifting of alliances would only be temporary and that their political line (world view) was still secure. In an important article published in the September 1971 issue of *Hung Ch'i* (the monthly CC theoretical journal), the Chinese justified their response to the Nixon initiatives by stating that: "Our principles must be firm, [but] we must also have all permissible and necessary flexibility to serve our principles." *Yearbook on International Communist Affairs, 1972*, p. 492.

[125] Conferences generally occur mid-way between party congresses. They offer a forum for discussing the development of domestic and foreign policies as outlined at the previous congress. They differ from party congresses in that normally new five-year plans are not introduced nor are elections held for top party posts. The next Romanian party congress, its eleventh, was held in November 1974.

considerably. While in 1969 Ceausescu had been forthright in his condemnation of the 1968 intervention in Czechoslovakia, his rhetoric in 1972 was less explicit, and he spoke only in general terms regarding what norms ought to operate in the relations among socialist states:

> . . . the relations among the Socialist countries must completely remove all inequality and national oppression, must be based upon full equality of rights, on the mutual observance of national independence and sovereignty. . . . The relations of solidarity and mutual assistance . . . should exclude any interference in the internal affairs; this is one of the basic principles of Marxism-Leninism. . . .[126]

The 1974 Yugoslavian Party Congress. This congress was in close agreement with the Romanian conference of 1972, and Yugoslavia exhibited a similar continuity in its policy by its participation in the Fourth Conference of Non-Aligned Nations, which was held in Algiers in September 1973. This marked twelve years that nonalignment had been at the heart of Yugoslavian policy.[127] In his May 1974 report to the Tenth LCY Congress, Tito again stressed this concept:

> Nonaligned policy . . . is playing a more meaningful role in international relations. At present, over two-thirds of the members of the United Nations are nonaligned and developing countries. . . . Acting in unity, they bring substantial influence to bear on the character and substance and decisions and directions in which the world organization engages its forces.
>
> In terms of its social-historical essence, nonaligned policy is anti-imperialist and anti-hegemonic; consequently it is not

---

[126] Nicolae Ceausescu, Report to the National Conference of the Romanian Communist Party, 19-21 July 1972 in: *Romania on the Way of Building Up the Multilaterally Developed Socialist Society* (Bucharest: Meridiane Publishing House, 1973), p. 517.

[127] What is most interesting to note about this conference is the position of Fidel Castro, which revealed the closeness that had developed between the Cuban CP and the CPSU over recent years. Here he explicitly rejected the position of Group III. Castro said, "The theory of 'two imperialisms,' one headed by the United States and the other allegedly by the Soviet Union . . . is fostered, of course, by those who regrettably betray the cause of internationalism from supposedly revolutionary positions. . . . The revolutionary government of Cuba will always oppose [those] who ignore the glorious, heroic and extraordinary services rendered to the human race by the Soviet people. . . ." See "Inventing a False Enemy Can Have Only One Aim, To Evade the Real Enemy." Document No. 20, p. 309.

and cannot be the instrument of anyone nor can it be something that is held in reserve by any one, or by any other policy.[128]

Clearly, Tito was attempting here to carve out an independent stance midway between the policy positions of the ruling Communist parties of Groups I and III. On the one hand, he assures the Soviets in their own rhetoric that nonalignment is "anti-imperialist"; on the other hand, he adopts Chinese rhetoric in describing his position as "anti-hegemonic." In actively attempting to ply an independent course between Groups I and III—while maintaining good relations with both—Tito showed a definite conciliatory shift from 1969, when the invasion of Czechoslovakia was a fresh memory and the LCY boycotted the Conference of Communist and Workers' Parties.[129]

After this effort toward compromise, Tito nevertheless distanced himself and the LCY from the CPSU in his stress on problems which still existed, and in his conception of the appropriate course for relations among socialist nations. In his emphasis on the "separate roads to socialism" approach, Tito made a criticism of the socialist system which had usually been reserved by the ruling CPs of Groups I and III for the capitalist world: the socialist countries face divisive contradictions. He explained that:

> . . . disproportions in the development of the modern world are manifest also in the development of the socialist countries. . . . Moreover, socialist production relations are also in greater or lesser measure interwoven with different elements of the old and the new. For these reasons, contradictions, and the possibility of conflict, are also present in socialist countries. . . .[130]

For Tito, the problem of overcoming these contradictions becomes the basis for his country's independent policy:

> Socialist countries cannot strengthen their position in the world . . . unless their own mutual relations are based on the principles of equality, independence, mutual respect and noninterference in the internal affairs of others. . . .[131]

---

[128] Report of the CC of the LCY to the Tenth Party Congress, delivered by Josip Broz Tito. Document No. 13, p. 222.

[129] In March-April 1971 they did send a delegation to the Twenty-fourth CPSU Congress, but they explicitly condemned the 1968 invasion of Czechoslovakia.

[130] Report to the Tenth LCY Congress. Document No. 13, p. 220.

[131] Ibid., p. 221.

Tito turned next to détente. In general he was positive about the change in world relations, but his statement also reflected caution:

> Relaxation of tension, negotiation and peaceful settlement of international problems is undoubtedly a positive process, although still very limited and unstable. . . . Détente cannot progress unless it encompasses and solves international economic problems.[132]

The 1974 Romanian Congress. By November 1974, the time of Romania's Eleventh Party Congress, Romanian policy had also become more favorably disposed toward détente, typically paralleling the Yugoslavian viewpoint. Ceausescu's address demonstrated this:

> True, the trend toward détente which has emerged in the past years is only at its beginnings. . . . There still exist zones of tension and conflict, which can lead to military confrontations and to wars with grave consequences for all mankind. . . .
>
> Proceeding from these considerations, we believe that highly responsible steps must be taken to consolidate the trend of détente, to find negotiated solutions to contentious and complex current problems, to promote a policy of peaceful cooperation and equality among all the peoples, to insure peace in the world . . . the events of the past years strongly confirm the real possibility of finding peaceful solutions even for the most complicated problems and situations.[133]

Romanian and Yugoslavian policies show the influence of détente also in the economic sphere. For example, in his address to the Eleventh Party Congress, Ceausescu spoke proudly of the development of new economic and political ties with the West European community as well as with the United States:

> Consistently acting in the spirit of peaceful coexistence, we have continued to expand our cooperation with all states, regardless of social system, including the developed capitalist countries. I want to emphasize with great satisfaction the great development of relations with the European countries, which, after the socialist countries, occupy the most important place in Romania's economic, scientific-technical, and cultural relations. . . . Romania's relations with the United States of America have also greatly developed. . . . Our country's relations with other developed capitalist countries

---

[132] Ibid., p. 132.

[133] Report of the CC RCP to the Eleventh Party Congress, delivered by Nicolae Ceausescu. Document No. 15, pp. 241-242.

have also powerfully developed, and we are determined to continue to expand our economic, cultural, and other exchanges with all these countries.[134]

As the Yugoslavian Tenth Party Congress took a similar policy stance, it would seem that both ruling CPs of Group II have been among the major benefactors of the new era of détente, as demonstrated by the increased substantive flexibility in their economic and political policies.

As the policies and world views of the two CPs of Group II have become more similar, there has been a parallel trend toward procedural coordination of the party congresses of the Romanian and Yugoslavian CPs. As is shown in Table 2, this is a new phenomenon, which only began to become perceptible in the mid-1960s—the timing being coincidental with the assertion of the LCY nonalignment policy and the 1965 change in the RCP political leadership. The Yugoslavs held their Eighth LCY Congress in November 1964, while the Romanians held their Ninth Congress five months later, in May 1965. In 1969 both CPs held congresses, the LCY Ninth Congress was in March and the Tenth RCP Congress five months later, in August. The most recent LCY congress, its tenth, occurred in late May-early June 1974. As might have been expected, the Romanian CP held its next congress, the eleventh, in November, again five months after the Yugoslav congress. This coordination is probably not a matter of conscious control by the LCY, but it is certainly no accident. Most probably it results from spontaneous independent initiatives by the RCP and LCY leaderships, growing out of recognition of the broad areas of common ground which have developed between them.

Increasing unity of purpose between the ruling CPs of Group II, along with the warming of relations of this group with the CPs of Group III, has had a significant effect upon the structure and nature of interparty relations among all three groups of ruling CPs. This has led to a greater fluidity in the nature of world order, resulting in turn in still greater flexibility for the ruling CPs of Group II. This seems to have been one of the more significant results of the new era of détente.

The Soviet Union and Recent Détente Developments

As testimony to the highly integrated nature of Group I, the ruling CPs of this group immediately echoed the Soviet policy shift reflected in the Soviet-American agreement of 1972 and gave unqualified public

---

[134] Ibid., p. 134.

support to the official Soviet position, which welcomed détente with the United States but condemned any Sino-American rapprochement.[135]

Several key developments occurred in 1973, the full consequences of which are yet to be seen. For the Soviets, there were important structural changes at the highest level of government. Though no firm conclusions can be drawn, we can make some suppositions as to the implications of these events. The CC plenum of 26–27 April 1973 seems to have been marked by an intense internal struggle, which was most likely over the direction of Soviet foreign policy and whether Brezhnev would prevail in his determination to lead his country towards détente. The announcement at the end of the plenum of changes in both the size and membership of the Politburo, the organizational pinnacle of Soviet political leadership,[136] indicated that Brezhnev prevailed, and that he had fully consolidated his rule.

Though Brezhnev's plenum report was never published, a lead article appearing in *Pravda* two days after the meeting ended contained a lengthy discussion and summary of the plenum. In addition to general approval of the successful foreign policy that had been pursued by the CPSU under the leadership of Brezhnev since the Twenty-fourth Party Congress, there was specific reference to the new relationship with the United States:

> The Moscow meeting marked a turning point in the development of Soviet-American relations. . . . The document . . . signed . . . on May 29, 1972, lays down a basis for bilateral mutually beneficial cooperation in different fields. It also contains commitments by both sides to do everything possible to avoid military confrontations and avert the outbreak of nuclear war.[137]

In spite of the reiteration of this line towards the United States, in other significant policy areas the Soviet position maintained con-

---

135 For evidence of this, see the various *Foreign Broadcast Information Service* supplements for May and June 1972.

136 Of the fifteen-member Politburo, Shelest and Voronov were retired. There were three promotions to membership status, bringing the size to sixteen. Promoted from candidate membership was Yuri Andropov (chairman of the Committee for State Security, KGB). Also added were Andrei Gromyko (foreign affairs minister) and Andrei Grechko (defense minister), who had not even been candidate members. Such by-passing of normal procedural channels could only have been done under the authority of the general secretary, and testifies to the consolidation of Brezhnev's rule. This was the first time in almost two decades that members of these strategic functional institutions had Politburo membership. The last previous representatives of these institutions on the Politburo were Beria, Molotov, and Zhukov, who left in 1953, 1955, and 1957, respectively.

137 "By the Leninist Course of Peace and Socialism." Document No. 4, pp. 131-132.

tinuity with the past. For example, further on, the same article states:

> The plenary meeting of the CPSU Central Committee drew attention to the necessity of displaying permanent vigilance and readiness and to give a rebuff to the intrigues of the aggressive imperialist circles, of waging a consistent struggle against reactionary ideology and propaganda.[138]

Other CPSU policies receiving continuing support included pursuit of unity among socialist states with emphasis on economic cooperation, as well as condemnation of the anti-Soviet line of the P.R.C.

Having fully consolidated his power within the CPSU and increased the stature of the CPSU among the other ruling CPs of Group I, while simultaneously improving relations with the ruling CPs of Group II, Brezhnev could again be confident of his position as he traveled to Washington in June 1973. From this summit there emerged the Agreement on the Prevention of Nuclear War, as well as a pledge to prevent the outbreak of war generally.

Whatever its concrete achievements, this summit clearly marked a dramatic and symbolic breach with the bipolar era. As the leader of America's chief adversary, it would have been highly unlikely a few years earlier that a general secretary of the CPSU would be allowed to address the American people on national television. In 1973 Brezhnev was encouraged to do so. In his talk, he stressed the special and common responsibilities of the United States and the U.S.S.R.:

> The general atmosphere in the world depends . . . on . . . our two countries. Neither economic nor military might, nor international prestige, gives our countries special privileges; but they do invest them with special responsibility for the destinies of universal peace and for preventing war.[139]

In his turn, President Nixon addressed the Soviet public on their national television. This was a dramatic departure, revealing the extent of the Soviet response to American détente initiatives. Together these speeches symbolized a break with the cold war era.

The Future

It is a premise of this analysis that the world order that emerged at the end of World War II has been breaking down and that we are

---

[138] Ibid., p. 132.

[139] *Pravda* (25 June 1973), translated in *Reports from the Soviet Press*, vol. 16, no. 13 (29 June 1973), p. 18.

now moving into an indeterminate future. Structural factors at work in the Communist world—intra-bloc fluidity, periods of succession crisis, and generational conflict—insure that the future course of behavior of the ruling CPs is open and unpredictable. This is particularly true at present, because the long-time—in fact, original —leaders of the leading CPs of Groups II and III have reached ages which make their replacement likely in the very near future.

The process of détente operating simultaneously with these structural factors has greatly contributed to the demise of the bipolar norm, which had been unquestioned by both sides during the cold war. While structural factors are indeterminate in effect, in that their impact on the future cannot be known, they can nonetheless be recognized, studied, and incorporated into American policy. Still, no matter how consciously we strive to adapt to such identifiable factors, there will always be influences and events which cannot be anticipated and whose true impact will not be recognized until long after they have occurred. For the United States, the events of 1974 are compelling testimony to this.

Within weeks after completing a dramatic round of summitry in Moscow, President Nixon was forced from office because of the Watergate scandal. His resignation, and the subsequent succession of Gerald Ford to the presidency, have created a situation unique to the American experience. For the first time in history there is a man in the White House who has never acquired a national electoral mandate.

While no one questions the legitimacy of his succession, the situation still places a great burden of responsibility on President Ford to build a national constituency. As a result, the United States finds itself in a position which, though fundamentally different in kind, is similar in some respects to those experienced by a Communist state during a period of succession. The problem of consolidation has been compounded for President Ford by the November 1974 elections, which returned large Democratic majorities to both houses of Congress.

As far as détente and relations with the Soviet Union are concerned, it seems clear that Brezhnev and perhaps some of his supporters in the Politburo underestimated the threat Watergate posed to the Nixon presidency. This may explain why they entered into a summit conference with Nixon at what now seems such a late stage of the Watergate crisis.

The mutual need of Brezhnev and Ford to disassociate the policy of détente from the Nixon presidency led to the quickly planned conference at Vladivostok in November 1974 and the announcement of plans for a full-scale summit in the fall of 1975. Brezhnev's interest in continuing the policy of détente must have been reinforced by his desire to mitigate any loss of prestige he may have suffered among top Soviet political leadership through too close an association with a fallen American President. Ford's interest was in demonstrating his capability in foreign affairs and making détente a policy of his presidency.

Whatever the implications within the top Soviet political leadership of Nixon's demise, in early 1975 rumors began to circulate that Brezhnev was in poor health, leading to speculation regarding his possible replacement. The persistence of these rumors suggests several hypotheses: (1) Any weakening of Brezhnev's position could be due to health alone, and if he is indeed in poor health, this would not necessarily mean that any policy shift will accompany his succession. (2) Whether Brezhnev's health is at issue or not, it may be that a deep-seated reaction to the fall of Nixon and/or a belief within the Soviet leadership that a more hostile President may soon occupy the White House has undermined détente and Brezhnev's political base. (3) These rumors may be without basis and Brezhnev may continue at the same level of political power he was enjoying as 1974 began.

Thus the events of 1974 raise serious questions about what can be gained by further negotiation with the Soviets in the present climate of uncertainty. If Brezhnev maintains his position of strength within the CPSU, while President Ford is unable to overcome the problems of his succession, it might perhaps be wiser not to pursue détente initiatives while the United States remains in this comparatively weaker position. On the other hand, if Brezhnev is replaced and a new succession crisis ensues, the American position could become stronger.

If this is the case, the U.S. could capitalize on the workings of the generational factor, which insures that several other successions within the ruling CPs will soon be taking place, increasing fluidity among the ruling CPs. Under any circumstances, the United States could make economic and political overtures [140] to the other ruling CPs, much as the Soviet Union has pursued the policy of détente not just with the U.S., but also with the countries of Western Europe and Japan.[141]

---

[140] See Kaplan, *Rationale for NATO, passim.* Here Kaplan makes the case for a dissuasion strategy in regard to the Warsaw Treaty Organization.

[141] See Vladimir Petrov, *U.S.-Soviet Détente* (Washington, D. C.: American Enterprise Institute, 1975), pp. 26-27.

The importance of economic considerations to Yugoslavia, for instance, has been discussed above. This kind of diplomacy is not as dramatic as great-power summitry, but it potentially could, in the long run, have a more significant impact upon the direction of world order. The Communist states with which such a policy would most likely bear fruit would be those in Group II, Romania and Yugoslavia, and those in Group I, most notably Poland, Hungary, and Czechoslovakia. By pursuing economic and political initiatives with these countries, it might be possible to encourage further fluidity among the ruling CPs, thus preventing them from becoming hardened into immobile economic, political, and military structures, as occurred immediately after World War II.

These policies can only be pursued with a full awareness of the indeterminate nature of world order. The shifts that have occurred so far may be primarily symbolic, but they are significant nonetheless, a fact which must be recognized.[142] Any artificial adherence to the deterministic policies of the cold-war era and the paradigm of rigid bipolarity will blind policy makers to the areas of flexibility and opportunity in a changing world.

It would, of course, be equally dangerous to raise any popular expectations which under present conditions are unlikely to be fulfilled. What is important is realistically to determine what is possible, and from this to determine how to pursue our national interests responsibly. The essential need is for a creative rather than a passive response to a changing world. In light of global economic problems and political tensions in various areas of the world, this is our only hope for making the last quarter of the twentieth century "a generation of peace."

---

[142] An excellent study examining the role of symbolism in politics is Robert J. Pranger's *Action, Symbolism, and Order* (Nashville: Vanderbilt University Press, 1968). See especially Chapters 4-6.

PART TWO
THE DOCUMENTS

2
GROUP ONE

UNION OF SOVIET SOCIALIST REPUBLICS

Document 1: Excerpts from the Report of the CC CPSU to the Twenty-third Congress of the CPSU, Delivered 29 March 1966 by Leonid Brezhnev, First Secretary of the CC CPSU*

THE INTERNATIONAL STATUS OF THE U.S.S.R. THE ACTIVITIES OF THE CPSU IN THE SPHERE OF FOREIGN POLICY

1. The World Socialist System, the Efforts of the CPSU to Strengthen Its Unity and Might

Comrades, work to strengthen the might and cohesion of the socialist community occupies an extremely important place among the multifarious activities of our party and state in the sphere of foreign policy. We regard the socialist community as one of the greatest historical achievements of the world working class; we regard it as the main revolutionary force of our time, the most reliable support for all peoples struggling for peace, national liberty, democracy, and socialism. During the period under review the world socialist system has grown substantially stronger; it has increased its international prestige and its impact on world affairs.

In the sphere of political cooperation between the socialist countries during the period under review, the relations between fraternal

---

*Source: *23rd Congress of the CPSU*, 29 March–8 April 1966 (Moscow: Novosti Press Agency Publishing House, 1966), pp. 11–57.

parties have developed on the basis of Marxism-Leninism, socialist internationalism and mutual support; on the principles of equality, noninterference and mutual respect; and on the principle of the independence of parties and states. In this period our relations with the Communist and workers' parties of the countries of the socialist community and with the socialist states have undoubtedly become better, closer, and more cordial. We have good fraternal relations with the People's Republic of Bulgaria, the Republic of Cuba, the Czechoslovak Socialist Republic, the German Democratic Republic, the Hungarian People's Republic, the Korean People's Democratic Republic, the Mongolian People's Republic, the Polish People's Republic, the Socialist Republic of Romania, the Democratic Republic of Vietnam, and the Socialist Federative Republic of Yugoslavia. Treaties of friendship, cooperation and mutual assistance play a great role in the development of relations between the Soviet Union and other socialist states. . . .

The world socialist system is making steady progress. The basic laws of socialist construction are common to all countries, they are well known and have been tested in practice. Nevertheless, as the socialist countries develop, they are constantly coming up against new problems engendered by the realities of life in all its complexity and variety. It stands to reason that there are no ready-made solutions to these problems, nor can there be any. The development of the world socialist system, therefore requires a constantly creative approach, on the tried and tested basis of Marxism-Leninism, to the problems that arise, [and] it requires the pooling of experience and opinions.

Business-like contacts and political consultations between the leaders of the fraternal parties of socialist countries have developed into a system. During the year and a half that have elapsed since the October (1964) plenum of the CC, members of the Presidium and secretaries of the CC, and many members of the CC CPSU have, on a number of occasions, met leaders of the Communist and workers' parties of almost all the socialist countries for negotiations and detailed talks. . . . Such meetings make it possible to summarize and use, in good time and more fully, all that is worthwhile in the practical activities of each country and of the entire socialist system, to elaborate more successfully the policy of Communist and socialist construction in all our countries and the most correct line in international affairs. . . .

In the sphere of the economic cooperation between socialist countries, our relations have developed and reached a higher level in recent years. Bilateral and multilateral economic relations have been substantially expanded. Trade turnover between socialist countries has greatly increased. Trade turnover with the countries belonging to the Council for Mutual Economic Assistance alone has increased from 5,600 million rubles to 8,500 million rubles in the period under review. A number of measures have been carried out for specialization and cooperation in production on mutually beneficial terms. In the interest of our peoples scientific, technical, and cultural contacts are constantly being multiplied and strengthened. . . .

The economy of the socialist countries is developing more rapidly than that of the countries of the bourgeois world. Suffice it to say that in the period 1961–65, the industrial output of the world socialist system increased by 43 percent and that of the capitalist system by 34 percent. As you see, the difference is substantial and apart from that, industrial growth figures in capitalist countries are not an indicator of higher living standards as they are in the socialist countries, but are primarily evidence of the growing profits of the monopolies and the progressing militarization of capitalist economy.

*   *   *

As far as the CPSU is concerned we shall continue to do all we can to ensure that economic relations with the fraternal socialist countries are extended and strengthened.

In the sphere of military cooperation, there has been a further consolidation of our relations with the socialist countries in the face of growing aggressive acts on the part of the imperialist forces headed by the U.S.A., [and there has been] a strengthening and improvement of the mechanism of the Warsaw Pact. . . . As far as the CPSU is concerned we shall continue to do all we can to extend and consolidate military cooperation of the fraternal socialist countries.

Comrades, cooperation and solidarity are the main sources of the strength of the socialist system. The development and deepening of this cooperation is in accordance with the vital interests of each individual country and of the socialist system as a whole, it promotes the cohesion of our ranks in the struggle against imperialism.

Such cohesion is particularly necessary in the present situation when the U.S. imperialists are escalating their aggression against the Vietnamese people. They have launched an unprovoked attack on the Democratic Republic of Vietnam (D.R.V.), a socialist country. The CPSU is working consistently for united action by all socialist countries in assisting the D.R.V. . . .

The CPSU and the Soviet people fully support the fraternal Korean people who are fighting against U.S. imperialism to unify Korea on a democratic basis. . . .

The heroic people of Cuba, the first American country to carry out a socialist revolution, are fighting and building socialism under difficult circumstances. Cuba is not alone: she is a member of the mighty community of socialist states. . . .

While speaking of the consolidation of the world socialist system, comrades, we must at the same time note that our relations with the parties of two socialist countries, with the Communist party of China and the Albanian Workers' party unfortunately remain unsatisfactory.

Our party and the Soviet people sincerely desire friendship with People's China and its Communist party. We are prepared to do everything possible to improve relations with People's Albania and the Albanian Workers' party.

* * *

We are convinced that our parties and our peoples will ultimately overcome all difficulties and will march side by side in the fight for our common, great revolutionary cause.

The CC CPSU puts forward for the future as *one of the main orientations of the party and the Soviet state in the sphere of foreign policy the development and consolidation of ideological, political, and organizational bonds with the Communist parties of all the socialist countries based on the principles of Marxism-Leninism; the development and consolidation of political, economic, and other bonds between the U.S.S.R. and the socialist states; [and] the promotion in every possible way of the cohesion of the socialist community and the strengthening of its might and influence. The CPSU will do everything in its power to ensure that the world socialist system becomes still more powerful and advances from victory to victory.*

2. Exacerbation of the Contradictions of the Capitalist System. Development of the Class Struggle of the Proletariat

Comrades, in its foreign policy the CC CPSU has paid regard to the processes taking place in the capitalist world. The capitalist system as a whole is gripped by a general crisis. Its inherent contradictions are growing more acute. In their efforts to surmount these contradictions and hold their ground in the struggle against socialism, the bosses of the bourgeois world pinned strong hopes on state regulation of the economy, scientific and technical progress and on greater military production. However, this has not, nor could it [ever] have cured capitalism of its basic ailments. . . .

*   *   *

The law of the uneven economic and political development of capitalist countries is operating implacably; the contradictions between the capitalist states are growing more acute. . . . The U.S. monopolies have taken advantage of this and mounted a fresh offensive in the world markets. . . . The competitive struggle in Western Europe, including the Common Market and other state-monopoly associations, has also become sharper. A process of disintegration has set in the imperialist blocs, as a consequence of the contradictions among the member countries. The United States is no longer able to direct the latters' policy as sweepingly as before. . . . The allies of the United States are becoming increasingly conscious of the dangers involved in blind conformance with Washington policies. Thus, a new area of contradiction and rivalry is appearing within the capitalist world.

Militarization of the economy, the most abhorrent development in the bourgeois world today, must not be overlooked. National riches created by workingmen are being increasingly used for the manufacture of death-dealing weapons, rather than for improving people's lives. . . .

Since NATO was founded, more than $1,000 billion have been spent in building up and improving its war machine. In the twenty postwar years U.S. military expenditures have exceeded those of the twenty years preceding the Second World War forty-eight times over. Today, more than three-quarters of all U.S. federal budget expenditures are being spent directly or indirectly for military purposes. . . . The imperialists would like nothing better than to subjugate many of the independent states and erect barriers to the social progress of mankind. Time and again the course of history is bearing out Lenin's description of American imperialism as a predatory, piratical, and hateful oppressor of the peoples.

As before, the contradiction between labor and capital—the main contradiction of capitalist society—operates to the full extent in the capitalist world. The monopolies are trying to impose greater burdens on the working class and other sections of working people. Never before has the degree of exploitation been so high as now. . . .

*   *   *

Mounting exploitation of the working people is giving impetus to the class struggle. The social battles in capitalist society are growing more bitter. The proletarians of Italy, Japan, France, Belgium, the United States, Great Britain, and other countries have been fighting back staunchly in recent years with strike actions against the monopoly offensive on their standard of living, and on many occasions they have been victorious. Suffice it to say that in the last ten years, the number of people involved in strikes has doubled and now totals some 55 to 57 million annually.

*   *   *

Headed by the Communist parties, who are their vanguard, the proletariat of the capitalist countries are waging an active struggle against war, against the colonial policy of the imperialists, and in support of peoples who have become victims of imperialist aggression. The resounding political successes scored lately by the working class and all the "left" forces of France speak plainly of their increasing influence on the country's social life, and of the growing political maturity of the masses. The working class of Italy is frustrating reactionary attempts at encroaching on the democratic gains of the people. During the period under review there has been a great upsurge in the United States, in the fight against racial discrimination, in the campaign for the civil rights of the 20 million American Negroes. Large sections of the American nation are protesting more and more vigorously against the U.S. aggression in Vietnam.

*   *   *

Times are becoming increasingly difficult for capitalism. Its doom is becoming more and more obvious. . . .

3. The CPSU Works for the Unity of the World Communist Movement

Comrades, a century ago, when Marx and Engels raised the banner of scientific communism, there were no more than a few dozen people in the international organization of the proletariat. [The] Communist League which they founded, was the world's first. That was the time when the world heard the proud word Communist imbued with such deep meaning. This word connotes the supreme truth, the supreme purpose of millions upon millions of workingmen.

Half a centry ago, when our party, led by Vladimir Lenin, marshalled the people to assault capitalism, there were 400,000 Communists in the world. Today, eighty-eight Communist parties in all continents have a membership of nearly 50 million. What is the reason for the steady growth of the Communist ranks, and for their influence? The reason is that the Communists express the basic interests of the working people more fully than anybody else. . . .

Armed with a scientific theory of social development, communism is the only political movement in the world that is able to see clearly the historic prospects of mankind. The general line of the Communist movement, worked out collectively by the fraternal parties at the 1957 and 1960 meetings, is a line for achieving the triumph of peace, democracy, national independence and socialism. It accords with the interests of all mankind. . . .

In the period under review the international activities of the CC CPSU have been imbued with the unchanging desire to strengthen unity and fraternal solidarity with the other Communist and workers' parties and to work with them for implementation of the general line of the world Communist movement.

*   *   *

The Communist parties of the socialist countries are doing immense constructive work. They are resolving the difficult problems of economic development, new social relations and the Communist education of the people, and are providing for the defense of their socialist gains. This work is of historic significance. . . .

The Communist parties in the capitalist countries are heading the struggle of the masses against the monopolies and forging a political revolutionary army in class battles. Today, Communist parties are exerting a strong influence on the entire national life in many of these countries. . . .

In France, Italy, Finland, Belgium, Great Britain, Austria, Denmark and Cyprus, Australia and Canada, India, Ceylon, Syria, Iraq, the Sudan, and the South African Republic, Chile, Uruguay, Argentina, Colombia, Brazil, Ecuador, Mexico and Guatemala, and other countries—wherever Communist parties exist, they are waging a determined struggle for greater influence on the masses, for the interests of the working class and all other working people. More and more, the Communists are winning the sympathies of the people. . . .

The Communists are the most active fighters for the unity of the working-class movement. Lately, distinct headway has been made in the struggle for such unity, although it still encounters considerable difficulties. These are due above all to the right-wing leaders of the social-democratic parties. But it is not these leaders who represent the true interests of the working-class movement. The working class is becoming increasingly conscious of the dangers implicit in the policy of the right-wing social-democratic leaders, who are bent on safeguarding capitalism and maintaining the division in the working-class movement. . . .

The collapse of imperialism's colonial system and the emergence of a large group of young independent states on the world scene confronts the *Communist movement in Asia, Africa, and Latin America* with new tasks. . . .

The Communists tread a thorny path in the countries of the capitalist world, falsely styled "free." Every step made by the Communist movement there involves grim struggle against an experienced, treacherous, and ruthless foe. . . . For many years now, the Communist parties of Spain, Portugal, Greece, West Germany, Venezuela, Peru, the South African Republic, and a number of other countries have had to operate underground. The Communist party of the United States is fighting gallantly in most difficult conditions, withstanding the assault of a giant coercive policy machine, and hounded continuously by anti-Communist ideologists in the pay of the bourgeoisie.

Unable to defeat the Communists in politico-ideological combat, bourgeois reaction resorts to terrorism against the Communist parties and to physical violence against loyal sons of the proletariat and all the working people. The whole of our party and all our nation condemn the anti-Communist terror in Indonesia. . . .

*   *   *

Giving leadership to the class struggle is a great and complicated art; today, it is probably more intricate than ever before. . . . The experience of the revolutionary movement during the last few years has again demonstrated that success is achieved by parties that adhere to the tried and true Leninist principles of strategy and tactics, and take account of the existing situation. Experience shows that deviations from the Marxist-Leninist line either to right or "left" become doubly dangerous when they are combined with nationalism, great-power chauvinism and hegemonic ambition. Communists cannot help drawing the proper conclusions from this.

Comrades, you know that the world Communist movement has run into serious difficulties over the last few years. The attitude of the CPSU on this score is well known to the Congress delegates. We regret deeply that the differences from which none but our common adversaries benefit have not been overcome to this day. This, we believe, goes against the interest of every fraternal party, and against the common interest of the entire world Communist movement. The CPSU believes that it is the duty of all Communists to work for the consolidation of the ranks of our movement. . . .

What concrete ways does our party conceive in the present situation for strengthening the unity of the Communist movement?

In the opinion of the CC CPSU, there is good common Marxist-Leninist ground for closing the Communist ranks, namely, the general line worked out by the 1957 and 1960 meetings of the fraternal parties. Developments since then have put this line to the most exacting test and it has withstood that test. Today there is every reason for saying that loyalty to this line is a dependable guarantee of unity and of new successes in the revolutionary movement.

Greater unity calls for the observance of the collectively defined rules governing relations between parties: those of complete equality and independence, noninterference in each other's internal affairs, mutual support, and international solidarity. . . . The CPSU is opposed to any and all hegemonic trends in the Communist movement. The CPSU stands for truly internationalist relations between all the parties on the basis of equality.

Like the other Marxist-Leninist parties, the CPSU believes that, despite differences, it is possible and necessary to work for united action by the Communists of all countries in the struggle against imperialism, in order to repel its aggressive actions more strongly, in the name of freedom and independence of the nations. The more closely united the worldwide army of Communists, the greater success will be achieved in such important tasks in the contemporary anti-imperialist struggle as the fight to end the U.S. aggression in Vietnam, support of the progressive forces of Africa, Asia, and Latin America against imperialist intrigues, and defense of our brother Communists from reactionary terrorism in some countries.

The conferences and meetings held lately by representatives of Communist parties have served to strengthen the unity of the world Communist movement. Our party attaches great importance to such contacts. In the last eighteen months alone, we have had meetings with more than 200 delegations from sixty fraternal parties. . . . The Central Committee of the CPSU fully shares and supports the fraternal parties' view that international conferences of Communist parties are an important and tested form of securing the international unity of Communists, and holding collective discussions of new problems. We stand for a new conference when the conditions for it are ripe.

. . . Today, at this congress, the CPSU again repeats the appeal to all Communists: Close the ranks tighter for the struggle against the common enemy—imperialism!

Comrades, *the Communist party of the Soviet Union is unswervingly loyal to its internationalist revolutionary duty. From the rostrum of our Congress we assure the representatives of the world*

Communist movement, and through them the Communists of the whole world, that:

The CPSU will work steadfastly for stronger international unity of all the fraternal parties on the basis of the great teaching of Marx-Engels-Lenin in accordance with the line worked out collectively by the world Communist movement.

We shall continue our determined struggle against revisionism, dogmatism, and nationalist tendencies, and shall promote the creative development of the Marxist-Leninist teaching.

Our party will continue to promote the creative development of the Marxist-Leninist teaching.

Our party will continue to promote the line for joint action by the Communist parties of the world in the struggle against imperialism for the great goals of peace, democracy, and national independence, for socialism and communism.

4. Development of the National Liberation Movement. Our Party's Support of the National Liberation Struggle

Comrades, all these years the CC CPSU has consistently followed a policy of giving every possible support to the struggle of the peoples against colonial oppression and promoting all-round cooperation with the newly free countries on a basis of equality, strict respect for sovereignty and noninterference in one another's internal affairs.

In the past few years the cause of national liberation has made considerable progress. The world has witnessed the emergence of another seventeen independent states, including the Algerian People's Democratic Republic, Kenya, Uganda, Tanzania, and Zambia. Almost the whole of Asia and Africa have now shaken off the yoke of colonial slavery. This is a great gain in the peoples' liberation struggle against imperialism.

But there are still countries in the world today where the imperialists are seeking by force of arms to preserve the shameful colonial system. In Angola and Mozambique, in "Portuguese" Guinea and in South Arabia patriots are heroically fighting the foreign enslavers and invaders. In South Africa and in Southern Rhodesia the resistance of the people to the racist regimes is mounting. Our party and the entire Soviet people actively support this struggle; we are giving effective all-round assistance to peoples fighting against foreign invaders for freedom and independence and shall continue to do so. We are firmly convinced that the day is not far distant when the last remnants of colonialism will be destroyed and the peoples will raise the banner of national freedom in the liberated territories. That is the sentence passed by history, and it is irrevocable.

The peoples of the countries that have won state independence are working to abolish the grim aftermaths of colonial rule. These countries have vast natural resources. Nevertheless, on a population basis, output is only one-fortieth to one-twentieth that of the economically developed countries. But the peoples who have achieved independence are fully determined to overcome their age-old backwardness.

The new life in the liberated countries is burgeoning in fierce combat with imperialism, in a sharp struggle between the forces of progress and the forces of internal reaction. Some social strata, supported by imperialism, are trying to direct the development of the liberated countries along the capitalist road. Others, expressing the interests of the bulk of the people, are working to promote development along the road of social progress and genuine national independence.

*   *   *

It should be borne in mind that to this day many of the newly free countries are subjected to economic exploitation and political pressure by imperialism, which has not reconciled itself to its defeats. It is doing everything it can to preserve the possibility of exploiting the peoples, and is resorting to new and craftier methods.

The capitalist monopolies still have considerable control over the economy and resources of many of the developing countries in Asia, Africa, and Latin America and are continuing ruthlessly to pillage them. The U.S.A., Great Britain, and other Western powers are draining nearly $6,000 million a year out of these countries as profits on capital investments.

Wherever they can, the imperialists try to utilize the internal contradictions in the newly free countries. . . . The imperialists ignore the national sovereignty of the newly free countries. They cynically lay claim to the right of intervening, by force of arms, in the internal affairs of other peoples. . . .

All this is a manifestation of the policy of neocolonialism, the struggle against which the whole of progressive mankind regards as one of its cardinal tasks. There is no doubt whatever that the people who have risen to fight for independence will carry this struggle on until final victory is achieved, and will oppose all attempts to reenslave them.

The CC CPSU informs the Congress with satisfaction that in the past few years our relations with the overwhelming majority of the independent countries of Asia and Africa have developed success-fully. There has been a considerable extension of trade, economic, and cultural cooperation between the U.S.S.R. and these countries. Nearly 600 industrial, agricultural, and other projects are being built in Asian and African countries with the aid of our design organizations and with the participation of Soviet building specialists. Soviet geological surveying teams are working in many of these countries, in jungles and sun-scorched deserts, helping the young countries to explore their mineral resources and make them serve their national economies.

More than 100 educational and medical institutions, as well as research centers, have been built or are under construction in these countries with Soviet assistance. The number of students from Asian, African, and Latin American countries studying at Soviet institutions of higher learning and technical schools has almost doubled in the past five years. The number of Soviet teachers, doctors, and other specialists in the cultural field now working in twenty-eight Asian and African countries has increased fourfold. . . .

Our party and government are also rendering all possible sup-port to the newly free countries in the international arena as well. The U.S.S.R. actively opposes imperialist interference in the internal affairs of the young national states. . . .

Comrades, an important development of the past few years has been the emergence of a number of newly free countries on the road of progressive social development. Experience has thereby confirmed the conclusion drawn by the 1960 Moscow meeting of Communist and workers' parties, and recorded in its statement: the masses "are beginning to see that the best way to abolish age-old backwardness and improve their living standard is that of noncapitalist develop-ment. Only in this way can the peoples free themselves from exploita-tion, poverty, and hunger."

Major social reforms have been carried out in such countries as the United Arab Republic, Algeria, Mali, Guinea, the Congo (Brazza-ville) and Burma. Foreign monopolies are being driven out. . . . The revolutionary creative work of the peoples who have proclaimed socialism as their objective is introducing features of its own into the forms of the movement towards social progress.

We have established close, friendly relations with the young countries steering a course towards socialism. Naturally, the further these countries move towards the objective they have chosen, the more versatile, profound, and stable our relations with them will become. The relations between the CPSU and the revolutionary democratic parties of these countries are likewise developing.

. . . Recent developments show that the reactionary forces have become more active, particularly in the African continent. . . . Special mention must [also] be made of the courageous liberation struggle of the peoples of Latin America. Only recently the U.S.A. regarded Latin America as a reliable bastion. Today in every country in that continent the people are waging a struggle against U.S. imperialism and its accomplices. . . .

An important factor of our day is the consolidation of the unity of the Asian, African, and Latin American peoples in the struggle against imperialism. . . .

Comrades, *the Communist Party of the Soviet Union regards as its internationalist duty [the] continued all-around support of the peoples' struggle for final liberation from colonial and neocolonial oppression.*

Our party and the Soviet state will continue to:

Render the utmost support to the peoples fighting for their liberation and work for the immediate granting of independence to all colonial countries and peoples.

Promote all-around cooperation with countries that have won national independence and help them to develop their economy, train national cadres and oppose neocolonialism.

Strengthen the fraternal links of the CPSU with the Communist parties and revolutionary democratic organizations in Asian, African, and Latin American countries.

The successes of the national liberation movement are inseparably bound up with the successes of world socialism and the international working class. The firm and unbreakable alliance of these great revolutionary forces is the guarantee of the final triumph of the cause of national and social liberation.

5. Struggle of the Soviet Union Against the Aggressive Policy of Imperialism for Peace and World Security

Comrades, in foreign relations the Soviet Union has consistently pursued a policy of peace—a policy that springs from the very nature of our state which always acts in the interests of the people. The foundation for this policy was laid by Lenin, and we steadfastly adhere to the Leninist approach to foreign affairs.

The years that have elapsed since the Twenty-second Congress of the CPSU [1961] have witnessed a tense struggle between two opposing trends in the international arena: the peace-loving and the aggressive. Alongside other socialist countries, the Soviet Union has pursued a policy aimed at relaxing tension, strengthening peace, [and] achieving peaceful coexistence of states with different social systems. . . .

On the other hand, these years have seen a still more glaring manifestation of the aggressive nature of imperialism, and the threat it constitutes to peace and to the freedom and independence of nations. The imperialists have brazenly interfered in the affairs of other countries and peoples, even going so far as to engage in armed intervention. As a result there has been an exacerbation of world tension. The threat of war from the aggressive acts of the imperialists, particularly the U.S. imperialists, has increased.

* * *

We have always sided with peoples subjected to imperialist aggression and have rendered them political, economic and, when necessary, military aid; we have exposed the perfidious designs of the aggressors. . . .

In speaking of mounting world tension and of the threat of a world war, special mention must be made of U.S. imperialist aggression against Vietnam. In flagrant violation of the Geneva Agreements, the U.S.A. has piratically attacked the Democratic Republic of Vietnam and is waging a barbarous war against the people of South Vietnam. . . . More than 200,000 U.S. troops, U.S. aircraft carriers, huge bombers, poison gases, and napalm are being used against the heroic patriots of Vietnam. Irresponsible statements threatening to escalate military operations still further are being made in Washington. Recently the U.S. State Department officially declared that there is a program for destroying vegetation and crops in Vietnam with chemicals in order to deprive the Vietnamese of food sources. Such is the real face of U.S. imperialism. Through its aggression in Vietnam the U.S. has covered itself with shame which it will never live down.

* * *

The Soviet Union and the peace-loving peoples of the whole world demand that the U.S.A. stop its aggression against Vietnam and withdraw all interventionist troops from that country. Continuation of this aggression, which the American military are seeking to extend to other Southeast Asian countries, is fraught with the most dangerous consequences to world peace.

* * *

As a consequence of U.S. aggression in Vietnam and other aggressive acts of American imperialism our relations with the United

States of America have deteriorated. The U.S. ruling circles are to blame for this.

The U.S.S.R. is prepared to live in peace with all countries, but it will not reconcile itself to imperialist piracy with regard to other peoples. We have repeatedly declared that we are prepared to develop our relations with the U.S.A., and our stand in this has not changed. But for these relations to develop, the U.S.A. must drop its policy of aggression. Good fruit of peaceful cooperation cannot be grown on the poisonous soil of aggression and violence. Our party and our government categorically reject the absurd standpoint that the great powers can develop their relations at the expense of the interests of other countries and peoples. All countries, big and small, have the same right to respect of their sovereignty, independence and territorial integrity. And nobody has the liberty to violate this right.

Comrades, the Soviet Union is vitally interested in ensuring European security. Today West German imperialism is the U.S.A.'s chief ally in Europe in aggravating world tension. West Germany is increasingly becoming a seat of war danger where revenge-seeking passions are running high. West Germany already has a large army in which officers of the Nazi Wehrmacht form the backbone. Many leading posts in the government are occupied by former Nazis and even war criminals. The policy pursued by the Federal Republic of Germany is being increasingly determined by the same monopolies that brought Hitler to power.

*   *   *

U.S. and West German imperialism are a peculiar sort of partners. Each wants to make use of the other for his own designs. Both seek to aggravate tension in Europe—each in accordance with his own considerations. The West German militarists entertain the hope—an unrealizable hope of course—that this will enable them to carry out their revenge-seeking plans. The U.S.A., for its part, wants some pretext to enable it, more than twenty years after the war, to continue keeping its troops and war bases in Europe and thereby have the means of directly influencing the economies and policies of the West European countries.

*   *   *

. . . Today, therefore, the struggle against the threat of another war is the vital affair of all European peoples. Even in West Germany itself more and more people are protesting against the bellicose policy of the Bonn rulers. . . . The balance of forces in Europe today is not at all what it was like on the eve of the Second World War. Nobody will succeed in changing the present frontiers of the European countries. . . .

*   *   *

We will never agree to, nor reconcile ourselves to the West German militarists obtaining nuclear weapons. . . . Nobody has the right to forget that after the defeat of the Nazi aggressors, the participants in the anti-Hitler coalition—the Soviet Union, the U.S.A., Great Britain, and France—solemnly pledged themselves under the Potsdam agreement to do everything necessary to prevent Germany from ever again threatening her neighbors and to preserve peace throughout the world. The Soviet Union will always honor this commitment.

We highly value the fact that our friend and ally, the German Democratic Republic, the first socialist state of the German working people, is vigilantly defending peace in the heart of Europe. It has implemented in practice the peace-loving and democratic principles of the Potsdam agreement and is consistently pursuing a policy of peace and advocating the strengthening of security in Europe.

As a whole, comrades, the positions of the socialist community in Europe are now firm and reliable. This is an important factor helping to consolidate socialism throughout the world and ensuring the security of all peoples. As a counterbalance to the bellicose and the revenge-seeking policy of U.S. and West German imperialism in Europe the Soviet Union is consistently advocating the strengthening of European security and peaceful, mutually advantageous cooperation among all European states.

*   *   *

Comrades, while exposing the aggressive policy of imperialism we are consistently and unswervingly pursuing a policy of peaceful coexistence of states with different social systems. This means that while regarding the coexistence of states with different social systems as a form of the class struggle between socialism and capitalism, the Soviet Union consistently advocates normal, peaceful relations with capitalist countries, and a settlement of controversial interstate issues by negotiation, not by war. The Soviet Union firmly stands for noninterference in the internal affairs of other countries, for respect of their sovereign rights and the inviolability of their territories.

It goes without saying that there can be no peaceful coexistence where matters concern the internal processes of the class and national liberation struggle in the capitalist countries or in the colonies. Peaceful coexistence is not applicable to the relations between oppressors and the oppressed; [it is not applicable] between colonialists and the victims of colonial oppression.

As regards state relations of the U.S.S.R. with capitalist countries, we want these relations to be not only peaceful, but also to include the broadest mutually advantageous contacts in the economic, scientific, and cultural fields.

* * *

The U.S.S.R. has always attached great importance to relations with neighboring countries and we are pleased to note that our good-neighbor policy has yielded beneficial results Our relations with Finland and Afghanistan are characterized by trust, friendship, and cooperation. Normal relations are taking shape with the Scandinavian countries, although it cannot be said, of course, that there are no obstacles to their further development. The Soviet people welcome the certain turn for the better that has taken place in recent years in the Soviet Union's relations with Turkey and Iran.

The CC CPSU and the Soviet government have always paid great attention to improving relations with such major Asian countries as India and Pakistan, which can virtually be considered our neighbors as well. In the period under review, our traditional, time-tested friendship with India and her great people has been further consolidated. There has likewise been an improvement in our relations with Pakistan.

* * *

The Soviet Union has always favored the development of friendly relations with Indonesia. The Indonesian revolution made a noteworthy contribution to the anti-imperialist struggle of the peoples. . . .

The Soviet Union supports Cambodia, a country friendly to us, in her just struggle to preserve and strengthen her independence, neutrality and territorial integrity.

There has been a considerable improvement in our relations with France. . . . Further development of Soviet-French relations may serve as an important element in strengthening European security.

In recent years our relations, particularly in the economic field, with such a major European country as Italy have begun to improve. We are prepared to develop these relations. An activation of Soviet-British relations would [also] undoubtedly be useful. . . .

We can note that lately there has been a certain advance in our relations with Japan, with whom we are developing mutually advantageous economic ties. But we cannot help taking into account the fact that there are U.S. troops and war bases on Japanese territory in the immediate proximity of Soviet frontiers. . . . All this, of course, hampers the development of our relations with Japan.

The dismantling of foreign military bases on alien territory and the withdrawal of foreign troops from such territory have been and remain a major international issue. The imperialist powers, primarily the United States of America, have established numerous military bases scattered throughout the world and have stationed contingents of their armed forces on the territories of other countries. . . . The Soviet Union considers that it is high time to end this situation which threatens the peace and security of countries, high time to dismantle military bases on foreign territory and withdraw foreign armed forces from this territory. . . .

In furtherance of the vital interests not only of the Soviet people but also of the broadest masses in all countries the Soviet Union is waging a consistent struggle to slow down and stop the arms race started by the imperialists, to reach agreement on practical steps towards general and complete disarmament. . . .

In the period under review the U.S.S.R. has continued to take an active part in the work of the United Nations. The admittance of many newly free countries to U.N. membership has substantially changed the situation in that organization, and the change has not been in favor of the imperialists. . . . We shall continue to regard the U.N. as an arena of active political struggle against aggression, for peace and the security of all peoples.

The Communist party of the Soviet Union considers that at this stage in the struggle for an improvement of the international situation, and for the consolidation of peace and the development of peaceful cooperation among nations it would be most important to achieve the following:

> To put an end to U.S. aggression in Vietnam, . . .
> To ensure strict adherence to the principle of noninterference in the internal affairs of states.
> To conclude an international treaty on the nonproliferation of nuclear weapons; to completely remove the question of the nuclear armament of the F.R.G. or of giving it access to nuclear weapons in any form; to implement the aspiration of the peoples for setting up nuclear-free zones in various parts of the world; to secure a solemn obligation on the part of the nuclear powers to refrain from using nuclear weapons first; to reach an agreement on the banning of underground nuclear tests. . . .

To initiate talks on European security; to discuss the proposals of socialist and other European countries for a relaxation of military tension and a reduction of armaments in Europe, and the development of peaceful, mutually advantageous relations between all European countries; to convene an appropriate international conference for this purpose; to continue to look for ways to a peaceful settlement of the German problem—one of the cardinal problems of European security. . . .

Such are our proposals. Many of them have been put forward earlier. Naturally, we do not regard them as all-embracing and are prepared to give our closest attention to all other proposals aimed at improving the international situation and strengthening peace.

Comrades, we have every reason to declare that our country's international position is stable. . . . The quicker our country moves forward in building the new society the more successfully will our international tasks be resolved. By the will of history the Land of Soviets was the first in the world to raise the banner of Communist construction. The Soviet people led by their Leninist Communist party will continue with honor to hold aloft this great, invincible banner.

Document 2: Excerpts from "Tasks at the Present Stage of the Struggle Against Imperialism and United Action of the Communist and Workers' Parties and All Anti-Imperialist Forces," the Main Report of the Conference of Communist and Workers' Parties, Adopted 17 June 1969*

The Conference of representatives of Communist and Workers' parties took place in Moscow at a very important juncture in world development. Powerful revolutionary processes are gathering momentum throughout the world. Three mighty forces of our time—the world socialist system, the international working class, and the national liberation movement—are coming together in the struggle against imperialism. The present phase is characterized by growing possibilities for a further advance of the revolutionary and progressive forces. At the same time, the dangers brought about by imperialism, by its policy of aggression, are growing. Imperialism, whose general crisis is deepening, continues to oppress many peoples and remains a constant threat to peace and social progress.

The existing situation demands united action of Communists and all other anti-imperialist forces so that maximum use may be made of the mounting possibilities for a broader offensive against imperialism—against the forces of reaction and war.

The conference discussed urgent tasks of the struggle against imperialism and problems of united action by Communists and all other anti-imperialist forces. As a result of the discussion, held in a spirit of democracy, equality, and internationalism, the participants in the conference reached common conclusions concerning the present world situation and the tasks arising from it.

I

Mankind has entered the last third of our century in a situation marked by a sharpening of the historic struggle between the forces of progress and reaction, between socialism and imperialism. This clash is worldwide and embraces all the basic spheres of social life: economy, politics, ideology, and culture.

. . . It has been possible to prevent the outbreak of a world war thanks to the growing economic, political, and military might, and the peace-loving foreign policy of the Soviet Union and other socialist

---

* Source: *Conference of Communist and Workers' Parties* (Moscow: Novosti Press Agency Publishing House, 1969), pp. 9-68.

states; [thanks] to the actions of the international proletariat and of all fighters against imperialism; to the struggle for national liberation; and also to the massive peace movement. . . . The events of the past decade bear out that the Marxist-Leninist assessment of the character, content, and chief trends of the present epoch is correct. Ours is an epoch of transition from capitalism to socialism.

At present there are real possibilities for resolving key problems of our time in the interests of peace, democracy, and socialism, [and] to deal imperialism new blows. However, while the world system of imperialism has not grown stronger, it remains a serious and dangerous foe. The United States of America, the chief imperialist power, has grown more aggressive.

* * *

The spearhead of the aggressive strategy of imperialism continues to be aimed first and foremost against the socialist countries. Imperialism does not forego open armed struggle against socialism. It ceaselessly intensifies the arms race and tries to activate the military blocs organized for aggression against the Soviet Union and other socialist countries. It steps up its ideological fight against them and tries to hamper the economic development of the socialist countries.

In its actions against the working-class movement imperialism violates democratic rights and freedoms and uses naked violence, brutal methods of police persecution and antilabor legislation . . . and is constantly in quest of new methods to undermine the working-class movement from within and "integrate" it into the capitalist system.

In its struggle against the national liberation movement, imperialism stubbornly defends the remnants of the colonial system on the one hand, and on the other, uses methods of neocolonialism in an effort to prevent the economic and social advance of developing states—countries which have won national sovereignty. . . .

The gulf between the highly developed capitalist states and the majority of the other countries of the capitalist world is growing wider; hunger is an acute problem in a number of the latter. Imperialism provokes friction in developing countries and sows division between them by encouraging reactionary nationalism. . . .

Through military-political blocs, military bases in foreign countries, economic pressure, and trade blockades, imperialism maintains tension in some areas of the world. . . .

In face of the strengthening of the international positions of socialism, imperialism tries to weaken the unity of the world socialist system. It uses the differences in the international revolutionary movement in an effort to split its ranks. It places its ideological apparatus, including mass media, in the service of anti-communism and its struggle against socialism [and] all progressive forces.

In these past years, imperialism has time and again provoked sharp international crises which have pushed humanity to the brink of a thermonuclear conflict. However, U.S. imperialism has to take into account the relationship of forces in the world, the nuclear potential of the Soviet Union, and the possible consequences of a nuclear-missile war, and it is becoming more and more difficult and dangerous for it to gamble on another world war. Therefore the ruling circles of the United States, without abandoning preparations for such a war, lay emphasis on local wars.

However, the contradiction between the imperialist "policy of strength" and the real possibilities for imperialism is becoming ever more evident. *Imperialism can neither regain its lost historical initiative nor reverse world development. The main direction of mankind's development is determined by the world socialist system, the international working class, [and] all revolutionary forces.*

The war in Vietnam is the most convincing proof of the contradiction between imperialism's aggressive plans and its ability to put these plans into effect. In Vietnam, U.S. imperialism, the most powerful of the imperialist partners, is suffering defeat, and this is of historic significance. The armed intervention in Vietnam holds a special place in the military and political designs of U.S. imperialism. . . .

*   *   *

. . . The criminal intervention in Vietnam has resulted in considerable moral and political isolation of the United States. It has turned ever broader masses of people, new social strata and political forces against imperialism, and speeded up the involvement of millions of young people in many countries in the anti-imperialist struggle. It has aggravated existing contradictions between the imperialist powers and created new ones. . . .

In the *Middle East* a grave international crisis has been precipitated by the Israeli aggression against the United Arab Republic, Syria, and Jordan. Through this aggression, imperialism—that of the U.S. above all—tried to crush the progressive regimes in the Arab countries, undermine the Arab liberation movement, and preserve or regain its positions in the Middle East. This it has failed to do. Nevertheless, supported by world reaction, including Zionist circles, the ruling forces of Israel continue to ignore the demands of the Arab states and of the peace-loving peoples, and the U.N. decisions on the withdrawal of Israeli troops from the occupied territories, persist in their policy of expansion and annexation, and ceaselessly commit fresh armed provocations. This policy is opposed by the Communist party and other progressive forces within Israel. . . .

*   *   *

U.S. imperialism has not abandoned its plans to strangle revolutionary *Cuba*. It continues to threaten the independence of the Republic of Cuba and in flagrant contravention of international law, tries to blockade it economically, and carries on provocative and subversive activity against it. . . .

In *Europe*, the North Atlantic bloc, the chief instrument of imperialist aggression and adventurism, continues to be active. The axis of this bloc is the alliance between Washington and Bonn. . . . West German militarism, the main source of the war danger in the heart of Europe, was revived and grew strong mainly with NATO assistance. . . .

The *Mediterranean* countries occupy an important place in the plans of imperialism. U.S. imperialism, which has important military bases in Spain, continues to support the Franco regime, thereby helping it to survive in opposition to the struggle of the fighting Spanish people. . . . The repeated exacerbation of the situation in Cyprus and the fascist coup in Greece are likewise the handiwork of the imperialists, who support the colonels' junta.

Southeast Asia and the Far East are one of the main areas of imperialist aggression and military gambles. In addition to SEATO, ANZUS, and the so-called Security Treaty between the United States and Japan, there is the virtual occupation of the Southwest Pacific and the Indian Ocean by U.S. armed forces. This entire system is spearheaded primarily against the national liberation movement, as well as against the neutral and nonaligned states in this area. The U.S. imperialists continue to occupy Taiwan, which is an integral part of the People's Republic of China, and obstruct the restoration of China's lawful rights in the United Nations. The U.S. imperialists continue armed provocations against the Korean People's Democratic Republic and the military occupation of South Korea. They exercise arbitrary rule, suppressing [the] progressive forces striving for freedom and the unification of the country. They commit acts of aggression against Laos and provocations against Cambodia. They have set up and are enlarging strong military bases in Thailand. They persist in their attempt to pressure India into abandoning her path of nonalignment and independent economic development. The imperialists supported the anti-popular coup in Indonesia. . . .

Imperialism has become more active in a number of *African* countries. It tries to halt the growth of the liberation struggle and preserve and strengthen its positions in that continent. . . . The armed intervention in the Congo (Kinshasa), the reactionary coups in Ghana and some other countries, moves designed to dismember Nigeria, [and] support for the fascist and racialist regimes in the Republic of South Africa and southern Rhodesia . . . all serve to further imperialist plans. The Portuguese colonialists, backed by NATO, try to keep their possessions by force of arms.

U.S. imperialism continues to step up its economic penetration, as well as its political, ideological and cultural intervention in the *Latin American* countries. . . . To promote this policy the U.S. imperialists put forward the Alliance for Progress program and resort to new, camouflaged forms of domination [such as] the Organization of American States and the Inter-American military alliance, and the proposed "Inter-American Peace Forces," and have arrogated the right to military intervention against any Latin American country as they have done against the Dominican Republic and against Panama. . . .

* * *

This policy of imperialist aggression which threatens world peace and the security and independence of nations is facing growing resistance in the capitalist countries from the working class, peasantry, young people, [and] students—from the broadest masses irrespective of their political views and ideology. . . .

* * *

In Western Europe the movement against the aggressive NATO bloc, for the normalization of relations and the development of cooperation between states and for safeguarding European security, encompasses ever wider strata of the population. . . .

The Latin American peoples are fighting against oppression and brazen interference of U.S. imperialism in their internal affairs. The strike movement of the workers, the actions of peasants, students and other strata show that broad masses throughout the continent are intensifying resistance to the dictates of the U.S.A. and its military designs. . . .

* * *

The events of the past decade have laid bare more forcefully than ever the nature of U.S. imperialism as a world exploiter and gendarme, as the sworn enemy of liberation movements. The U.S. monopolies have penetrated the economies of dozens of countries, where they are increasing their capital investments and seeking to gain control of key positions.

West German imperialism is increasing its economic strength, building up its war machine, reaching out for nuclear weapons and intensifying its drive for domination over Western Europe . . . [moreover,] despite the weakening of British imperialism, Britain remains one of the major imperialist powers and strives to maintain its positions in Africa, Asia, the Caribbean, and the Middle East by neo-colonialist methods and sometimes by direct military intervention. . . .

Japanese imperialism is [also] gaining in strength, intensifying its expansion, especially in Asia. Militarism is again rearing its head in Japan. . . .

French imperialism tries to maintain and consolidate its positions in world economy and politics. It persistently continues to build up a nuclear strike force and refuses to join in measures that would promote disarmament. . . . Italian monopoly capital is likewise stepping up its expansion.

Economic development is becoming more uneven among the various imperialist powers and in the capitalist world as a whole. Life demonstrates the correctness of the Marxist-Leninist theory of struggle between the imperialist powers and between the capitalist monopolies for spheres of influence. Industrial and commercial competition is growing sharper, and the financial war is spreading. . . .

The inter-imperialist contradictions are manifest not only in the economic sphere. NATO is also undergoing a serious crisis. The aggressive blocs established in Asia—CENTO and SEATO—are beginning to crack up. Western Europe is becoming an arena of discord among the capitalist countries. This weakens the world system of imperialism and upsets U.S. imperialism's plans for hegemony.

Contradictions are also growing deeper within the ruling circles of the imperialist countries. . . . The ruling circles of some countries realize the need to reckon with the real situation which has taken shape in Europe as a result of the war and of postwar development and are beginning to see that the German Democratic Republic must be recognized. A number of countries have recognized the Democratic Republic of Vietnam and the People's Republic of China despite U.S. pressure. The Communist and workers' parties, the working class, and the anti-imperialist forces take into account all the contradictions in the enemy camp and strive to deepen and utilize them in the interest of peace and progress.

Each imperialist power pursues its own aims. At the same time, together they form the chain of the world system of imperialism. Present-day imperialism . . . has some new features. Its state-monopoly character is becoming more pronounced. It resorts ever more extensively to such instruments as state-stimulated monopolistic concentration of production and capital, redistribution by the state of an increasing proportion of the national income, allocation of war contracts to the monopolies, government financing of industrial development and research programs, the drawing up of economic development programs on a countrywide scale, the policy of imperialist integration, and new forms of capital export.

... Practically no capitalist state has been able to avoid considerable cyclical fluctuations and slumps in its economy; in some countries, periods of rapid industrial growth alternate with periods in which there is a slowdown and often a drop in production. The capitalist system is in the grip of an acute monetary and financial crisis.

* * *

The scientific and technological revolution accelerates the socialization of the economy; under monopoly domination this leads to the reproduction of social antagonisms on a growing scale and in a sharper form. . . .

* * *

The instability of the capitalist system has increased. Sociopolitical crises are breaking out in many countries, in the course of which the working masses are becoming aware of the necessity of deep-going and decisive changes.

This became primarily evident from the events in France in May and June 1968, from the powerful strike movement there, in which the Communists played an important role and the working people made considerable gains. . . .

In Italy, [there has been] the steady growth of the strike movement on a national scale. . . .

In Spain, the struggle of the masses continues to undermine the fascist dictatorship of Franco. . . .

In Great Britain, major class battles are unfolding, including political strikes in defense of the trade unions and of the right to strike, which are under attack by the Labor government.

Class battles, strikes, and other actions by the working people, students, and other social segments have been stepped up in Japan, Mexico, Brazil, Argentina, the Federal Republic of Germany, Uruguay, Belgium, Portugal, Chile, India, Pakistan, Turkey, and other countries and also in West Berlin. . . . Democratic front governments with the participation of Communists, have been formed in some states of India. In Finland, the Communists take part in the government.

Moreover, the depth of the crisis in the capitalist world is also strikingly revealed by the advance of the mass struggle in the United

States itself—that main pillar of world imperialism. A wave of rebellions against racial discrimination, poverty, starvation, and police brutality has swept the Negro ghettoes. . . .

In the U.S.A. militant strikes for economic demands take place often in defiance of government pressure and threats, and contrary to the will of reactionary trade union officials. . . .

Intellectual, professional and religious circles in the U.S.A. are becoming more and more active in the movement of social protest and for peace. Young people, students in particular, black and white, are in revolt in different ways against the Vietnam War, military conscription, racism, and monopoly control of universities. Reaction replies to this with the assassination of public figures, mounting repression, and massive violence. The notorious "American way of life" is being discredited in the eyes of the world.

Everywhere the monopoly bourgeoisie tries to create the illusion that everything the working people aspire to can be achieved without a revolutionary transformation of the existing system. To conceal its exploiting and aggressive nature, capitalism resorts to theoretical whitewash—"people's capitalism," the "welfare state," the "affluent society," et cetera. . . .

The conscience and intellect of mankind cannot be reconciled with the crimes of imperialism. Imperialism bears the guilt for two world wars which snuffed out the lives of tens of millions of people. It has created a gigantic military machine which devours tremendous human and material resources. . . . Imperialism gave birth to fascism— the system of political terror and death camps. . . .

Imperialism is responsible for the hardship and suffering of hundreds of millions of people. It is chiefly to blame for the fact that vast masses of people in Asian, African and Latin American countries are compelled to live in conditions of poverty, disease, and illiteracy and under archaic social relations, [as well as for the fact] that entire nationalities are doomed to extinction.

*   *   *

The working class, the democratic and revolutionary forces, [and] the peoples must unite and act jointly in order to put an end to imperialism's criminal actions which can bring still graver suffering to mankind. To curb the aggressors and liberate mankind from imperialism is the mission of the working class—of all the anti-imperialist forces fighting for peace, democracy, national independence and socialism.

95

II

The world socialist system is the decisive force in the anti-imperialist struggle. Each liberation struggle receives indispensable aid from the world socialist system, above all from the Soviet Union.

The Great October Socialist Revolution; the building of socialism in the Soviet Union; the victory over German fascism and Japanese militarism in the Second World War; the triumph of the revolution in China and in several other countries in Europe and Asia; the emergence of the first socialist state in America, the Republic of Cuba; the rise and development of the world socialist system, comprising fourteen states; and the inspiring influence of socialism on the entire world have created the prerequisites for accelerating historical progress and opened new prospects for the advance and triumph of socialism throughout the world.

Socialism has shown mankind the prospect of deliverance from imperialism. . . . The contribution of the world socialist system to the common cause of the anti-imperialist forces is determined primarily by its growing economic potential. The swift economic development of the countries belonging to the socialist system at rates outpacing the economic growth of the capitalist countries, the advance of socialism to leading positions in a number of fields of scientific and technological progress, and the blazing of a trail into outer space by the Soviet Union—all these tangible results, produced by the creative endeavors of the peoples of the socialist countries, decisively contribute to the preponderance of the forces of peace, democracy, and socialism over imperialism.

The socialist world has now entered a stage of its development when the possibility arises of utilizing on a scale far greater than ever before the tremendous potentialities inherent in the new system. This is furthered by developing and applying better economic and political forms corresponding to the requirements of mature socialist society, which already rests on the new social structure. . . .

Practice has shown that socialist transformations and the building of the new society are a long and complex process, and that the utilization of the tremendous possibilities opened up by the new system depends on the [ruling] Communist parties [and] on their ability to resolve the problems of socialist development in the Marxist-Leninist way.

The application of science in various social and economic fields and the full utilization of the potentialities opened up by the scientific and technological revolution for speeding up economic development and for satisfying the needs of all members of society are made possible by socialist ownership, the planned organization of production, and the active participation of workers by hand and by brain in guiding and managing the economy. An important requisite for the development of socialist society is to give full scope to the scientific and technological revolution, which has become one of the main sectors of the historic competition between capitalism and socialism.

*   *   *

The defense of socialism is an internationalist duty of Communists. The development and strengthening of each socialist country is a vital condition of the progress of the world socialist system as a whole. Successful development of the national economy, improvement of social relations and the all-round progress of each socialist country conform both to the interests of each people separately, and [to] the common cause of socialism.

One of the most important tasks before the Communist and workers' parties of the socialist countries is to develop all-embracing cooperation between their countries and ensure fresh successes in the decisive areas of the economic competition between the two systems, in the advance of science and technology. . . .

Relying on its steadily growing economic and defense potential, the world socialist system fetters imperialism, reduces its possibilities of exporting counterrevolution, and in fulfillment of its internationalist duty, furnishes increasing aid to the peoples fighting for freedom and independence, and promotes peace and international security. So long as the aggressive NATO bloc exists, the Warsaw Treaty Organization has an important role to play in safeguarding the security of the socialist countries against armed attack by the imperialist powers, and in ensuring peace.

The successes of socialism . . . largely depend on the cohesion of the socialist countries. Unity of action of the socialist countries is an important factor in bringing together all anti-imperialist forces.

The establishment of international relations of a new type and the development of the fraternal alliance of the socialist countries is a complex historical process. . . . Successful development of this process implies strict adherence to the principles of proletarian internationalism, mutual assistance and support, equality, sovereignty, and noninterference in each other's internal affairs.

Socialism is not afflicted with the contradictions inherent in capitalism. When divergences between socialist countries do arise owing to differences in the level of economic development, in social structure, in international position, or because of national distinctions, they can and must be successfully settled on the basis of proletarian internationalism, through comradely discussion and voluntary fraternal cooperation. They need not disrupt the united front of socialist countries against imperialism.

*   *   *

In the citadels of capitalism, the working class, as recent events have shown, is the principal driving force of the revolutionary struggle, [and] of the entire anti-imperialist democratic movement. The present period is characterized by a sharpening of the struggle of the working class and of the broad masses of working people not only for an improvement of their economic conditions but also for [satisfaction of] political demands. . . . These demands are increasingly directed against the system of domination by monopoly capital, [and] against its political power. The desire of the working masses to effect a radical change in the economic and social system based on the exploitation of man is growing ever stronger. . . .
. . . The radical democratic changes which will be achieved in the struggle against the monopolies and their economic domination and political power, will promote among the broad masses awareness of the need for socialism.

In the new situation, the need for working-class unity has become even more urgent. . . . A differentiation is taking place in the ranks of Social Democracy, and this is also reflected in the leadership. Some of the leaders come out in defense of monopoly capital and imperialism. Others are more inclined to reckon with the demands of the working masses in the economic and social fields, and in the questions of the struggle for peace and progress.

Communists, who attribute decisive importance to working-class unity are in favor of cooperation with the socialists and Social-Democrats to establish an advanced democratic regime today, and to build a socialist society in the future. They will do everything they can to carry out this cooperation. . . .

*   *   *

The Communist policy of united action by all the parties of the working class and the trade unions draws growing support. This policy of unity affords the working-class movement greater opportunities in the anti-imperialist struggle and makes it possible to bring into this struggle that section of the proletariat which is still unorganized or still follows bourgeois parties. Communists will improve their political and ideological work with an eye to securing working-class unity.

Domination by finance capital and the realization of "agrarian programs" by the monopolist states lead to the ruin of ever larger sections of the small and middle farmers. Lately, the farmers have been putting up growing resistance to these measures, conducting mass actions supported by urban working people. The strengthening of the alliance of workers and farmers is one of the basic prerequisites of the success of the struggle against the monopolies and their power.

Big capital tramples on the vital interests of the majority of the urban middle strata. Therefore, despite their lack of unity and special susceptibility to bourgeois ideology, large masses of the middle strata are coming forward in defense of their interests. . . .

In this age, when science is becoming a direct productive force, growing numbers of intellectuals are swelling the ranks of wage and salary workers. Their social interests intertwine with those of the working class; their creative aspirations clash with the interests of the monopoly employers, who place profit above all else. . . .

The convergence of interests of the working class, farmers, urban middle strata and intellectuals, as well as their growing cooperation, reduce the social foundations of monopoly power, sharpen its internal contradictions, and promote the mobilization of broad masses of people for the struggle against monopolies and imperialism. The numerical growth and mounting political activity of young people have become an important factor in social affairs in Western Europe, America, Japan, Turkey and other countries.

*　　*　　*

Communists think highly of the upsurge of the youth movement and actively participate in it. . . . An important feature of our epoch is the large-scale participation of women in the class struggle, the anti-imperialist movement and, in particular, the struggle for peace. This is strikingly demonstrated in the massive protest campaigns against the U.S. aggression in Vietnam. . . .

Owing to the considerable aggravation of social contradictions, conditions have arisen in many capitalist countries for an anti-monopoly and anti-imperialist alliance of the revolutionary working-class movement and broad masses of religious people. The Catholic Church and some other religious organizations are experiencing an ideological crisis, which is shattering their age-long concepts and existing structures. Positive cooperation and joint action between Communists and broad democratic masses of Catholics and followers of other religions are developing in some countries. The dialogue between them on issues such as war and peace, capitalism and social-ism, and neocolonialism and the problem of the developing countries, has become highly topical; their united action against imperialism, for democracy and socialism, is extremely timely. . . .

In the course of antimonopolist and anti-imperialist united action, favorable conditions are created for uniting all democratic trends into a political alliance capable of decisively limiting the role played by the monopolies in the economies of the countries concerned, of putting an end to the power of big capital and of bringing about such radical political and economic changes as would ensure the most favorable conditions for continuing the struggle for socialism. The main force in this democratic alliance is the working class. . . .

The collapse of the colonial system has considerably weakened the position of imperialism. *In the past decade the role of the anti-imperialist movement of the peoples of Asia, Africa and Latin America in the world revolutionary process has continued to grow.* In some countries, this movement is acquiring an anticapitalist content.

In many *Asian and African* countries the national liberation movement has entered a new phase. A large number of national states has emerged in this area, substantially altering the world political structure and changing the balance of power to the detriment of imperialism. . . .

Of great importance for the future of Africa and the cause of peace is the liberation of southern Africa, one of the last areas of colonial domination. The armed struggle which is being waged in this area by the peoples of Angola, Mozambique, Guinea-Bissau, Zimbabwe, Namibia, and South Africa is inflicting heavy blows on the coalition of fascist and racialist regimes. . . .

The Arab liberation movement is playing an outstanding role in the battle waged against world imperialism. . . . The growth of the movement for national liberation, and the social progress of the peoples in this strategically important and oil-rich area, evoke the violent hatred of the imperialists and the oil monopolies which are weaving a web of intrigues and plots against this movement, and resorting to wars and aggressive actions.

*   *   *

Social differentiation is developing in the newly independent countries. . . . In a number of young states the social role and political activity of the working class have increased. The importance of international ties between the young proletariat of the countries of Asia and Africa and the working class of the socialist countries and the capitalist states is growing.

The toiling peasantry has great revolutionary potential. It is taking an active part in the struggle against imperialism, for the national liberation of peoples, and for consolidating the independence of the young states. . . .

In most of the independent Asian and African states, along with the task of consolidating and safeguarding political independence and sovereignty, the central problems of social progress are to overcome economic backwardness, set up an independent national economy, including their own industry, and raise the people's standard of living. The solution of these problems involves far-reaching socioeconomic changes, the implementation of democratic agrarian reforms in the interests of the working peasantry and, with its participation, the abolition of outdated feudal and prefeudal relations, the liquidation of oppression by foreign monopolies, the radical democratization of social and political life and the state apparatus, regeneration of national culture and the development of its progressive traditions, the strengthening of revolutionary parties, and the founding of such parties where they do not yet exist. The pressing problems of social development of these states are the object not only of sharp struggle between the peoples of these countries and the neocolonialists, but also of internal social conflicts. The establishment of relations of friendship and effective cooperation with socialist countries is of great importance for independent Asian and African countries.

. . . Some young states have taken the noncapitalist path, a path which opens up the possibility of overcoming the backwardness inherited from the colonial past and creates conditions for transition to socialist development. In these countries the socialist orientation is making headway, overcoming great difficulties and trials. These states are waging a determined struggle against imperialism and neocolonialism. Countries which have taken the capitalist road have been unable to solve any of the basic problems facing them. . . .

*   *   *

The way to carry out the tasks of national development and social progress, and effectively rebuff neocolonialist intrigues is to raise the activity of the people, enhance the role of the proletariat and the peasants, [and] rally working youth, students, intellectuals, urban middle strata and democratic army circles—all patriotic and progressive forces. It is this kind of unity the Communist and workers' parties are calling for.

. . . The social progress of the peoples in the newly liberated countries demands close cooperation between the Communist and workers' parties and the other patriotic and progressive forces. A hostile attitude to communism, and persecution of Communists, harms the struggle for national and social emancipation.

Most of the *Latin American* countries won state independence early in the last century. They have, by and large, travelled a long way along the road of capitalist development; a large proletariat has emerged, is growing and becoming steeled in struggle both in town and country, and there are Communist parties in practically all these countries. The Latin American peoples are struggling against a common oppressor and exploiter, U.S. imperialism, which has placed the entire continent in a position of dependence, regarding it as its strategic hinterland. Some of them are still fighting colonial domination. . . .

The Cuban revolution has broken the chain of imperialist oppression in Latin America and has led to the establishment of the first socialist state on the American continent, marking a historic turning point and opening in this region a new phase of the revolutionary movement. . . . The proletariat and the Communist and workers' parties play an increasingly important role in the anti-imperialist movement in Latin America. . . .

*   *   *

It is of paramount importance for the prospects of the anti-imperialist struggle to strengthen the alliance between the socialist system, the forces of the working-class movement, and national liberation.

III

The social and political situation in the world today makes it possible to raise the anti-imperialist struggle to a new level. Decisive superiority over imperialism and the defeat of its policy of aggression and war can be secured by intensifying the offensive against it. This insistently demands concrete practical steps and actions on all continents in order to give a clear perspective to the democratic and progressive forces, and all the forces desiring a positive solution of the major problems worrying mankind today—the problems of the peace and the security of nations.

The Communist and workers' parties represented at the conference, aware of their historic responsibility, propose united action to all Communists of the world, to all opponents of imperialism, to all who are prepared to fight for peace, freedom, and progress.

(1) A primary objective of united action is to give *all-round support to the heroic Vietnamese people.* The conference calls on all who cherish peace and national independence to intensify the struggle in order to compel U.S. imperialism to withdraw its interventionist

troops from Vietnam, cease interfering in the internal affairs of that country, and respect the right of the Vietnamese people to solve their problems by themselves. . . .

(2) *The main link of united action of the anti-imperialist forces remains the struggle against war—against the menace of a thermonuclear world war and mass extermination which continues to hang over mankind.* . . .

(3) *The defense of peace is inseparably linked up with the struggle to compel the imperialists to accept peaceful coexistence of states with different social systems,* which demands observance of the principles of sovereignty, equality, territorial inviolability of every state—big and small—and noninterference in the internal affairs of other countries, respect for the rights of every people freely to decide their social, economic and political system, and the settlement of outstanding international issues by political means through negotiation.

The policy of peaceful coexistence facilitates the positive solution of economic and social problems of the developing countries. [It] does not contradict the right of any oppressed people to fight for its liberation by any means it considers necessary—armed or peaceful. This policy in no way signifies support for reactionary regimes.

* * *

Communists regard it as their duty to combat the imperialist policy of whipping up international tension and any attempt aimed by them at bringing back the cold war, and to work for a relaxation of tension, which is one of the most insistent and urgent demands of the peoples.

(4) *To preserve peace, the most urgent task is to prevent the spread of nuclear weapons* and to enforce the nuclear nonproliferation treaty. . . . The setting up of nuclear-free zones in various parts of the world would be of great practical importance in improving the international atmosphere and strengthening trust between states. *The main effort should be directed toward the prohibition of nuclear weapons. Nuclear energy should be used exclusively for peaceful purposes.*

It is [also] necessary to step up the struggle for an effective ban on bacteriological and chemical weapons, which have been extensively used by the U.S. forces in Vietnam.

* * *

Alongside its universal tasks, the struggle for peace has very important tasks of a more specific or more regional nature whose aim is to assure security in some continents or geographic zones. . . .

The interests of world peace call for the disbandment of military blocs. . . . In this light the socialist countries have already declared for the simultaneous dissolution of NATO and the Warsaw Treaty. The conference emphatically condemns the provocative attempts of the imperialist powers, particularly the U.S.A., the Federal Republic of Germany, and Britain, to step up the activity of NATO. The disbandment of NATO would be a decisive step towards the dissolution of all blocs, the dismantling of all military bases on foreign soil and the establishment of a reliable system of collective security. . . .

Attainment of lasting security in this continent is a problem which holds a paramount place in the minds and aspirations of the European peoples. The conferences of the Warsaw Treaty member countries in Bucharest in 1966 and in Budapest in 1969, and also the Karlovy Vary conference in 1967 charted a concrete program of action and measures to create a system of European security.

It is imperative to secure the inviolability of the existing frontiers in Europe, in particular the frontiers along the Oder-Neisse and the frontier between the Federal Republic of Germany and the German Democratic Republic, and to work for the international legal recognition of the German Democratic Republic. It is also imperative to work to prevent West Germany from securing atomic weapons in any form, for the renunciation by the Federal Republic of Germany of her claim to represent the whole of Germany, the recognition of West Berlin as a separate political entity, the recognition that the Munich diktat was invalid from the very outset, and the banning of all neo-Nazi organizations. . . .

The principle of the inviolability of neutral states must be respected unconditionally. These states can make a major contribution to the policy of peaceful coexistence if they take advantage of every opportunity to act in a spirit of détente and peace. To achieve these aims energetic steps have to be taken in this direction and the problem of European security approached with initiative, with a will to achieve concrete practical measures.

The organization of a broad congress of European peoples, which would prepare for, and facilitate the holding of a conference of states, is the most important of all these peace initiatives.

(5) *The conference calls on world public opinion to display unflagging and active solidarity with the peoples and countries which are constant objects of aggressive encroachments by imperialism*—the German Democratic Republic, the Korean People's Democratic Republic, and the entire Korean people. The conference calls for the restoration of the lawful rights of the People's Republic of China in the United Nations and the return of Taiwan at present under United

States military occupation. It remains the duty of Communists and all other revolutionary and anti-imperialist forces in Latin America and throughout the world to defend the Republic of Cuba.

We Communists call for united action against all imperialist acts of aggression, against recourse to local wars and other forms of intervention by imperialism in any area of the world. In face of the aggressive policy pursued by the imperialists and the ruling circles of Israel, we pledge solidarity with the Arab peoples who demand the return of the territories occupied by the Israeli invaders, . . .

(6) *Communists reiterate their solidarity with the struggle of the peoples of Asia, Africa and Latin America. . . .*

The demand of our epoch is to rid our planet completely of the curse of colonialism, destroy its last centers, and prevent its revival in new camouflaged forms. . . . We urge effective international measures in support of the patriots of Angola, Mozambique, Guinea-Bissau, Zimbabwe, Namibia and South Africa, [and] in support of all oppressed peoples.

*   *   *

(7) *We consider it imperative to step up the fight against the fascist menace and relentlessly to rebuff profascist sorties.* Fascism is intensifying its activity at a time when the crisis of imperialism is growing sharper, . . . In Greece neofascism has seized power. In Spain the ultras are trying to return to fascist methods of repression. . . . In Portugal, fascism, . . . is resorting to demagogy in an effort to cover up its terroristic policy. In West Germany the neo-Nazis have laid open claim to power. Neofascist forces are also becoming more active in other countries. . . .

All these manifestations of fascism are coming up against growing resistance from the people, and this demands united action by all the antifascist forces, and also greater international support from the Communist and workers' parties, from all democratic and progressive movements in every country.

*   *   *

(8) We Communists again call on all honest men in the world to unite their efforts in the struggle against the *man-hating ideology and practices of racialism.* We call for the broadest possible protest movement against the most ignominious phenomena of our time, the barbarous persecution of the 25 million Negroes in the U.S.A., the racialist terror in South Africa and Rhodesia, the persecution of the Arab population in occupied territory and in Israel. We call for protest against racial and national discrimination, against Zionism,

and [against] anti-Semitism, all of which are fanned by reactionary capitalist forces and which are used to mislead the masses politically.

* * *

(9) The interests of the struggle against imperialism, which attempts to stifle basic human freedoms, demand a tireless fight to defend and win freedom of speech, freedom of the press, freedom of assembly, freedom of demonstration and association, [and] the equality of all citizens. [They demand] *to democratize every aspect of social life.* A firm rebuff must be administered to any attempt and any legislation by reaction designed to nullify the democratic rights and freedoms won in the course of hard class battles. . . . We Communists oppose all forms of oppression of nations and national minorities. We want to see every nation or national group develop its own culture and language, and we firmly defend the right of all nations to self-determination.

* * *

The present situation demands greater militant solidarity of the peoples of the socialist countries, [and] of all contingents of the international working-class movement and national liberation in the struggle against imperialism.

The participants in the conference call on all organizations representing workers, peasants, office employees, youth, students, intellectuals, women, [and] various groups and social strata with different political, philosophic and religious convictions and views—to pool their efforts with those of the Communist parties for concerted action in the anti-imperialist struggle for a relaxation of tensions and in defense of peace. We invite them all to join in a broad and constructive exchange of opinion on the widest possible range of issues bearing on the anti-imperialist struggle.

* * *

IV

The participants in the conference consider that the most important prerequisite for increasing the Communist and workers' parties contribution to the solution of the problems facing the peoples is to raise the unity of the Communist movement to a higher level in conformity with present-day requirements. This demands determined and persistent effort by all the parties. *The cohesion of the Com-*

munist and workers' parties is the most important factor in rallying together all the anti-imperialist forces.

The participants in the conference reaffirm their common view that relations between the fraternal parties are based on the principles of proletarian internationalism, solidarity, and mutual support; respect for independence and equality, and noninterference in each other's internal affairs. Strict adherence to these principles is an indispensable condition for developing comradely cooperation between the fraternal parties and strengthening the unity of the Communist movement. Bilateral consultations, regional meetings and international conferences are natural forms of such cooperation and are conducted on the basis of the principles accepted in the Communist movement. These principles and these forms give the Communist and workers' parties every possibility to unite their efforts in the struggle for their common aims, under conditions of the growing diversity of the world revolutionary process. All parties have equal rights. As there is no leading center of the international Communist movement, voluntary coordination of the actions of parties in order effectively to carry out the tasks before them acquires increased importance.

United action by Communist and workers' parties will promote cohesion of the Communist movement on Marxist-Leninist principles. Joint action aimed at solving vital practical problems of the revolutionary and general democratic movements of our time promote a necessary exchange of experience between the various contingents of the Communist movement. They help to enrich and creatively develop Marxist-Leninist theory, to strengthen internationalist revolutionary positions on urgent political problems.

The participants in the conference proclaim their parties' firm resolve to do their utmost for the working people and for social progress, with a view to advancing toward complete victory over international capital. . . .

[They] are convinced that the effectiveness of each Communist party's policy depends on its successes in its own country, on the successes of other fraternal parties, and on the extent of their cooperation. Each Communist party is responsible for its activity to its own working class and people and, at the same time, to the international working class. The national and international responsibilities of each Communist and workers' party are indivisible. . . .

The Communist and workers' parties are conducting their activity in diverse, [and] specific conditions, requiring an appropriate approach to the solution of concrete problems. Each party, guided by the principles of Marxism-Leninism and in keeping with concrete national conditions, independently elaborates its own policy, determines the directions, forms, and methods of struggle, and, depending on the circumstances, chooses the peaceful or nonpeaceful way of transition to socialism, and also the forms and methods of building socialism in its own country. At the same time, the diverse conditions in which the Communist parties operate, the different approaches to practical tasks, and even differences on certain questions must not hinder concerted international action by fraternal parties, particularly on the basic problems of the anti-imperialist struggle. The greater the strength and the unity of each Communist party, the better can it fulfill its role both inside each country and in the international Communist movement.

Communists are aware that our movement, while scoring great historical victories in the course of its development, has recently encountered serious difficulties. Communists are convinced, however, that these difficulties will be overcome. This belief is based on the fact that the international working class has common long-term objectives and interests, on the striving of each party to find a solution to existing problems which would meet both national and international interests, and the Communists' revolutionary mission; it is based on the will of Communists for cohesion on an international scale. The Communist and workers' parties, regardless of some difference of opinion, reaffirm their determination to present a united front in the struggle against imperialism.

Some of the divergences which have arisen are eliminated through an exchange of opinion or disappear as the development of events clarifies the essence of the outstanding issues. Other divergences may last long. The conference is confident that the outstanding issues can and must be resolved correctly by strengthening all forms of cooperation among the Communist parties, by extending interparty ties, mutual exchange of experience, comradely discussion and consultation, and unity of action in the international arena. It is an internationalist duty of each party to do everything it can to help improve relations and promote trust between all parties, and to undertake further efforts to strengthen the unity of the international Communist movement. This unity is strengthened by a collective analysis of concrete reality.

*　　*　　*

Loyalty to Marxism-Leninism and to proletarian internationalism, and dedicated and devoted service in the interests of their peoples and the common cause of socialism, are a requisite for the efficacy and correct orientation of united action by the Communist and workers' parties, a guarantee that they will achieve their historic goals.

The Communist movement is an integral part of modern society and is its most active force. Hence, the banning of Communist parties is an attack on the democratic rights and vital interests of the peoples. The participants in the conference support all the Communist parties of the world, without exception, which fight for their right of legal participation in the political life of their countries. We emphatically condemn the brutal repressions and terror which have claimed the lives of thousands upon thousands of Communists and other democrats and revolutionaries in Indonesia, Spain, Portugal, Greece, Bolivia, Brazil, Colombia, Mexico, Venezuela, Panama, Paraguay, Guatemala, South Africa, Thailand, Haiti, Malaysia, Iran, the Philippines and some other countries. We proclaim our solidarity with our fellow fighters in the common struggle who are lying in the jails of fascist and dictatorial regimes, [and] in prisons in the capitalist countries, and we work for their release.

The participants regard this conference as an important stage in the cohesion of the world Communist movement. They consider that the absence of certain Communist parties should not hinder fraternal ties and cooperation between all Communist parties without exception. They declare their resolve to achieve joint action in the struggle against imperialism, for the common objectives of the international working-class movement, as well as with the Communist and workers' parties not represented at the present conference.

*　　*　　*

The struggle against imperialism is a long, hard and strenuous fight. Tense class battles lie ahead and they cannot be avoided. Let us step up the offensive against imperialism and internal reaction. The revolutionary and progressive forces are certain to triumph.

Peoples of the socialist countries, workers, democratic forces in the capitalist countries, newly liberated peoples, and those who are oppressed, unite in a common struggle against imperialism, for peace, national liberation, social progress, democracy, and socialism!

Document 3: Excerpts from the Report of the CC CPSU to the Twenty-fourth Congress of the CPSU, Delivered 30 March 1971 by Leonid Brezhnev, General Secretary of the CC CPSU*

THE INTERNATIONAL POSITION OF THE U.S.S.R. THE CPSU'S FOREIGN POLICY ACTIVITY

Comrades, our internal development is closely connected with the situation in the world arena. In view of this, the party's Central Committee has devoted much attention to international problems. Plenary meetings of the CC have repeatedly considered the most important and pressing problems of the U.S.S.R.'s foreign policy, and the CPSU's activity in the Communist movement.

The Soviet Union is a peace-loving state, and this is determined by the very nature of our socialist system. The goals of Soviet foreign policy, as formulated by the Twenty-third Congress of the CPSU, consist in ensuring, together with other socialist countries, favorable international conditions for the construction of socialism and communism; consolidating the unity and cohesion of the socialist countries, their friendship and brotherhood; supporting the national liberation movement and engaging in all-round cooperation with the young developing states; consistently standing up for the principle of peaceful coexistence between states with different social systems; giving a resolute rebuff to the aggressive forces of imperialism; and safeguarding mankind from another world war.

The whole of the CC's practical activity in the sphere of foreign policy has been designed to achieve these goals.

1. For the Further Development of the Friendship and Cooperation of the Socialist Countries

The CC's attention has been constantly centered on questions of further cohesion and development of the world socialist system, and relations with the fraternal socialist countries and their Communist parties.

The world socialist system has a quarter-century behind it. From the standpoint of development of revolutionary theory and practice these have been exceptionally fruitful years. The socialist world has

---

* Source: *24th Congress of the CPSU, 30 March-9 April 1971: Documents* (Moscow: Novosti Press Agency Publishing House, 1971), pp. 8-39.

given the Communist and working-class movement experience which is of tremendous and truly historic importance. This experience shows:

- Socialism, which is firmly established in the states now constituting the world socialist system, has proved its great viability in the historical contest with capitalism.
- The formation and strengthening of the world socialist system has been a powerful accelerator of historical progress which was started by the Great October Revolution. Fresh prospects have opened up for the triumph of socialism all over the world; life has provided confirmation of the conclusion drawn by the 1969 International Meeting of Communist and Workers' Parties that "the world socialist system is the decisive force in the anti-imperialist struggle."
- The world socialist system has been making a great contribution to the fulfillment of a task of such vital importance for all the peoples as the prevention of another world war. It is safe to say that many of the imperialist aggressors' plans were frustrated thanks to the existence of the world socialist system and its firm action.
- Successes in socialist construction largely depend on the correct combination of the general and the nationally specific in social development. Not only are we now theoretically aware but also have been convinced in practice that the way to socialism and its main features are determined by the general regularities, which are inherent in the development of all the socialist countries. We are also aware that the effect of the general regularities is manifested in different forms consistent with concrete historical conditions and national specifics. It is impossible to build socialism without basing oneself on general regularities or taking account of the concrete historical specifics of each country. Nor is it possible, without a consideration of both these factors, correctly to develop relations between the socialist states.

*　　*　　*

The experience accumulated over the quarter-century also makes it possible to take a more profound and more realistic approach in assessing and determining the ways of overcoming objective and subjective difficulties which arise in the construction of the new society and the establishment of the new, socialist type of interstate relations. . . .

The past five-year period has seen a considerable contribution to the treasure house of the collective experience of the fraternal countries and parties. In the last five years, the economic potential of the socialist states has increased substantially, the political foundations of socialism have been strengthened, the people's living standards have been raised, and culture and science have been further developed.

At the same time, it is known that some difficulties and complications have continued to appear in the socialist world, and this has also had an effect on the development of relations between individual states and the Soviet Union. However, this has not changed the dominant tendency of strengthening friendship and cohesion of the socialist countries. On the whole, our cooperation with the fraternal countries has been successfully developing and strengthening in every sphere.

The CPSU has attached special importance to developing *cooperation with the Communist parties of the fraternal countries*. . . . The period under review was marked by important successess in *coordinating the foreign policy activity* of the fraternal parties and states. . . .

The Warsaw Treaty Organization has been and continues to be the main center for coordinating the foreign policy activity of the fraternal countries. [Member] countries displayed the initiative of putting forward a full-scale program for strengthening peace in Europe, which is pivoted on the demand that the immutability of the existing state borders should be secured. . . . The Warsaw Treaty countries can also undoubtedly count among their political assets the fact that the plans which had existed within NATO to give the F.R.G. militarists access to nuclear weapons have not been realized.

Joint efforts by the socialist states have also made it possible to achieve substantial progress in . . . the strengthening of the international positions of the German Democratic Republic. The so-called Hallstein Doctrine has been defeated. The G.D.R. has already been recognized by twenty-seven states, and this process is bound to continue.

Active and consistent support from the Soviet Union and other socialist countries is vitally important for the struggle of the peoples of Vietnam and the other countries of Indochina against the imperialist interventionists. The steps taken by the socialist states in the Middle East have become one of the decisive factors which have frustrated the imperialist plans of overthrowing the progressive regimes in the Arab countries.

*   *   *

As a result of the collective formulation and implementation of a number of measures in recent years, the *military organization of the Warsaw Treaty* has been further improved. . . .

In short, comrades, the socialist countries' multilateral political cooperation is becoming ever closer and more vigorous. . . .

Of equal importance is *cooperation in the economic sphere*, and extension and deepening of national economic ties between the socialist countries. The period under review has also been fruitful in this respect.

Let us turn to the facts.

The Soviet Union and the fraternal states seek to help each other in every way to develop their national economies. In the last five years, over 300 industrial and agricultural projects have been built or reconstructed in the socialist countries with our technical assistance. We have been supplying our friends with many types of industrial products on mutually advantageous terms. . . .

*   *   *

The U.S.S.R. and other CMEA countries arrange their economic relations on a long-term basis. In particular, the fraternal countries have coordinated their national economic plans for 1971–1975. In the last few years, active work has been continued in developing the organizational structure and technical basis for multilateral economic cooperation.

*   *   *

All this has produced its results, helping to make social production more efficient, and to develop the national economy of each of our countries at a rapid pace. In the past five-year period, the CMEA countries' industrial production increased by 49 percent. Trade between them has also been growing.

However, like other members of CMEA, we believe that the possibilities of the socialist division of labor are not yet being fully used. Practice has led us up to this common conclusion: it is necessary to deepen specialization and cooperation of production, and to tie in our national economic plans more closely, that is, to advance along the way of the socialist countries' economic integration. Comrades, this is an important and necessary endeavor.

The economic integration of the socialist countries is a new and complex process. It implies a new and broader approach to many economic questions, and the ability to find the most rational solutions, meeting the interests not only of the given country but of all the cooperating participants. It requires firm orientation on the latest scientific and technically advanced lines of production.

*   *   *

In the period between the Twenty-third and the Twenty-fourth Congresses, our party has displayed much concern for strengthening *bilateral relations between the Soviet Union* and the socialist countries. Close and diverse cooperation, friendship, and cordiality are characteristic of our relations with the Warsaw Treaty countries—Bulgaria, Hungary, the German Democratic Republic, Poland, Romania and Czechoslovakia.

New treaties of friendship, cooperation, and mutual assistance have been concluded with Bulgaria, Hungary, Czechoslovakia, and Romania, together with the treaties with the G.D.R., Poland and Mongolia, . . . Our friendship with the Polish People's Republic is unshakable. We note with deep satisfaction that the difficulties which arose in fraternal Poland have been overcome. . . .

Our party and the Soviet people have relations of socialist solidarity and strong and militant friendship with the Working People's Party of Vietnam and the Democratic Republic of Vietnam. . . . Also over these years, the Central Committee has devoted constant attention to strengthening cooperation with the Republic of Cuba and the Communist Party of Cuba. . . .

For half a century now, the CPSU and the Soviet state have had bonds of strong and time-tested friendship with the Mongolian workers' party and the Mongolian People's Republic. . . .

In the last few years, our ties with the Democratic People's Republic of Korea [D.P.R.K.] and the Korean workers' party have grown, and this, we are sure, meets the interests of the peoples of both countries. The Soviet Union has supported and continues to support the proposals of the D.P.R.K. government on the country's peaceful, democratic unification, and the Korean people's demands for a withdrawal of U.S. troops from the south of Korea.

In the period under review, Soviet-Yugoslav relations have continued to develop. The Soviet people want to see socialism in Yugoslavia strengthened, and her ties with the socialist community growing stronger. . . .

Concerning our relations with the People's Republic of China, it will be recalled that the Chinese leaders have put forward an ideological-political platform of their own which is incompatible with Leninism on the key questions of international life and the world Communist movement, and have demanded that we should abandon the line of the Twentieth Congress and the program of the CPSU. They unfolded an intensive and hostile propaganda campaign against our party and country, made territorial claims on the Soviet Union, and in the spring and summer of 1969 brought things to the point of armed incidents along the border.

*   *   *

In the last eighteen months, as a result of the initiative displayed on our part, there have been signs of some normalization in relations between the U.S.S.R. and the P.R.C. A meeting of the heads of government of the two countries took place in September 1969, and this was followed by negotiations in Peking between government delegations on a settlement of the border issues. These negotiations are proceeding slowly, and it goes without saying that their favorable completion calls for a constructive attitude not only of one side.

*   *   *

. . . We cannot . . . fail to see that the anti-Soviet line in China's propaganda and policy is being continued, and that the Ninth Congress of the CCP [April 1969] has written this line, which is hostile to the Soviet Union, into its decisions.

*   *   *

We shall never forsake the national interests of the Soviet state. The CPSU will continue tirelessly to work for the cohesion of the socialist countries and the world Communist movement on a Marxist-Leninist basis. At the same time, our party and the Soviet government are deeply convinced that an improvement of relations between the Soviet Union and the People's Republic of China would be in line with the fundamental, long-term interests of both countries, the interests of socialism, the freedom of the peoples, and stronger peace. . . .

*   *   *

As regards Albania, we are prepared, as in the past, to restore normal relations with her. This would be beneficial to both countries and to the common interests of the socialist states.

Comrades, the political crisis in Czechoslovakia has been fairly prominent in the international events of recent years. . . . The Czechoslovak events were a fresh reminder that in the countries which have taken the path of socialist construction the internal anti-socialist forces, whatever remained of them, may, in certain conditions, become active and even mount direct counterrevolutionary action in the hope of support from outside—from imperialism—which, for its part, is always prepared to form blocs with such forces.

*   *   *

The Czechoslovak events showed very well how important it is constantly to strengthen the party's leading role in socialist society, steadily to improve the forms and methods of party leadership, and to display a creative Marxist-Leninist approach to the solution of pressing problems of socialist development.

* * *

In view of the appeals by party and state leaders, Communists, and working people of Czechoslovakia, and considering the danger posed to the socialist gains in that country, we and the fraternal socialist countries then jointly took a decision to render internationalist assistance to Czechoslovakia in defense of socialism. In the extraordinary conditions created by the forces of imperialism and counterrevolution, we were bound to do so by our class duty, loyalty to socialist internationalism, and the concern for the interests of our states and the future of socialism and peace in Europe.

You will recall that in its document, "Lessons of the Crisis Development," a plenary meeting of the CC of the Czechoslovak Communist party gave this assessment of the importance of the fraternal states' collective assistance:

> The entry of the allied troops of the five socialist countries into Czechoslovakia was an act of international solidarity, meeting both the common interests of the Czechoslovakian working people and the interests of the international working class, the socialist community, and the class interests of the international Communist movement. This internationalist act saved the lives of thousands of men, ensured internal and external conditions for peaceful and tranquil labor, strengthened the Western borders of the socialist camp, and blasted the hopes of the imperialist circles for a revision of the results of the Second World War.

We fully agree with the conclusion drawn by the Czechoslovak Communist party. . . . The peoples of the socialist countries have clearly demonstrated to the whole world that they will not give up their revolutionary gains, and that the borders of the socialist community are immutable and inviolable.

We are sincerely glad that the Communists of Czechoslovakia have successfully stood the trials that fell to their lot. Today the Czechoslovak Communist party is advancing toward its Fourteenth Congress, which we are sure will be a new and important stage in strengthening the positions of socialism in Czechoslovakia.

* * *

The Communist Party of the Soviet Union has regarded and continues to regard as its internationalist duty in every way to promote the further growth of the might of the world socialist system. . . .

... We want the world socialist system to be a well-knit family of nations, building and defending the new society together, and mutually enriching each other with experience and knowledge, a family, strong and united, which the people of the world would regard as the prototype of the future world community of free nations.

Allow me to assure our friends, our brothers, and our comrades-in-arms in the socialist countries that the Communist Party of the Soviet Union will spare no effort to attain this lofty goal!

2. The Peoples Against Imperialism. Imperialism, Enemy of the Peoples and Social Progress

Comrades, at its Twenty-third Congress and then in a number of its documents our party has already given a comprehensive assessment of modern imperialism. A Marxist-Leninist analysis of its present-day features is contained in the material of the 1969 International Communist meeting. Allow me, therefore, in the light of the experience of the last few years to deal only with some of the basic points which we must take account of in our policy.

The features of contemporary capitalism largely spring from the fact that it is trying to adapt itself to the new situation in the world. In the conditions of the confrontation with socialism, the ruling circles of the capitalist countries are afraid more than they have ever been of the class struggle developing into a massive revolutionary movement. Hence, the bourgeoisie's striving to use more camouflaged forms of exploitation and oppression of the working peoples, and its readiness now and again to agree to partial reforms in order to keep the masses under its ideological and political control as far as possible. . . .

However, adaptation to the new conditions does not mean that capitalism has been stabilized as a system. *The general crisis of capitalism has continued to deepen.*

Even the most developed capitalist states are not free from grave economic upheavals. The U.S.A., for instance, has been floundering in one of its economic crises for almost two years now. . . .

The contradictions between the imperialist states have not been eliminated either by the processes of integration or the imperialists' class concern for pooling their efforts in fighting against the socialist world. By the early 1970s, the main centers of imperialist rivalry have become clearly visible: these are the U.S.A., Western Europe (above all, the six Common Market countries), [and] Japan. The economic and political competitive struggle between them has been growing ever more acute. . . .

In the past five-year period, imperialist foreign policy has provided fresh evidence that imperialism has not ceased to be reactionary and aggressive.

In this context, one must deal above all with U.S. imperialism, which . . . seeks to dominate everywhere, interferes in the affairs of other peoples, highhandedly tramples on their legitimate rights and sovereignty, and seeks by force, bribery and economic penetration to impose its will on states and whole areas of the world.

Needless to say, the forces of war and aggression also exist in the other imperialist countries. In West Germany, these are the revanchists, who have been increasingly ganging up with the neo-Nazis; in Great Britain, these are the executioners of Northern Ireland, the suppliers of arms to the South African racists, and the advocates of the aggressive U.S. policy; in Japan these are the militarists who, in defiance of the constitution, which prohibits war "for all time," seek once again to push the country onto the path of expansion and aggression.

Another fact, comrades, that should also be borne in mind is that since the war militarism in the capitalist world has been growing on an unprecedented scale. This tendency has been intensified in the recent period. In 1970 alone, the NATO countries invested $103 billion in war preparations. Militarization has acquired the most dangerous nature in the U.S.A. In the last five years, that country has spent almost $400 billion for military purposes.

The imperialists have been systematically plundering the peoples of dozens of countries in Asia, Africa, and Latin America. . . . They are prepared to commit any crime in their efforts to preserve or restore their domination of the peoples in their former colonies or in other countries which are escaping from the grip of capitalist exploitation. The last five-year period has provided much fresh evidence of this. The aggression against the Arab states, the colonialist attempts to invade Guinea, and the subversive activity against the progressive regimes in Latin America—all this is a constant reminder that the imperialist war against the freedom-loving peoples has not ceased. The continuing U.S. aggression against the peoples of Vietnam, Cambodia and Laos is the main atrocity committed by the modern colonialists; it is the stamp of ignominy on the United States.

*　　*　　*

Comrades, we have no doubt at all that the attempts of imperialism to turn the tide of history, to make it flow in its favor, are bound to fail. However, we Communists are well aware that there is no room for passivity or self-complacency. . . .

* * *

The *international working-class movement* continues to play, as it has played in the past, the role of time-tested and militant vanguard of the revolutionary forces. The events of the past five-year period in the capitalist world have fully borne out the importance of the working class as the chief and strongest opponent of the rule of the monopolies, and as a center rallying all the antimonopoly forces.

In countries like France and Italy, where the traditions of the class struggle are more developed, and where strong Communist parties are active, the working people, headed by the working class, have attacked not only individual groups of capitalists, but the whole system of state-monopoly domination. In Great Britain, the class struggle has reached a state of high tension, and the current strikes are comparable in scale and in the numbers involved only with the general strike of 1926. In the U.S.A., working-class action against the monopolies has assumed great scope, and the struggle of the Negro people for equality, and of youth against the war in Vietnam is spreading with unprecedented acerbity. The mass working-class movement in the F.R.G. is gathering momentum. For the first time in many decades, large-scale class clashes have taken place in the Scandinavian countries and in Holland. The sociopolitical crisis in Spain continues to sharpen. In all the class battles of the recent period, the working people's trade unions, especially those brought together within the World Federation of Trade Unions, have played a considerable and increasingly important role.

The meeting of the fraternal parties, it will be recalled, drew the conclusion that the current large-scale battles of the working class are a harbinger of fresh class battles which could lead to fundamental social change, to the establishment of the power of the working class in alliance with other sections of the working people.

At the same time, comrades, imperialism is being subjected to ever greater pressure by the forces which have sprung from the national liberation struggle, above all by the young, independent, and anti-imperialist minded states of Asia and Africa. The main thing is that *the struggle for national liberation in many countries has in practical terms begun to grow into a struggle against exploitative relations, both feudal and capitalist.*

Today, there are already quite a few countries in Asia and Africa which have taken the noncapitalist way of development, that is, the path of building a socialist society in the long term. Many states have now taken this path. . . .

The offensive by the forces of national and social liberation against domination by imperialism is expressed in various forms.

119

Thus, in the countries oriented towards socialism, the property of the imperialist monopolies is being nationalized. This makes it possible to strengthen and develop the state sector, which is essential as an economic basis for a revolutionary democratic policy. In a country like the United Arab Republic, the state sector now accounts for 85 percent of total industrial production, and in Burma, the state sector controls over 80 percent of the extractive and almost 60 percent of the manufacturing industry. New serious steps in nationalizing imperialist property have been taken in Algeria. Many foreign enterprises, banks, and trading companies have been handed over to the state in Guinea, the Sudan, Somalia and Tanzania.

Serious steps have also been taken to solve the land problem, which is complicated and has a bearing on the lot of many millions of peasants. Taking the past five-year period alone, important agrarian transformations have been carried out in the U.A.R. and Syria, and have been started in the Sudan and Somalia. An agrarian reform has been announced for this year in Algeria. In the People's Republic of the Congo (Brazzaville) all the land and its minerals are now state owned.

Needless to say, it is no easy thing to bring about a radical restructuring of backward social relations on noncapitalist principles, and in an atmosphere of unceasing attacks by the neocolonialists and domestic reactionaries. This makes it all the more important that, despite all these difficulties, the states taking the socialist orientation have been further advancing along their chosen path.

*   *   *

As to our country, it fully supports this just struggle. The U.S.S.R.'s political and economic cooperation with the liberated countries has been further developed in the last few years. Our trade with them is growing. Dozens of industrial and agricultural enterprises have been built in many countries of Asia and Africa with our participation. We have also been making a contribution to the training of personnel for these countries. All this is being done in the mutual interest.

Great changes have been taking place in a number of Latin American countries. The victory of the Popular Unity forces in Chile was a most important event. . . .

The great Lenin's prediction that the peoples of the colonies and dependent countries, starting with a struggle for national liberation, would go on to fight against the very foundations of the system of exploitation, is coming true. . . .

Comrades, success in the struggle against imperialism largely depends on the cohesion of the anti-imperialist forces, above all of *the world Communist movement,* their vanguard. In the last five years, our party together with the other fraternal parties, has done much to strengthen this cohesion and the unity of the Communist ranks.

*   *   *

The main aim has been to secure a turn toward the cohesion of the Communist movement and consolidation of its ideological basis. An important stage in these efforts was the 1967 Conference of European Communist Parties at Karlovy Vary and also a number of other international meetings of Communists.

As a result the question of calling an international meeting of Communist and workers' parties was placed on the order of the day. . . . The meeting was a major step forward in strengthening the international unity of the Communists and in consolidating all the anti-imperialist forces. It has done a great deal for developing a number of propositions of Marxist-Leninist theory as applied to the present-day situation. . . .

*   *   *

On the whole there is ground to say that cohesion in the international Communist movement is being increasingly strengthened, and that fruitful bilateral and multilateral interparty ties are becoming ever more active. Our party welcomes this. . . .

However, comrades, another fact we cannot afford to lose sight of is that negative phenomena have not yet been overcome everywhere. The fight against right- and "left"-wing revisionism, against nationalism, continues to be urgent. It is precisely the nationalistic tendencies, especially those which assume the form of anti-Sovietism, that bourgeois ideologists and bourgeois propaganda have placed most reliance on in their fight against socialism and the Communist movement. They have been trying to induce the opportunist elements in the Communist parties to make something of an ideological deal. They appear to be telling them: just give us proof that you are anti-Soviet, and we shall be prepared to proclaim that you are the true "Marxists," and that you are taking completely "independent attitudes." The course of events has shown, incidentally, that such men also take the way of struggle against the Communist parties in their own countries. Examples of this are renegades of the types of Garaudy in France, Fischer in Austria, Petkov in Venezuela, and the "Manifesto" group leaders in Italy. The fraternal parties regard the fight against such elements as an important condition for strengthening their ranks. Consequently, even these examples—and their number could easily be multiplied—testify that the struggle against revisionism and nationalism continues to be an important task of the Communist parties.

*   *   *

We maintain and have been developing relations with the Left Socialist parties in some countries of the West, East and Latin America. . . .

In accordance with the line laid down by the 1969 international meeting, the CPSU is prepared to develop cooperation with the Social-Democrats both in the struggle for peace and democracy, and in the struggle for socialism, without, of course, making any concessions in ideology and revolutionary principles. However, this line of the Communists has been meeting with stubborn resistance from the right-wing leaders of the Social-Democrats. . . .

Comrades, to the lot of the Communists have fallen the hardest trials of any that have ever fallen to the lot of fighters for the people's cause. We remember these words of Lenin's: "Selfless devotion to the revolution and revolutionary propaganda among the people are not wasted even if long decades divide the sowing from the harvest." (Lenin, *Collected Works*, vol. 18, p. 31.) The ideas of the Communists have sprouted remarkable shoots in the practice of real socialism, and in the thoughts and deeds of millions upon millions of men.

*   *   *

Conscious of its internationalist duty, the Communist Party of the Soviet Union will continue to pursue a line in international affairs which helps further to invigorate the worldwide anti-imperialist struggle, and to strengthen the fighting unity of all its participants.

The full triumph of the socialist cause all over the world is inevitable, and we shall not spare ourselves in the fight for this triumph, for the happiness of the working people!

3. Rebuff to the Imperialist Policy of Aggression.
The Soviet Union's Struggle for Peace
and the Security of Peoples

Comrades, in the period under review the Central Committee and the Soviet government did their utmost to ensure peaceful conditions for Communist construction in the U.S.S.R., to expose and frustrate action by the aggressive imperialist forces, and to defend socialism, and the freedom of peoples and peace.

Our policy has always combined firm rebuffs to aggression with the constructive line of settling pressing international problems and maintaining normal, and wherever the situation allows, good relations with states belonging to the other social system. As in the past, we have consistently stood up for the Leninist principle of peaceful coexistence of states, regardless of their social system. This principle has now become a real force of international development.

Let me deal with the most important international problems. . . . To start with the events in Southeast Asia . . . anyone capable of taking a realistic view of things must realize that neither direct armed intervention, nor torpedoing of negotiations, nor even the ever wider use of mercenaries will break down the Vietnamese people's determination to become master of [their] own country. The so-called Vietnamization [policy] . . . will [not] get the U.S.A. out of the bog of its dirty war in Indochina or wash away the shame heaped on that country by those who started and are continuing the aggression. . . . The Soviet Union resolutely demands an end to the imperialist aggression against the peoples of Vietnam, Cambodia and Laos. . . .

The Middle East is another "hot spot" in world politics. The crisis which has arisen as a result of Israel's attack on the U.A.R., Syria, and Jordan has been one of the most intense in the development of international relations over the past period. . . . Together with the fraternal socialist countries we did everything necessary to stop and condemn the aggression. . . . Our country has helped to restore the defense potential of the Arab states which were subjected to invasion, the U.A.R. and Syria, with whom our cooperation has been growing stronger from year to year.

. . . The attitude of the Arab side provides a real basis for settling the crisis in the Middle East. The Israeli government's rejection of all these proposals, and Tel Aviv's now openly brazen claims to Arab lands, clearly show who is blocking the way to peace in the Middle East, and who is to blame for the dangerous hotbed of war being maintained in that area. At the same time, the unseemly role of those who are instigating the Israeli extremists—U.S. imperialism and international Zionism as an instrument of the aggressive imperialist circles—is becoming ever more obvious.

. . . The longer the delay in reaching a political settlement in the Middle East, the stronger will be the indignation of world public opinion, and the Arab people's hatred of the aggressor and its patrons; and the greater the harm the Israeli rulers will inflict on their people and their country. The Soviet Union will continue its firm support of its Arab friends. . . .

* * *

Comrades, Europe has been one of the most important lines in our foreign policy activity all these years. The improvement in Soviet-French relations has had important positive consequences for the whole course of European affairs. . . . We stand for the further development and deepening of relations between the U.S.S.R. and France, and regard this as an important factor of international security.

New prospects in Europe are opening up as a result of a substantial shift in our relations with the F.R.G. . . . Now, the treaties of the Soviet Union and Poland with the F.R.G. have confirmed with full certainty the inviolability of borders, including those between the G.D.R. and the F.R.G., and the western border of the Polish state.

* * *

. . . We are prepared to cover our part of the way towards normalization and improvement of relations between the F.R.G. and the socialist part of Europe, provided, of course, the other side acts in accordance with the letter and spirit of the treaty.

The positive changes that have recently taken place in Europe do not mean that the problems Europe inherited from the Second World War have been fully solved. What is to be done to continue the improvement in the European situation, to make headway in ensuring collective security in Europe, and in developing cooperation both on a bilateral and on an all-European basis?

The situation in Europe as a whole would be improved by the convocation of an all-European conference. . . . [Furthermore,] an improvement of the situation on the continent naturally requires that the Soviet-West German and the Polish-West German treaties should enter into force as soon as possible. There should also be a settlement of the problems connected with West Berlin. . . .

Another pressing task is establishment of equitable relations between the G.D.R. and the F.R.G., based on the generally accepted rules of international law, and also admission of both these states to the United Nations. [Also,] considerable importance should also be attached to the satisfaction of the legitimate demand of the Czecho-slovak Socialist Republic that the Munich agreement should be recognized as having been invalid from the outset.

124

Comrades, disarmament is one of the most important international problems of our day. . . . A treaty on the nonproliferation of nuclear weapons was prepared and has entered into force in the period under review. . . . The important point now is to have the F.R.G., Japan, Italy, and other countries back up their signatures to the treaty with its ratification. Treaties banning the stationing of nuclear weapons in outer space and on the sea and ocean floor have been concluded. But what has been achieved constitutes only the first few steps. It is our aim to bring about a situation in which nuclear energy shall serve peaceful purposes only.

We are engaged in negotiations with the U.S.A. on a limitation of strategic armaments. Their favorable outcome would make it possible to avoid another round in the missile-arms race, and to release considerable resources for constructive purposes. We are seeking to have the negotiations produce positive results. . . . The struggle for an end to the arms race, both in nuclear and conventional weapons, and for disarmament—all the way to general and complete disarmament—will continue to be one of the most important lines in the foreign policy activity of the CPSU and the Soviet state.

In recent years, the U.S.S.R.'s relations with the countries of the capitalist world have been fairly active and diverse. . . . For instance, we have been cooperating—on mutually advantageous terms, of course—with Italy in building the Volzhsky Auto Works, and with Austria and several other countries in developing the gas industry, including the laying of gas pipelines from the Soviet Union to Western Europe. Agreement was recently reached on the Soviet Union's participation in setting up an iron-and-steel complex in France. Also, Japanese companies are to cooperate in building a new port in the Far East. . . .

As usual, we have devoted much attention to our relations with our neighbors. Good neighborly relations and cooperation with Finland have continued to grow stronger; our relations with Afghanistan and Iran have been developing successfully; we have normal relations with Pakistan and Turkey; [and] our ties with Sweden are stable. Our friendly relations with India have developed considerably. . . . [And] we believe there are considerable possibilities for further extending mutually advantageous cooperation with Japan. . . .

Now about the Soviet Union's relations with the United States of America. An improvement in Soviet-American relations would be in the interests of the Soviet and the American peoples, [and] the interests of stronger peace. However, we cannot pass over the aggressive U.S. actions in various parts of the world. In the recent period, the U.S. administration has taken a more rigid stance on a number of international issues, including some which have a bearing on the interests of the Soviet Union. The frequent zigzags in U.S. foreign policy, which are apparently connected with some kind of domestic political moves dictated by short-term considerations, have also made dealings with the United States much more difficult.

We proceed from the assumption that it is possible to improve relations between the U.S.S.R. and the U.S.A. Our principled line with respect to the capitalist countries, including the U.S.A., is consistently and fully to practice the principles of peaceful coexistence, to develop mutually advantageous ties, and to cooperate with states prepared to do so, in strengthening peace, [and] making our relations with them as stable as possible. But we have to consider whether we are dealing with a real desire to settle outstanding issues at the negotiation table or attempts to conduct a "positions-of-strength" policy.

Whenever the imperialists need to cover up their aggressive schemes, they try to revive the "Soviet menace" myth. . . . But the peoples will not be deceived by the attempts to ascribe to the Soviet Union intentions which are alien to it. We declare with a full sense of responsibility: we have no territorial claims on anyone whatsoever; we threaten no one, and have no intention of attacking anyone; we stand for the free and independent development of all nations. But let no one, for his part, try to talk to us in terms of ultimatums and strength.

We have everything necessary—a genuine peace policy, military might, and the unity of Soviet people—to ensure the inviolability of our borders against any encroachments, and to defend the gains of socialism.

Comrades, the period under review marked the end of the quarter-century since the rout of Hitler Germany and militarist Japan. The fruits of that great victory still live in international realities today. The Soviet people cherish everything that has been attained at such great cost.

For more than twenty-five years now, our people have lived in peace. We regard this as the greatest achievement of our party's foreign policy. . . . [However, it is not] possible to consider the threat of another world war as having been completely eliminated. It is the vital task of all the peaceable states, of all the peoples, to prevent this threat from becoming reality.

The Soviet Union has countered the aggressive policy of imperialism with its policy of active defense of peace and strengthening of international security. . . . The CPSU regards the following as the *basic* concrete tasks of this struggle in the present situation.

First

To eliminate the hotbeds of war in Southeast Asia and in the Middle East and to promote a political settlement in these areas on the basis of respect for the legitimate rights of states and peoples subjected to aggression.

To give an immediate and firm rebuff to any acts of aggression and international arbitrariness. For this, full use must also be made of the possibilities of the United Nations.

Repudiation of the threat or use of force in settling outstanding issues must become a law of international life. For its part, the Soviet Union invites the countries which accept this approach to conclude appropriate bilateral or regional treaties.

Second

To proceed from the final recognition of the territorial changes that took place in Europe as a result of the Second World War. To bring about a radical turn towards détente and peace on this continent. To ensure the convocation and success of an all-European conference.

To do everything to ensure collective security in Europe, we reaffirm the readiness expressed jointly by the participants in the defensive Warsaw Treaty to have a simultaneous annulment of this treaty and of the North Atlantic alliance, or—as a first step —to dismantle their military organizations.

Third

To conclude treaties putting a ban on nuclear, chemical, and bacteriological weapons.

To work for an end to the testing of nuclear weapons, including underground tests, by everyone everywhere.

To promote the establishment of nuclear-free zones in various parts of the world.

We stand for the nuclear disarmament of all states in possession of nuclear weapons, and for the convocation for these purposes of a conference of the five nuclear powers—the U.S.S.R., the U.S.A., the P.R.C., France, and Britain.

Fourth

To invigorate the struggle to halt the race in all types of weapons. We favor the convocation of a world conference to consider disarmament questions to their full extent.

We stand for the dismantling of foreign military bases. We stand for a reduction of armed forces and armaments in areas where the military confrontation is especially dangerous, above all in Central Europe.

We consider it advisable to work out measures reducing the probability of accidental outbreak or deliberate fabrication of armed incidents and their development into international crises and into war.

The Soviet Union is prepared to negotiate agreements on reducing military expenditure, above all by the major powers.

Fifth

The U.N. decisions on the abolition of the remaining colonial regimes must be fully carried out. Manifestations of racism and apartheid must be universally condemned and boycotted.

Sixth

The Soviet Union is prepared to expand relations of mutually advantageous cooperation in every sphere with states which for their part seek to do so. Our country is prepared to participate with the other states concerned in settling problems like the conservation of the environment, development of power and other natural resources, development of transport and communications, prevention and eradication of the most dangerous and widespread diseases, and the exploration and development of outer space and the world's oceans.

Such are the main features of the program for the struggle for peace and international cooperation, [and] for the freedom and independence of nations, which our party has put forward.

* * *

Of course, in international affairs not everything depends on us or our friends alone. We have not advanced in every sphere as fast as we should like toward the goals we set ourselves. A number of important acts have yet to be brought to completion, and their importance will become fully evident later. But the overall balance is obvious: great results have been achieved in these five years. Our country's international position has become even stronger, its prestige has been enhanced, and the Soviet people's peaceful endeavor has reliable protection.

Document 4: Excerpts from "By the Leninist Course of Peace and Socialism"*

The CPSU Central Committee held a plenary meeting on 26 and 27 April 1973, and heard and discussed a report by Leonid Brezhnev on the international activities of the CPSU Central Committee to implement the decisions of the Twenty-fourth Congress of the party. The plenary meeting unanimously passed a decision in which it approved wholly and entirely the work done by the political bureau to ensure a lasting world peace and reliable security for the Soviet people who are building communism. Speakers at the meeting . . . noted the great personal contribution made by Leonid Brezhnev toward accomplishing these tasks.

*   *   *

At its Twenty-fourth Congress, our party put forward a concrete and realistic program for placing international relations on a healthier basis and strengthening peace. The Soviet peace program, as it is now called everywhere, was acclaimed by the peoples and seriously interested the governments of many countries. The CPSU Central Committee and the political bureau of the Central Committee, being guided in all their foreign policy activities by the behests of the great Lenin about the peaceable and at the same time revolutionary character of the foreign policy of our socialist state, a policy reflecting the vital interests of the working masses, have carried out a great amount of work to implement the decisions of the Twenty-fourth Congress of the party.

The active international policy of the CPSU which relies on the great strength and prestige of the Soviet state and the support of the entire people, is conducive to positive changes in the world situation. The plenary meeting outlined further prospects and tasks in our struggle for a lasting peace and international cooperation. "The plenary meeting of the Central Committee," the decision says, "instructs the Political Bureau to follow undeviatingly, as before, the foreign policy course laid down by the Twenty-fourth Congress of the CPSU and, taking as a guide the propositions and conclusions of Leonid Brezhnev's report at this plenary, meeting, to fight for the full implementation of the peace program and work [so that the] favorable changes which have been achieved in the international situation become irreversible."

*Source: *Pravda* (29 April 1973) as translated in: *Foreign Broadcast Information Service, Soviet Union, Daily Report* (30 April 1973), pp. J1-J5.

A major direction of the CPSU's foreign policy activities is its struggle for strengthening the positions of world socialism and developing all-round cooperation with the socialist countries. By the joint efforts of the CPSU and the fraternal parties of the socialist community the might and unity of the fraternal countries are being strengthened, as is the concertedness of their policy, which is playing an increasingly great part in positive changes in the international arena.

The most important event of the recent period was the victory of the Vietnamese people. The will of the heroic Vietnamese people to freedom and the great power of solidarity of the socialist countries have led to the termination of the imperialist aggression against Vietnam. The Soviet Union, being loyal to internationalism and the interests of world socialism, has given all-round assistance to Vietnam. Our Leninist party and the Soviet state have carried high the banner of revolutionary solidarity; they reiterate this solidarity and will facilitate in every way the establishment of peace in Indochina.

The end to the political blockade of the German Democratic Republic and the recognition of the G.D.R. by most of the states of the world was a major success for the concerted policy of the fraternal countries. The international position of Cuba, the first socialist state in the Western Hemisphere, has grown stronger. All the countries of the socialist community have scored historic successes in building a new society. All-round cooperation between fraternal socialist countries is being developed and deepened. Their cooperation in the economic field, which is determined by the implementation of the comprehensive program of socialist economic integration, is now in a qualitatively new stage.

The CPSU will contribute in every way toward further strengthening the unity of the socialist states, toward strengthening and expanding fraternal ties with them. Of special importance is the development of economic cooperation with CMEA countries, cooperation which calls today for a maximum use of the possibilities of socialist economic integration [and] which leads to the further strengthening of [the] economic and defense might of the socialist community.

Since the Twenty-fourth Congress of the CPSU the principles of peaceful coexistence have won broad recognition as a norm of relations between states with different social systems, and a turn from the cold war to détente is taking place. There is a favorable objective basis for the further development of these positive changes. The peaceable foreign policy of the Soviet Union has been and remains a major factor of change in the international situation.

Favorable conditions have also emerged for the development of peaceful cooperation between European states. The Soviet Union and the fraternal socialist countries have broken through the cold war front and laid the foundation for détente in relations between states in the East and the West of the European continent.

A great part in this respect was played by the work done by the Political Bureau of the CPSU Central Committee in connection with the conclusion and ratification of the treaty with the F.R.G. . . . The signature of the treaties by the U.S.S.R. and Poland with the F.R.G., the Four-Power agreement on West Berlin, and the conclusion of the treaty on the principles of relations between the G.D.R. and the F.R.G. have created realistic prerequisites for the further development of mutually beneficial relations by the Soviet Union and other socialist countries with the F.R.G. in the fields of economy, science and technology, and cultural ties.

The steady development of Soviet-French relations, which rests on the traditions of friendship of long standing between the peoples of the U.S.S.R. and France, is having a positive effect on improving the European situation. . . .

The Soviet Union is developing good neighborly relations with other European countries as well. This finds expression not only in the sphere of trade and economics but also in the expansion of interstate contacts, [and] in political consultations on major international issues.

Our party proceeds from the historical need for bringing about a radical turn toward détente and peace in the European continent, and for creating such a system of interstate relations that could become a living and attractive example of peaceful coexistence. All European peoples are longing for a lasting peace. They solidarize ever more actively with the struggle of the Soviet Union for European security.

The task of holding an all-European conference on security and cooperation has moved to the forefront of European politics today. The Soviet Union, jointly with other socialist countries, wants the all-European conference to help ensure reliable security and peaceful cooperation between all European countries. The U.S.S.R. also attaches great importance to the question of force reductions in central Europe.

The Moscow meeting between the Soviet leaders and the U.S. President in 1972 marked a turning point in the development of Soviet-American relations. The well-known document Basic Principles of Relations Between the Union of Soviet Socialist Republics and the United States of America, signed by General Secretary of the CPSU Central Committee Leonid Brezhnev and U.S. President Richard Nixon in Moscow on 29 May 1972, formulates the starting points of principle for the development of Soviet-American relations in the new conditions.

This document lays down a basis for bilateral, mutually beneficial cooperation in different fields. It also contains commitments by both sides to do everything possible to avoid military confrontations and avert the outbreak of a nuclear war. Thus, a foundation was laid for the further development of Soviet-American relations. A number of agreements were concluded between the U.S.S.R. and the U.S.A., resulting in achievements in the field of political and economic relations, scientific-technological and cultural ties. The CPSU and the Soviet state proceed from the belief that it is advisable to ensure durable peaceful relations between the U.S.S.R. and the U.S.A. on the basis of the principles of peaceful coexistence. It goes without saying that a similar approach is also required from the United States.

An improvement of Soviet-Japanese relations has begun to take shape recently. The development of large-scale, long-term, and mutually advantageous cooperation between the U.S.S.R. and Japan accords with the interests of both countries. As far as the political aspect is concerned, full normalization of relations through the conclusion of an appropriate agreement will meet the interests of the two countries.

Carrying out work for the development of relations between the Soviet Union and states with a differing social system along the principles of peaceful coexistence, the CPSU considers to be an important condition for the expansion and strengthening of positive trends in world politics. . . .

*   *   *

The plenary meeting of the CPSU Central Committee drew attention to the necessity of displaying permanent vigilance and readiness to give rebuff to the intrigues of the aggressive imperialist circles, of waging a consistent struggle against reactionary ideology and propaganda. It is necessary [to] inform the world public about the life of the Soviet land—its ideals, achievements, and its international activities. This is a powerful means of winning to our side the minds and hearts of millions of people.

Our party devotes great attention to the development of relations of the U.S.S.R. with the countries of Asia, Africa and Latin America. The Soviet Union consistently pursues a line of support for the legitimate rights of Arab peoples in their struggle against the Israeli aggression, for the settlement of the Middle East crisis in accordance with the resolution of the U.N. Security Council. Basing itself on the Soviet-Indian treaty of friendship and cooperation, our country develops friendly, mutually advantageous relations with India and actively contributes to relaxation of tensions in South Asia.

The Soviet Union ever more widely develops relations with the countries of Latin America. Recent facts have borne out that the trend toward liberation from the yoke of monopolies, [and] toward freedom and democratic development is strengthening in that part of the world. This is seen from the course of events in Chile and Peru, as well as in a number of other countries of the continent.

The invariable line of the Soviet Union towards the countries of Asia, Africa, and Latin America—fighting for freedom, for consolidation of independence, [and] for economic and social progress—is that of active support for this just struggle.

The plenary meeting of the Central Committee noted with satisfaction the solidarity of Marxist-Leninist parties and mass public movements with the activities of the CPSU and the Soviet state for the implementation of the peace program.

Positive processes are under way in the international Communist movement. They lead to its further cohesion, enhancing its activeness in the revolutionary struggle, [the] growth of its role in world development, [and] in defense of the peace and security of nations. All these developments are inseparably linked with the International Conference of Communist and Workers' Parties of 1969.

*　　*　　*

The world congress of peace-loving forces to be held in Moscow in the current year will be an important international public event. It is called upon to become a real factor in the mobilization of the popular masses in all continents for struggle for consolidation of peace and relaxation of tensions. We attach great significance to the congress and will work for its success.

The plenary meeting stressed that the persistent struggle waged by the P.R.C. leadership, against the cohesion of socialist countries and the world Communist movement, against the efforts of peace-loving states and [against] peoples striving for international détente, [is] detrimental to the cause of peace and international socialism. The plenary meeting reaffirmed the resoluteness of our party to further pursue in relations with China the line of the Twenty-fourth Congress of the CPSU.

The international policy of the CPSU is closely linked in all its versatile activities with the leadership of Communist construction in the U.S.S.R. A successful fulfillment and overfulfillment of the Ninth Five-Year Economic Development Plan is of tremendous significance today both for our internal life and for ensuring further successes in the international scene.

Guided by the directives of the December 1972 plenary meeting of the CPSU Central Committee, the propositions and conclusions of Leonid Brezhnev's report on the fiftieth anniversary of the U.S.S.R., the party and the entire people have spread socialist emulation for the successful fulfillment of the targets of the five-year plan. The plenary meeting of the Central Committee has called upon the Communists and all the working people of the U.S.S.R. to lay, by shock work in the third decisive year of the five-year-plan period, a firm foundation for the fulfillment and overfulfillment of all the targets outlined by the Twenty-fourth Congress of the CPSU, [in order to achieve] a considerable increase in the effectiveness of all the branches of national economy, and improvement of the quality of manufactured products.

The April plenary meeting of the CPSU Central Committee reaffirmed with full unanimity that our party's Leninist strategic line is a correct one. "The basic principles of our socialist revolutionary course in international policy were laid down by great Lenin," Leonid Brezhnev stressed in his address at the plenary meeting of the CPSU Central Committee. "We undeviatingly preserve loyalty to his instructions and his behests. And this loyalty to the creative spirit of Marxism-Leninism [and] its principled purposefulness is an earnest reason for our new successes [and the] new victories of our just cause."

*   *   *

The Soviet people unanimously and fully support the Leninist home and foreign policy of the CPSU. The decisions of the plenary meeting of the CPSU Central Committee are a new proof of the fact that the party justifies with honor the high confidence of the people. By their selfless labor for the good of the homeland, [and by their] high consciousness and cohesion around the Leninist party, the Soviet people will make a new, great contribution to safeguarding [the] peace and social progress of mankind.

BULGARIA

Document 5: Excerpts from the Report of the CC BCP to the Tenth Congress of the BCP, Delivered 20 April 1971 by Todor Zhivkov, General Secretary of the CC BCP*

1. The International Situation and the Tasks of the Party and the State in the Sphere of Foreign Policy

Comrades, during the period under review the activities of our party and our state were conducted in the conditions of a complicated international situation. The basic contradiction of our era—the contradiction between capitalism and socialism—has deepened still further. The socialist countries have scored new successes in their all-round progressive development. Their international prestige has grown, as has their role in determining the fate of mankind. A number of countries, which freed themselves from colonial domination, have taken new steps in their progressive social development. The process of the general crisis of capitalism has grown deeper. The struggle of the working class and of the other democratic and progressive social strata against the exploitation and the aggressive policy of the capitalist monopolies has become more active. The international Communist and working-class movements have grown stronger. The aggressive nature of imperialism has become more pronounced; the brutal acts of provocation and military adventures are aggravating the international situation.

Vladimir Ilyich Lenin once predicted that "the socialist revolution will not be only first and foremost a struggle of the revolutionary proletariat in each country against their own bourgeoisie—no, it will also be a struggle against imperialism, of all colonies and countries oppressed by imperialism, and of all dependent countries" (V. I. Lenin, *Works*, Bulg. ed., vol. 30, p. 149).

Our times, comrades, prove convincingly the correctness of the predictions of our leader. For the first time in its struggles for freedom and a good life over thousands of years mankind is marching against slavery, exploitation, and poverty, along with enormous organized forces such as the world socialist system, the international working class, and the national liberation movement—the three powerful streams in the revolutionary process today.

The world socialist system—the main force of the international revolutionary process in the era of transition from capitalism to social-

---

*Source: *Under the Banner of Internationalism* (Sofia: Sofia Press, 1971), pp. 8-25.

ism—considerably increased in might during the period under review. Its connections with the international working class and the national liberation movement grew stronger, as did its influence in international affairs.

As regards rates of development the socialist countries have dynamically outstripped the capitalist world. For the period of 1951–1969, the average annual growth of industrial production of the member countries of the Council for Mutual Economic Assistance was 10.5 percent, while it was 5.6 percent for the developed capitalist countries. The member countries of the Council for Mutual Economic Assistance embrace 18 percent of the territory of the world and only 10 percent of its population, while they turn out about one-third of the world's industrial production. . . .

The successes scored by the Soviet Union, the country of Lenin and the October Revolution, the country which is tracing the road to communism for mankind, are outstanding, and constitute a great part in the balance sheet of the successes of the socialist community. Having rendered inestimable service to mankind in the past, the Soviet Union is today the mainstay of world socialism, and of the struggle for peace, a good life, for understanding and cooperation among the nations. . . .

That is why the eyes of all mankind were turned toward Moscow and the Kremlin, where the Twenty-fourth Congress of the great Communist Party of the Soviet Union was in session. The Soviet Union has always justified the world's hopes. The Eighth Five-Year Plan has been fulfilled. A great stride has been taken in the direction of communism. Enormous successes have been scored in every field— in economy, in science and technology, in culture, and in defense. The remarkable Report of the General Secretary of the Central Committee of the Communist Party of the Soviet Union [at the Twenty-fourth Congress] outlined a new, impressive program for the development of the Soviet Union, and put forward a comprehensive program for the consolidation of world peace, which our party and our people hail and support completely. . . .

Once more from the rostrum of the Tenth Congress, the Bulgarian Communists with deep feelings of fraternal pride cordially greet the Soviet Communists, workers, members of collective farms and the intelligentsia. . . .

Comrades, the People's Republic of Bulgaria builds her relations with the fraternal socialist countries on the firm foundations of socialist internationalism. During the period under review, we renewed our treaties of friendship, cooperation, and mutual assistance with the Soviet Union, Poland, Hungary, Czechoslovakia and Romania.

We signed a treaty of this kind with the German Democratic Republic for the first time. We concluded a treaty of friendship and cooperation with Mongolia. Our relations with Cuba and the Democratic Republic of Vietnam were further developed; bilateral relations with the People's Democratic Republic of Korea were expanded. Following this line of policy the party and the government are making efforts to normalize our interstate relations with the People's Republic of China in spite of the serious ideological and political differences between us.

In the past few years the development of cooperation between the member countries of the Council for Mutual Economic Assistance entered upon a new stage. Our countries intensified the coordination of their national economic plans, intensified the specialization and cooperation in the fields of production and research, and entered upon a new stage in the process of bringing their economies together on the basis of socialist integration. Cooperation in the field of ideology and culture, and our united action in the international arena have expanded. The resistance of imperialism against our peaceful policy, and the renewed activity of NATO and the other aggressive blocs have brought about the strengthening and perfecting of the Warsaw defense system, which is a powerful protective shield of our socialist achievements.

* * *

The socialist system is a young system. As they advance along the road of building the new society, the different countries experience some difficulties and temporary setbacks.

Encouraged and supported by international reaction, antisocialist and right-wing revisionist forces tried, during the period under review, to force a breakthrough in the world of socialism and push Czechoslovakia out of the world socialist community. As is well known, the People's Republic of Bulgaria fulfilled its international duty and its obligations as an ally, and together with the other socialist allied countries rendered internationalist assistance to the fraternal Czechoslovak people. We are genuinely happy that the Czechoslovak Communists overcame the period of trial, that they freed their ranks of the right-wing revisionists and united the party under the banner of Marxism-Leninism. . . .

* * *

No doubt the fraternal parties in the socialist countries will use the lesson drawn from the experience of our common development and will continue to play their responsible leading role ever more successfully. The world socialist system will continue to overcome all difficulties, it will continue to flourish and grow stronger, multiplying its ranks as it marches forward ever more confidently!

I avail myself of the high rostrum of the Tenth Congress to extend our most cordial greetings to the delegations of the Communist and workers' parties from the fraternal socialist countries and. . . .

. . . to express our fraternal solidarity with the heroic peoples of the Democratic Republic of Vietnam, the Republic of Cuba, and the Korean People's Democratic Republic which have been successfully building socialism under the leadership of their glorious parties, despite the provocations and open acts of aggression of the imperialist forces!

Comrades, as noted by the Moscow conference [1969], a *distinctive feature of present-day capitalism* is the intensification and acceleration of the process of its transformation into state-monopoly capitalism. This process has further aggravated all contradictions inherent in capitalism and has led to the emergence of new contradictions stemming from the scientific and technological revolution under capitalism. During the last few years, the situation in the capitalist countries has deteriorated still further, and their contradiction-ridden economy is now being shaken by new and serious difficulties: financial and currency crises, economic stagnation and recession, mass unemployment, and soaring inflation.

The working class is the main revolutionary force in present-day capitalist society. The range of the social battles in the capitalist countries has shown the high level of class consciousness and unity of the working-class movement. Never before in the capitalist countries have there been such big strikes and other mass movements of the working class. If in 1958 the number of the strikers in the advanced capitalist countries was 26 million people, in 1966 their number rose to 44 million, while in 1970 the number was over 63 million people. The economic struggle engages the working people in clashes with the bourgeois state. [These clashes] assume an ever clearer political character. Proof of this is the powerful struggle of the working class in Great Britain which has lately gained in momentum against the anti-working-class legislation. . . .

The farmers, the petite bourgeoisie and part of the middle bourgeoisie are rising against the power of the monopolies. The level of political activity is rising among large sections of intellectuals, university students, office workers, and of some religious groups, and others. Various sections and groupings of young people are vehemently reacting against the bourgeois order, although they do not always have the right political orientation in the complex social

138

and political conflicts of today. Some of the young people are still held captive by bourgeois reformist illusions, while others take ultra-leftist positions. But the revolutionization of the youth within the citadels of capitalism is a phenomenon of enormous importance. . . . What binds these groups together with the working class is the striving to fight against reaction, to defend and extend democratic liberties and to stop the drive toward war.

. . . The achievement of unity of action between socialists and Communists is an important step in this direction and in overcoming the split in the working-class movement. The recent municipal elections in France have shown once again that wherever the left-wing forces are united, they win the support not only of the working class but also of the broad masses of working people.

The most essential aspect in the development of the international working-class movement between the Ninth and the Tenth Congresses of the Bulgarian Communist Party was the *struggle for the restoration and consolidation of the unity of the international Communist movement on the basis of Marxism-Leninism and proletarian internationalism.*

*   *   *

Our ties with the fraternal parties, particularly with the parties in the socialist countries, were extended and deepened during that period of time. . . . During the 1967–1970 period, our country was visited by 315 delegations and working groups to exchange experience, as well as by 250 leading functionaries of Communist and workers' parties on various occasions. Three hundred thirteen Bulgarian delegations and working groups were guests of fraternal parties. . . .

No doubt in the past few years, one of the most important events not only in the life of our movement but also in international life as a whole was the *International Conference of Communist and Workers' Parties held in Moscow in 1969.* The Moscow conference became an important stage in strengthening the unity and solidarity of the Communist movement, and in consolidating the unity of action of the broad peoples' masses throughout the world in the struggle against imperialism. The documents adopted by the Moscow conference are exerting and will continue to exert a lasting influence upon the entire development of the international situation.

Recently the Chinese leaders took advantage of the celebrations of the glorious anniversary of the Paris Commune and renewed their slanders against the international Communist movement, against the countries of the socialist community and against the Communist

Party of the Soviet Union, the party which for seven decades has been the irreplaceable standard-bearer of the world Communist movement!

The Bulgarian Communist party most decisively condemns the attacks and slanderous inventions of the Chinese leaders and their efforts to create a split in our movement—in the ranks of the socialist countries—and to weaken the anti-imperialist front. Our party will continue to fight most energetically right and "left" revisionism, nationalism and anti-Sovietism. . . .

Comrades, life has once again shown that the *national liberation revolution* in our era is also a national democratic revolution. Its anti-imperialist character brings it closer to the struggle of the working class in the capitalist countries and makes it an integral part of the world socialist revolution.

The national liberation movement is continuing to drive imperialism out of a growing number of regions in the world. Seven more independent countries have appeared on the map of the world. The peoples are engaged in an armed struggle against the colonizers in Angola, Mozambique, Guinea-Bissau and other countries. The struggle against the racist regimes in South Africa, Zimbabwe and Namibia is also on the rise.

New anti-imperialist regimes were set up in a number of African and Asian countries during the past few years. The Arab national-liberation movement is expanding. The anti-imperialist struggle is gaining momentum in Latin America. Above all, we should stress the great importance of the recent victory of the people's forces in Chile. The governments of Peru and Bolivia have taken a stand against slavish dependence on the North American monopolies. The movement of national and social liberation in Latin America, which began with the victory of the Cuban revolution, is growing.

*   *   *

Imperialism has no desire to reconcile itself to the loss of its positions in those countries. Using more subtle and flexible forms and methods in pursuing a neocolonialist policy, it is trying to preserve its economic domination there and to stop the progressive development of those countries. It fans up nationalism, separatism, tribalism, and religious conflicts, while organizing counterrevolutionary coups d'état.

Irrespective of the fact that imperialism has scored partial successes, its positions in the countries of the "third world" are continuing to weaken. Many of the newly liberated countries have taken the road of radical social and economic changes and have given a socialist orientation to their development. The recent elections in India, one of the world's biggest countries, are an example of the fascination which the ideas of socialism hold for the masses of the people. . . .

*   *   *

The People's Republic of Bulgaria pursues an unswerving policy of friendship and cooperation with the developing countries which have embarked upon the road of independence. Our relations with these countries are based on complete equality and on mutual interests; they are guided by our striving to assist them in their efforts toward rapid economic, social and cultural upswing. . . .

Comrades, imperialism is enraged because it is doomed by history. This fact is pushing it towards adventurism, and it is intensifying its aggressive character which makes it a still more treacherous and dangerous enemy. In its efforts to hold back the progressive course of history and preserve and consolidate its positions on a world scale, imperialism, primarily U.S. imperialism, is grossly violating the norms of international law, trampling upon the independence and sovereignty of other nations, and resorting to open military interventions. . . .

The basic content of the aggressive policy of imperialism is spearheaded against the socialist community and, above all, against the Soviet Union—its powerful vanguard. Imperialism has not abandoned its preparations for all-out armed aggression against socialism. But being aware of the dangers to which a new world war will expose it at the present stage, imperialism is resorting to the tactics of ideological subversion, to "quiet counterrevolution" and "local wars," hoping in this way to achieve certain advantages without running risks.

The criminal war of United States imperialism in *Vietnam* most clearly shows the aggressive character and adventurist nature of its policy. . . . The American imperialists and their South Vietnamese puppets attacked Laos after attacking Cambodia. But their attempt to put the doctrine of "Asians to fight Asians" into practice suffered complete defeat. . . . The People's Republic of Bulgaria resolutely condemns American intervention in Laos and Cambodia. We are giving and will continue to give every necessary aid and support to the heroic struggle of the peoples of Indochina.

*   *   *

Imperialism has kindled a dangerous hotbed of war in the *Middle East*. The main responsibility for the alarming situation in this sensitive region falls on the U.S.A. which is giving its support to Israel, provides it with arms, encouraging its aggressive policy and predatory appetites as it tries to crush the Arab liberation movement in order to restore lost positions. This line is dangerous and has no future. It is risking an increase and extension of the military confrontation in the Middle East. . . . Our country hails the recent proposals of the United Arab Republic for the liquidation of the hotbed of war in the Middle East. These proposals are an expression of the moderate and realistic policy of the Egyptian government. . . .

The People's Republic of Bulgaria also condemns the aggressive and provocative acts of imperialism in other parts of the world, denounces the rude interference in the home affairs of sovereign countries, and is ready to join efforts with all peaceloving countries in the world to oppose firmly and promptly all arbitrary international acts. . . . We shall continue to take advantage of the possibilities offered by the United Nations Organization and other international organizations in attaining this goal.

Comrades, during the period after the Ninth Congress of the party *our relations with the capitalist countries* became more active and extensive. Political contacts on different governmental levels have increased. Top-level Bulgarian state and government delegations visited Turkey, Austria, Finland, Japan, Norway, Denmark and Iceland. State and government leaders of these and other countries visited Bulgaria. Along with the traditional trade relations which are especially active with France, Italy, Austria, the Federal Republic of Germany, and Great Britain, useful, mutually advantageous scientific, technical, and industrial cooperation with a number of capitalist countries has been developing. . . . Our relations with these countries are built on the principles of peaceful coexistence and on the basis of mutual interest. . . .

In recent years the problems of peace and European security have occupied a central position in the foreign policy of the People's Republic of Bulgaria. As is known, the proposal of convening an all-European conference on the problems of peace, security, and cooperation, which is one of the greatest initiatives in international life, was made by the Warsaw Pact member-states. . . .

The treaties signed between the Soviet Union and the Federal Republic of Germany, [and] between Poland and the Federal Republic of Germany in 1970 are of great importance for the further improvement of the situation in Europe. These treaties must come into force in order to play a positive role. Other problems that need a positive solution are those existing between the Federal Republic of Germany and the neighboring socialist countries, the German Democratic Republic and Czechoslovakia.

Of serious importance for the further improvement of the political climate in Europe is the legal international recognition of the German Democratic Republic, the normalization of its relations with the Western European countries, as well as its admission to the United Nations Organization and to the other international organizations.

*　　*　　*

One of the major strategic tasks in the program for consolidating world peace, worked out by the Twenty-fourth Congress of the Communist Party of the Soviet Union, is general and complete disarmament. We hail the realistic Soviet proposals for the conclusion of interstate agreements on specific problems connected with the fulfillment of this task, such as: simultaneous liquidation of the military organizations of NATO and the Warsaw Pact; banning of chemical and bacteriological weapons; convening a conference of the countries possessing nuclear weapons for the purpose of reaching an agreement on nuclear disarmament; creating zones free of nuclear arms in different parts of the world; liquidating foreign military bases; cutting down armed forces and arms in regions where confrontation of the war blocs is especially dangerous; taking measures to diminish the chances of having accidental or prearranged war conflicts break out; and decreasing war expenditures.

Comrades, the complex and controversial character of the world today is reflected in the *Balkan Peninsula.* . . . Not long ago we renewed the Treaty of Friendship, Cooperation, and Mutual Aid with our northern neighbor, the Socialist Republic of Romania. We coordinated our plans for the next five-year plan and envisaged a new sharp increase in trade. . . .

In our relations with the Socialist Federative Republic of Yugoslavia our country is being led by the consideration that cooperation between the two socialist countries corresponds to the interests of our peoples, and to the interests of peace [and] socialism. . . .

Our relations with the People's Republic of Albania do not correspond to the interests of the two countries. The Albanian leaders have sunk into the quagmire of opportunism and anti-Sovietism and are constantly pitting Albania against her natural allies. In spite of this we shall continue our efforts to normalize and improve relations between our two Balkan countries.

In recent years considerable improvement was scored in our relations with the Republic of Turkey. . . . [And] as is known, our relations with the kingdom of Greece were normalized by the signing of a number of bilateral treaties in 1964. . . . Since the very creation of the Republic of Cyprus our relations have been friendly. We are giving full support to the just aspirations of the people of Cyprus to preserve their territorial integrity, their independence and the sovereignty of their country.

Along with the development of bilateral relations with its neighbors, the People's Republic of Bulgaria will continue to support and actively participate in all multilateral Balkan initiatives which would extend economic, political, and cultural relations among the Balkan countries and turn the Balkan Peninsula into a zone of lasting peace and stability, of understanding and cooperation.

Comrades, the friendship and cooperation with the Soviet Union is the unshakeable granite basis on which the entire foreign policy of the People's Republic of Bulgaria rests. . . .

Our party, our country, and the Bulgarian people have adhered and will always adhere to the behest of Georgi Dimitrov: to consolidate the sacred Bulgarian-Soviet friendship, to extend and deepen our relations with the great country of communism under construction. Allow me, comrades, to assure the general secretary of the Central Committee of the Communist Party of the Soviet Union, a prominent figure in the world Communist and working-class movement, the great friend of Bulgaria, Comrade Leonid Ilyich Brezhnev, allow me to assure our dear comrades and brothers, the members of the Soviet delegation, allow me to assure the Soviet Communists and the Soviet people that we shall never under my circumstances fail to carry out this behest which is vital for the destinies of socialist Bulgaria. Today, expressing the innermost thoughts and feelings of the Bulgarian Communists, of our entire people, our party is solemnly inscribing these cherished words in its program:

"The Bulgarian Communist party and the Bulgarian people need Bulgarian-Soviet friendship the way all living things need the sun and air, it is a centuries-old friendship and a friendship to last centuries, it is one of the main motive forces of our development, it is a prerequisite and guarantee for the future upsurge of our socialist country and of its morrow."

Our foreign policy is not based on conjunctural considerations but on the lasting interests of our people, of the socialist community and of the interests of the international revolutionary movement. Its basic goal is to ensure maximum favorable international conditions for building a socialist society in our country, thus making its contribution to the consolidation of the positions of socialism, progress, and peace throughout the world.

*　　*　　*

With its loyalty to the internationalist traditions of Dimiter Blagoev and Georgi Dimitrov, the Bulgarian Communist party has gained high prestige within the international Communist movement. For us, Bulgarian Communists, the respect and trust of the fraternal parties is more valuable than all worldly wealth, and in the future as well, we shall cherish and consolidate them in our life through our labor and through our struggle for the victory of our great common cause.

CZECHOSLOVAKIA

Document 6: Excerpts from the Report of the CC CzCP to the Fourteenth Congress of the CzCP, Delivered 25 May 1971 by Gustav Husak, General Secretary of the CC CzCP*

OUR FOREIGN POLICY SERVES SOCIALISM AND PEACE

Comrades, the complicated development through which the Czechoslovak Communist party passed over the past five years has left its mark on the international activity of the party and the foreign policy of our state.

"The Lesson Drawn from the Crisis Development in the Party and Society after the Thirteenth Congress of the Communist Party of Czechoslovakia" presents an objective picture of one of the great battles fought between socialism and imperialism in the sixties. It shows to the full extent the interrelation between internal political disruption and imperialist subversion as well as the unavoidable need for close cooperation between the internal and internationalist socialist forces in the defense of the revolutionary gains of socialism in the C.S.S.R. It is an irrefutable fact that the rescue, strengthening, and present development of socialism in our country represents a remarkable victory for the world revolutionary forces, and a heavy loss and defeat for imperialism.

That is the foundation of the class truth on which we based our analysis of the recent past. We said already at the Moscow International Conference of Communist and Workers' Parties in June 1969, that by the Fourteenth Congress of the Czechoslovak Communist party we would prepare an evaluation of the Czechoslovak crisis into which the party and society got itself in 1968. This we have done. The conclusions reached by the Central Committee were unanimously approved by Czechoslovak Communists and they are supported also by the great majority of our working people.

We express our comradely gratitude to all the fraternal parties that have been observing our developments over the past two years with understanding and supporting with solidarity the efforts of Czechoslovak Communists to strengthen socialism in this country. We again express our readiness to welcome in a comradely way everyone who wishes to learn the objective truth about our situation, and

---

*Source: *14th Congress of the Communist Party of Czechoslovakia* (Prague: Orbis, 1971), pp. 74-80.

we shall acquaint him with all the facts which we have deduced from our present knowledge and evaluation. It is up to the fraternal parties to adjudge for themselves which of our experiences is significant for them too.

*　　*　　*

Our party considers its cardinal task to be to contribute with all its forces toward implementing the conclusions jointly adopted at the Moscow conference of representatives of Communist and workers' parties in 1969. . . . That is why we agree with the views of the fraternal parties, that a broadly based international meeting of Communists should become a permanent practice in our movement, which would promote its revolutionary ability to act. . . .

At the present time we have good comradely relations with the great majority of fraternal parties. We wish to assure them from the platform of this congress that Czechoslovak Communists, taking a lesson from recent experience, will vigilantly guard their socialist achievements and revolutionary workers' power in Czechoslovakia. . . . Our party will exert every effort to contribute in an all-round and effective manner to strengthen the political, economic and defense power of the socialist community.

We assure the fraternal Communist parties of the capitalist countries of our solidarity and support for them in this struggle with the bourgeoisie. . . .

We wish at the same time to assure the Communist and revolutionary democratic parties of the developing countries of Asia and Africa, that we shall support actively all their endeavors to overcome the social and economic heritage of colonialism. . . . We assure our support to all those countries which are still waging a national liberation struggle for release from the colonial yoke.

We also welcome the new progressive phenomena in the anti-imperialist movement on the Latin American continent, strong evidence of which is the victory of the forces of Popular Unity in Chile and the successes of the national democratic antimonopolistic advance in Peru and Bolivia.

We proudly endorse the fundamental mission of Communists to be the vanguard of all truly revolutionary and progressive events. . . . Developments throughout the world are confirming again and again the viability and correctness of the Marxist-Leninist teachings. . . . Our recent experience and the knowledge of other parties strongly confirms that revisionism must necessarily merge into open betrayal of socialism and the revolutionary workers' movement, and into the inevitable transference of its representatives to anti-Communist and anti-Soviet positions.

In the struggle against right-wing opportunism and international revisionism, however, we must not overlook the danger which the current theory and practice of the Chinese leadership entails for the interests of socialism, world communism and the common anti-imperialist struggle. It is based on anti-Sovietism. . . . The leadership of the Communist party of China refuses to establish any sort of relations with the great majority of the Communist and workers' parties, not excluding our own. We should like to express the conviction that the Chinese Communists and Chinese people will sooner or later realize this mistake. We are willing to discuss all problems which could contribute to a normalization of mutual relations, for we are convinced that this is in the interests not only of both countries but in the cause of socialism and peace in the world.

Comrades, with the passing of two years we can say that the results of our cooperation with the socialist countries, a bond which was restored after the April plenary session of the Communist party Central Committee in 1969 on the basis of mutual trust, are now very good and developing favorably. But this does not mean that we are fully satisfied. Particularly in the sectors of economic, scientific, and cultural relations there are many new possibilities and stimulants to still more effective expansion of our mutual relations.

*   *   *

In the future, the Czechoslovak Socialist Republic will contribute to seeing that the member countries of the Warsaw Treaty successfully coordinate their procedures on foreign political affairs, and secure the joint defense of revolutionary achievements and the inviolability of the borders of the socialist community.

The main pillar of power of world socialism and also the most important source of its revolutionary energy is the Soviet Union, which also represents an impassable barrier against the expansionist and conquering character of imperialism. It is above all thanks to its tremendous economic and military power, its international authority, and Leninist peace program, which was once more summarized in the foreign political concept of the Twenty-fourth Congress of the CPSU, that socialism is now asserting its influence in solving all world problems.

We can say with pleasure and satisfaction at our congress that Czechoslovak-Soviet relations have not only been fully restored but have reached at the present time a qualitatively higher level and are recording also broader application. A symbol of these fraternal relations, in the true sense of the word, is the new Treaty of Friendship, Cooperation, and Mutual Assistance between Czechoslovakia and the Soviet Union, the first anniversary of which we commemorated on May 6th. Our relations and cooperation with the Polish People's Republic, the German Democratic Republic, the Hungarian People's Republic, the Bulgarian People's Republic, the Romanian Socialist Republic, and the Mongolian People's Republic, founded on common socialist interests and aims, are also developing successfully. Recent talks between representatives of the Communist party of Czechoslovakia and the League of Communists of Yugoslavia show that there are realistic conditions also for improving mutual relations between Czechoslovakia and the Socialist Federative Republic of Yugoslavia.

Comrades, we are certainly voicing the sentiments of all delegates to our congress when we assure the representatives of the Workers' Party of Vietnam and of the National Liberation Front of South Vietnam present here, that our party and all our people support from the bottom of their hearts the just cause of our Vietnamese friends, who have not relented in their heroic many-years-long struggle against the American aggressors and their Saigon lackeys. . . .

Our full sympathy and support goes to the first socialist country on the American continent—the Cuban Republic. . . . We also voice our full solidarity with the Korean People's Democratic Republic, unwaveringly striving for a peaceful unification of the country and for enforcing the withdrawal of the American occupation troops from South Korea. . . .

At the present time international attention is directed toward the Middle East region where, as a result of the expansionist and aggressive policy of Israel, supported by American imperialism, a dangerous focal point of war has been created. We take an unqualified and resolute stand on the side of the United Arab Republic and the other Arab states striving to overcome the consequences of Israeli aggression. [We call] for the return of the occupied territory and the assertion of the just claims of the Palestinian people. A realistic way of establishing peace in this area would be the fulfillment of all the provisions of the resolution of the Security Council of the United Nations of November 1967.

*   *   *

In view of the geographical position of our country, we are interested in peaceful developments in Europe, [and] in an effective system of collective security. We are of the opinion that the constructive initiative of the socialist countries over many years has created favorable conditions for the all-round preparation of an All-European Conference on Security and Cooperation and for its convening without any preliminary conditions. There can be no doubt that every positive step in strengthening conditions of peace in Europe is of worldwide importance. . . .

An important step in this direction was the conclusion of a treaty between the U.S.S.R. and the Federal Republic of Germany [F.R.G.] and between the Polish People's Republic and the F.R.G. It is, however, regrettable that the Federal Parliament has not yet ratified these important documents. This only confirms that there are influential forces at work in the F.R.G. which prevent a real settlement of relations with the socialist states. Proof of this is also the negative stand on the recognition, according to international law, of the German Democratic Republic, even though this is an entirely justified and natural demand on the part of a sovereign state which has proved in its whole policy that it has made an end once and for all with the militarist and reactionary past of Germany and has accomplished much for peaceful development in Europe.

One of the unsolved problems which has an indisputable impact on the development of conditions in Europe are the still unsolved relations between the Czechoslovak Socialist Republic and the Federal Republic of Germany. The chief obstacle to this solution is the persistent attitude of the Federal Republic of Germany to the Munich Dictate, which maintains the untenable stand that it was a valid international treaty. Meanwhile it is generally known that Munich was negotiated without the participation of Czechoslovakia and against that country—that it was forced upon her by threats and violence. Our just demand to proclaim the Munich agreement as invalid from the very outset, with all the ensuing consequences, is based on the irrefutable fact that this so-called agreement was part of the criminal Nazi betrayal of peace and was a step that led to the Second World War, that it was a crime committed against Czechoslovakia. . . .

We want to reconfirm at our congress our firm determination to expand political, economic, and cultural relations, in the spirit of the Leninist policy of peaceful coexistence, with all capitalist countries on condition that their governments will respect the wish of our working people to live and work in a socialist society. We are convinced that this resolution of ours is in harmony with the aspirations of all nations and peoples of good will. But never for a moment should we forget the threat of world imperialism headed by the aggressive circles of the United States of America. It is essential to evolve a broadly based campaign with the progressive, democratic, national liberation and socialist forces against its expansive aggression and intentions of world domination. The Communist Party of Czechoslovakia takes it as its highest international obligation to play as large a share as possible in this common revolutionary struggle.

MONGOLIA

Document 7: Excerpts from the Report of the CC MWP to the Sixteenth Congress of the MWP, Delivered 7 June 1971 by Yumzhagiin Tsedenbal, First Secretary of the CC MWP *

The Sixteenth MWP Congress is beginning its work on the threshold of the glorious jubilee of the people's revolution, which brought the Mongolian people complete national and social liberation, happiness and optimism. High political and labor enthusiasm define the sentiments of the M.P.R. working people, who are greeting the party congress and the fiftieth anniversary of the people's revolution with new successes in the sphere of peaceful creative activity in the name of the further flourishing of their socialist motherland.

Exactly five years have elapsed since the Fifteenth party Congress, which adopted the new, fourth MWP program—a program for the completion of building socialism in our country. In implementing the previous party congress's decisions, the Mongolian people have achieved major successes in the years which have elapsed in resolving the economic and cultural building tasks and increasing their material prosperity. Our country's working people fulfilled the 1966–70 M.P.R. national economic and cultural development plan for the main indicators. A further important step forward was thereby made in creating the material and technical base of socialism in the M.P.R.

The period which has elapsed since the Fifteenth party Congress has been filled with most important events in the international sphere too. Among these the Fiftieth anniversary of the Great October Socialist Revolution, which opened a new era in world history, and also the birth centenary of the greatest thinker of our age—V. I. Lenin —stand out for their significance. The celebrations of these worldwide historic events in the M.P.R. merged into a striking demonstration of the unswerving loyalty of the Communists and all the Mongolian working people to the immortal Leninist doctrine, the principles of proletarian internationalism, and indestructible Mongolian-Soviet friendship.

Other outstanding events in the lives of all the countries' Communists and peoples were the 1969 Moscow Conference of Communist and Workers' Parties and the historic Twenty-fourth CPSU Congress, both of which are of great significance in the struggle for the

* Source: *Foreign Broadcast Information Service, Asia & Pacific Supplement*, no. 117, supp. 42 (17 June 1971), pp. 1-9.

unity of action of all revolutionary and anti-imperialist forces and for the triumph of the cause of peace and socialism.

* * *

. . . The past five-year period has been marked by a further consolidation of the M.P.R.'s external position, an increase in our country's authority in the world arena, and an activation of our participation in international affairs.

In its foreign policy activity the party Central Committee, as previously, has firmly and persistently followed a course aimed at consolidating the M.P.R.'s alliance, friendship, and cooperation with the Soviet Union and the other socialist countries in every possible way, and at strengthening the international positions and unity of action of the countries of the socialist community. This unwavering foreign policy course of ours is completely in keeping with the M.P.R.'s interests and enjoys the unanimous support of all the Mongolian people.

* * *

CPSU Central Committee General Secretary Comrade L. I. Brezhnev's words at the Soviet Communists' Twenty-fourth Congress about the strong and tested Mongolian-Soviet friendship, which has grown and become stronger over half a century, evoked an ardent response among the M.P.R. Communists and working people.

Mongolian-Soviet relations can be characterized as follows: Our friendship with the Soviet Union is socialist internationalism in action. This internationalism is manifested fully in our daily lives, in the Mongolian people's successes and achievements and in the development and further deepening of Mongolian-Soviet cooperation, which, becoming enriched with new experiences and new forms, is yielding rich fruit.

The 1966 visit to the M.P.R. by the Soviet party and government delegation led by CPSU Central Committee General Secretary Comrade L. I. Brezhnev constitutes a striking page in the annals of Mongolian-Soviet friendship. The new Treaty of Friendship, Cooperation, and Mutual Aid between the M.P.R. and the U.S.S.R.—a treaty forming the political and juridical basis of the indestructible alliance and brotherhood between the Mongolian and Soviet peoples —was signed during this historic visit.

The official friendly visit to our country by U.S.S.R. Supreme Soviet Presidium Chairman N. V. Podgorny in 1969 and also the M.P.R. party and government delegation's visit to the Soviet Union in October 1970 were of great significance for further consolidating and deepening the relations of friendship and cooperation between our countries. The negotiations held in Moscow last year resulted in the determination of the main directions of economic cooperation for the immediate future and in the outlining [of] specific measures to promote the further consolidation of our national economy's material and technical base.

The Soviet Union's genuinely internationalist aid in developing M.P.R. production forces and raising the Mongolian working people's material prosperity and cultural level is steadily growing with every passing year. Industrial enterprises and agricultural, housing, cultural, and everyday projects were constructed in various corners of our country during the years of the last five-year plan with Soviet technical and economic aid and direct participation by Soviet workers and specialists. In accordance with the task of further consolidating the defense might of the entire socialist community, the Soviet Union also renders invaluable aid in increasing the M.P.R.'s defense capability.

* * *

The Soviet people's magnificent successes in the building of communism and their outstanding scientific and technical achievements are increasing the might of the entire socialist community and exerting an enormous and inspiring influence on the development of the world revolutionary process.

* * *

It was with profound satisfaction that the M.P.R. Communists and working people received the magnificent program for building communism in the Soviet Union outlined by the Twenty-fourth CPSU Congress. Our party warmly welcomes and fully supports the constructive plan for safeguarding peace and international security formulated by the Leninist party's congress, a plan which is completely in keeping with the vital interests of the peoples of all the world's countries. . . .

* * *

The launching of the Soyuz spacecraft manned by remarkable Soviet cosmonauts provides new testimony to the Soviet people's creative brilliance. Permit me to offer sincere congratulations on this outstanding event, an event which is taking place during our Congress's work.

In its foreign policy activity, the party attaches great significance to consolidating friendship and cooperation with the other socialist countries and with [their] Communist and workers' parties. Close and multifaceted cooperation links the M.P.R. with Bulgaria, Hungary, the G.D.R., Poland, Romania, and Czechoslovakia. The M.P.R.'s relations of friendship and cooperation with the D.R.V., the D.P.R.K., Cuba, and Yugoslavia have enjoyed further development during the years which have elapsed.

* * *

The M.P.R. participates actively in CMEA activity. This enables us to accelerate the national economic development rate by utilizing the advantages of the socialist division of labor. At present, in jointly solving the problems of economic development, CMEA countries are implementing a course aimed at socialist integration. This is intended to promote a general upsurge in the socialist countries' economic potential and the implementation of the law concerning the equalization of their economic development levels, which results in the achievement of what V. I. Lenin spoke about—the actual equality of nations in economic and cultural development.

* * *

The formulation of a comprehensive program for the development of socialist economic integration on the basis of the Twenty-third and Twenty-fourth CMEA session decisions constitutes a major step forward along the path of further deepening the cooperation between the CMEA socialist states. . . . Our party and the M.P.R. government regard the further consolidation of all-round cooperation with the fraternal countries within the CMEA framework as one of the main directions of our foreign policy activity.

Strong fraternal friendship and ardent international solidarity link the Mongolian people with the heroic Vietnamese people, who are waging a courageous struggle against the imperialist aggressors. The M.P.R. warmly welcomed the formation of the PRGRSV. We are deeply convinced that the Vietnamese people's just cause, which relies on the international aid of the Soviet Union and the other countries in the socialist community, will be crowned with complete victory.

In consolidating its relations of friendship with the fraternal countries, the M.P.R. proceeds from the fact that the intensification and improvement of the socialist states' cooperation is completely in keeping with the interests of world socialism—the vanguard and nucleus of all the revolutionary and anti-imperialist forces of the present.

As practice has shown, building socialism is a complex and multifaceted process, in the course of which certain difficulties conditioned by circumstances of a domestic and external nature can and do arise. These difficulties and the concomitant problems are being successfully resolved by the Communist and workers' parties on the basis of unswerving observance of the principles of Marxism-Leninism and consolidation of international solidarity with the fraternal socialist countries. The Mongolian Communists warmly greet . . . the Polish working people, who, having overcome the difficulties which arose in their midst recently, are exerting great efforts to insure further rapid development for the whole country.

The 1968 political crisis, when internal counterrevolutionary forces and their accomplices launched frenzied attacks with the aid of imperialist reaction against socialism's position in Czechoslovakia with a view to restoring the capitalist system, was a serious test of the strength of the foundation of socialism in fraternal Czechoslovakia. It is with great satisfaction that we note that the healthy forces in the CzCP and Czechoslovak society, relying on the timely international assistance of the five Warsaw Pact countries, managed to deal a resolute rebuff to the forces hostile to socialism and to protect their people's interests and achievements.

*　　*　　*

The lessons of the Czechoslovak events confirm that the working people's socialist achievements are inviolable and that the defense of socialism is the vital concern of the fraternal Communist parties and the common international duty of the countries of world socialism.

Under present conditions, when the spearhead of imperialism's aggressive policy is aimed against the socialist states' unity, special urgency is attached to the cohesion in our ranks on the basis of the principles of Marxism-Leninism and to the need to act in a united front in the struggle against imperialism.

During the period under review the M.P.R., as previously, exerted its own efforts to normalize relations with the P.R.C., relations for whose serious disruption we were not to blame. We shall continue to pursue a course aimed at the restoration and development of friendly cooperation and good-neighborliness with the P.R.C.

Our party sees its task as constantly extending and defending all-round cooperation with the other socialist countries, developing and strengthening ideological-political ties with these countries' Marxist-Leninist parties, promoting in every possible way the consolidation of the unity and cohesion of the entire socialist community, and rearing the MWP working people in the spirit of friendship and international solidarity with the fraternal peoples building socialism and communism.

The MWP persistently pursues a course aimed at rendering all possible support to the peoples' international workers and national liberation movement, the struggle against colonialism and neocolonialism, and the consolidation and development of friendly relations with the states which have embarked on the path of independent development and will continue to support the Communists, the working class, and all the working people in the capitalist countries in their struggle for peace, democracy, and socialism, and against imperialism.

It must be stressed that the M.P.R.'s friendly relations with many Asian and African countries, including India, Algeria, Ceylon and others, are developing successfully in the interests of the peoples' struggle for peace and social progress. We note with profound satisfaction that a number of states on the Asian and African continents are now following a noncapitalist development path, implementing progressive transformations in their countries' socioeconomic lives. The M.P.R.'s experience convincingly confirms the historically promising nature of the noncapitalist development path for countries which have liberated themselves from colonial domination.

. . . In the Latin American countries the establishment of diplomatic relations between the M.P.R. and Chile at the beginning of this year constituted a favorable development. . . . Loyal to the ideas of peace and equal cooperation between the peoples, the M.P.R. will continue to develop and extend its friendly relations with the Asian, African, and Latin American countries in the interests of support for the anti-imperialist struggle of these countries' peoples and the interests of the triumph of the cause of peace and social progress.

*　　*　　*

The growth and extension of the MWP's cooperation with other detachments of the Communist movement is evidenced by the fact that our party now maintains close ties and contacts with more than seventy of the world's Communist and workers' parties. Unity of views and action, close fraternal cooperation, and mutual support have been and remain a norm and distinguishing feature of the mutual relations between the MWP and Lenin's great party—the CPSU—and the other Marxist-Leninist parties of the socialist countries. The Mongolian Communists and working people nurture feelings of special respect for, and profound sympathy with, the CPSU—the most highly tempered and experienced detachment of the world Communist movement which exemplifies unwavering loyalty to the great Marxist-Leninist banner.

Our party also pursues a course aimed at extending bilateral ties and contacts with the Communist, left socialist, and revolutionary democratic parties of the other countries of the world and at strengthening solidarity and cooperation with them in the struggle for the cohesion of the anti-imperialist forces.

*   *   *

The congresses of the fraternal Marxist-Leninist parties constitute a valuable contribution to the devolopment of Marxist-Leninist theory, the enrichment of the practice of building the new society, and the intensification of the struggle against all types of opportunism and revisionism. The historic Twenty-fourth CPSU Congress, the subsequent Tenth Bulgarian Communist Party Congress, and the Fourteenth CzCP Congress have again confirmed that the strength of the Marxist-Leninist parties and the Communist movement lies in boundless devotion to the principles of proletarian internationalism and the great doctrine of Marx, Engels, and Lenin.

*   *   *

The 1969 Moscow conference's evaluations and conclusions serve as a program of action for the Communist and workers' parties, including the MWP, in the struggle for the revolutionary principles of Marxism-Leninism and against right and "left" opportunism within our movement and bourgeois nationalism, anticommunism, and anti-Sovietism.

Our party is waging a principled struggle against the Chinese leaders' anti-Marxist political line. The Chinese leaders are attempting by their divisive actions to disunite the socialist countries, undermine and split the ranks of the Communist movement, and disarm the working class and working people of various countries in the face of frenzied attacks by imperialist reaction. The course pursued by the Chinese leaders, who have taken belligerent nationalism and anti-Sovietism into their armory, has led to China's isolation from the socialist countries and to armed provocations against Lenin's motherland—the U.S.S.R. Such a course is radically at variance with the interests of the peoples' revolutionary struggle, including the vital interests of the Chinese people themselves. Together with the fraternal parties, our party will continue to do everything to protect the purity of the Marxist-Leninist doctrine by joint efforts and to defend and constantly consolidate the unity and cohesion of all the fighters for the working-class cause and against imperialism and its henchmen.

*   *   *

From our congress rostrum we resolutely condemn the U.S. imperialists' criminal aggression against the Indochina peoples. Our party considers that the only feasible way to achieve both a rapid political settlement of the problems of Vietnam, Laos, and Cambodia and the establishment of peace in Southeast Asia, is an immediate end to the shameful colonial war and the unconditional and total withdrawal of U.S. forces from the countries in this region.

As an Asian socialist country, the M.P.R. has a vital interest in safeguarding peace and security in Asia and the Far East. It resolutely opposes the imperialist policy of perpetuating the partition of Korea and advocates the peaceful and democratic unification of this country in the interests of the entire Korean people and the interests of safeguarding peace in the Far East.

The Asian peoples are well aware that the essence of U.S. policy in Asia lies ultimately in establishing U.S. domination in Asia.

. . . The M.P.R. has a profound interest in peaceful Japanese development. However, the facts testify that Japanese monopoly capital, by extending the military-political alliance with the United States, is pushing the country onto the path of militarization to an ever-increasing extent.

The extension of ties between the Asian states and the development of fruitful cooperation on the basis of the principles of equal rights, mutual benefit, and noninterference in each other's internal affairs would undoubtedly serve the cause of the establishment of stable peace in this part of the world. In this connection the idea advanced by the Soviet Union in 1969, of creating a collective security system in Asia, enjoys support among the Asian peoples, who see the creation of such a system as a reliable guarantee safeguarding peace on the continent.

Like the other fraternal socialist countries the M.P.R. has been firmly on the Arab people's side since the very beginning of the Middle East crisis and expresses its ardent solidarity with their struggle for national independence, territorial integrity, and social progress. The M.P.R. believes that the establishment of genuine peace in the Middle East requires the liquidation of all the consequences of the Israeli aggression. Here consideration must be given to the rights and interests of all the Middle East peoples, including the Arabs of Palestine. U.S.S.R. Supreme Soviet Presidium Chairman Comrade N. V. Podgorny's recent visit to the U.A.R. and the signing of the friendship and cooperation treaty between the Soviet Union and the U.A.R. are of great significance for insuring a stable and just peace in the Middle East.

*   *   *

One of the most urgent and cardinal tasks of present-day international development—a task on which the attention of the world public is riveted—is the problem of safeguarding European security.

The M.P.R. established diplomatic relations with twenty states during the period under review. Our country now maintains diplomatic relations with fifty-three of the world's states. This fact testifies to the growth of socialist Mongolia's international authority and to the further steady extension of its foreign ties. During the period under review, the MWP acted in a united front with the fraternal socialist countries and all peace-loving forces in solving urgent problems of international life.

GERMAN DEMOCRATIC REPUBLIC (EAST GERMANY)

Document 8: Excerpts from the Report of the CC SED to the Eighth Congress of the SED, Delivered 15 June 1971 by Erich Honecker, General Secretary of the CC SED*

THE MAIN TRENDS IN THE INTERNATIONAL DEVELOPMENT AND THE FOREIGN POLITICAL LINE OF THE SED

Comrades, the G.D.R. is building up socialism in full conformity with those historical development processes which mark our epoch. If one looks at the worldwide movement for freedom, peace, and progress, then everyone feels that we are a part of a large struggling community for revolutionary renewal of the world. We are thus certain that our cause will be victorious; that the future will belong to our cause.

The four years full of struggle since our Seventh Party Congress clearly illustrate this. The socialist world system—the forces of peace, democracy, and national independence—have achieved important new successes. The course of international events fully proved the collective assessment worked out at the International Conference of the Communist and Workers' Parties in 1969. As a result of this and because of the constant growth, power, and strength of the Soviet Union; and because of the consolidation of the international position of the socialist community of states, the balance of power further shifted in favor of socialism and the anti-imperialist movement in the world.

If mankind has been successfully kept from a new world war, and if time and again the imperialist aggressors have been put in their place, it was due primarily to the Soviet Union and the entire socialist community of states. The role played by the international socialist system as the main revolutionary force of our time and as a reliable bastion of peace has been further intensified. Its influence on international developments is growing continuously.

Today the progress of mankind is advanced by three powerful revolutionary streams: the international socialist system, the international workers' movement, and the national liberation movement of the peoples. It has been and will continue to be the aim of our party to work together with the CPSU and the fraternal parties of the other socialist countries to consolidate the fighting alliance of

---

* Source: *Neues Deutschland* (16 June 1971), pp. 3-9A, as translated in: *Foreign Broadcast Information Service Supplement, Eastern Europe*, no. 122, supp. 43, (24 June 1971), pp. 10-22.

these main revolutionary forces of the present. Occasional difficulties and temporary setbacks in the international class struggle could not stop the advance of social progress and did not hamper the further curbing of imperialism, despite its unabated aggressive and dangerous nature.

Today the attack on the imperialist positions is continuously intensified. Imperialism's attempts to maintain and strengthen its positions by military aggression and counterrevolutionary actions, by growing exploitation of foreign peoples, and by ideological diversion has failed time and again. Under the pressure of the changed international balance of power in favor of socialism, imperialism is trying to adapt to the new conditions of the class struggle in order to achieve its old aims with other methods. But its lack of any prospects for the future is obvious already. . . .

1. The G.D.R. in the Community of Socialist States

Comrades, as a socialist state the G.D.R. represents a firm and immovable part of the socialist community. It is linked in close friendship with the country of Lenin—with the glorious Soviet Union. [Applause.] The firm rooting of the G.D.R. in this alliance is the basic condition for the implementation of the vital interests of the working class and all citizens of our G.D.R.

As a result of the pooling of the forces of the fraternal countries, the advantages of socialism for the working people in every socialist country, including the G.D.R., will most quickly and successfully become effective, notably:

> Because, through the collective defense alliance of the Warsaw Pact armed forces, peace and security are reliably protected for the people of the G.D.R.;
> Because, socialism by nature is internationalist and, through the cooperation of the socialist countries, the slogan expressed by Marx and Engels, "Proletarians of All Countries United," is fulfilled on a higher level.

In the period under review the party Central Committee based all its political decisions on this irrefutable fact. Herein lies the pledge for the further successful progress of our G.D.R. It is this adherence to the community of socialist states which definitely guarantees the sovereignty of the G.D.R. I want to make it quite clear once more that no one will ever succeed in tearing the G.D.R. away from the family of fraternal socialist countries. [Prolonged applause.]

Our course and its results and experience affirm this basic historic doctrine: Our relationship with the Soviet Union and with the

CPSU was, is, and will be, the decisive criterion for loyalty to Marxism-Leninism and to proletarian internationalism. [Applause.] Universal significance is attached to the guiding principles for the further building of communism which were decided on at the Twenty-fourth CPSU Congress. In more than fifty years of applying Marxist-Leninist theories to the problems of the universal revolutionary process and in the practice of building a new social order, the CPSU has proved to be the most experienced and most battle-tested party—the vanguard of the international Communist and workers' movement. We associate ourselves with the great theoretical and practical experiences of the Soviet Union and apply them to our concrete and historical conditions. For us, this spells full harmony between the priority of general principles for building socialism and the consideration of specific conditions in each country.

Our overall cooperation with the Soviet Union has developed in a way that increasingly meets the requirements arising from the social and economic goals of the Soviet Union and the G.D.R., as well as from the necessity to struggle against imperialism. Without exaggeration, one can say that this political, economic, and scientific-technological cooperation has reached a higher qualitative level since our previous congress. . . .

The Central Committee of our Socialist Unity Party of Germany values highly the fact that political consultation between the party and government leaders of the G.D.R. and the Union of Soviet Socialist Republics has been expanded. This is true of discussions of basic problems regarding the internal development of our countries and cooperation in the ideological sphere, as well as in the coordination of foreign policy. Once again it emerged that in all questions, there is perfect unanimity between our parties and states. In this spirit, our Eighth Party Congress sends fraternal greetings to the CPSU Central Committee, to all Soviet Communists, to the government of the Soviet Union, and to all peoples of the Soviet Union; and simultaneously declares that the Socialist Unity Party of Germany will imperturbably continue the course of our friendship and cooperation. [Applause.]

Dear comrades, we will never forget what the Soviet people and their glorious army did to free us from Hitlerite fascism. Eternal glory be to the Soviet soldiers fallen for our freedom and our future. We shall always honorably fulfill their legacy. [Applause.]

Comrades, we have always aimed our efforts at establishing ever closer relations with the other members of the Warsaw Pact treaty, and we are facing new and greater possibilities in this field in the future. . . . Relations with our fraternal neighbor states—with the

People's Republic of Poland and the Czechoslovak Socialist Republic —are developing successfully. Cooperation and friendly ties with the Hungarian People's Republic, the People's Republic of Bulgaria, the Socialist Republic of Romania, and the Mongolian People's Republic are also developing very well and cordially.

Our relationship with the D.R.V.—with the heroic struggle of the brave people against U.S. imperialism and its accomplices—are characterized by fraternal solidarity. Our relations with the Democratic People's Republic of Korea and the Republic of Cuba developed closer in the spirit of cooperation and friendship. It was possible to extend relations with the Socialist Federal Republic of Yugoslavia.

* * *

Our party also anticipates that in the future, too, the role of the CMEA council will increase in socialist economic integration and will be beneficial to all. . . . The directives for the coming five-year plan of our G.D.R., which are submitted to our party congress for adoption, make full allowance for this aim.

It is impossible to talk of cooperation within the socialist community of states without stressing the significance of the Warsaw Treaty for domestic and foreign policy and above all for the military protection of our community.

* * *

Comrades, the experience of the past years shows that the international forces of the counterrevolution have not abandoned their aim of preventing us from following our socialist path and of trying to restore capitalism. We must time and again recall Lenin's saying: Until the historic phase of transition from capitalism to communism is concluded, exploiters will inevitably hope for a restoration, this hope being then converted to attempts at restoration. Faced with a dangerous and perfidious imperialist opponent, we cannot permit ourselves to relax our vigilance even for a minute. Our alliance with the socialist countries is inviolable. It has proved its effectiveness in fending off all counterrevolutionary attacks of the imperialists. Only a few days ago, at the Fourteenth Party Congress of the Czechoslovak Communists, we expressed our full agreement with our Czechoslovak comrades, who have defeated the enemies of socialism after an involved struggle and have set the further course for the construction of socialism in their country. [Applause.] The lesson of the struggle of our Czechoslovak friends and comrades with the class enemy are undoubtedly of international importance. In the future we will strive

164

to prevent the imperialist opponent from attacking socialism in Europe, either by military pressure, or by open or covert counter-revolution.

*　　*　　*

At the Twenty-fourth CPSU Congress Comrade Leonid Brezhnev outlined the great goal of shaping the world system of socialism into a harmonious family of peoples which the people of the world will see as the example of a future worldwide community of free people. We wholeheartedly approve this, and we will do everything to make our contribution to this end. [Applause.]

2. The Struggle Against Imperialism

Comrades, in their pursuit of a peaceful life—of justice and social security and of freedom and democracy—the peoples are confronted with imperialism as the archenemy. As before, it is the main obstacle on the road to secure peace and social progress. If we make every effort to enforce the policy of peaceful coexistence between states with different social systems, then we do so in full awareness that imperialism has not changed its character. These dialectics of the international class struggle of our era must be fully understood.

Imperialism shows its true features anew every day. It wages barbaric wars, and the atrocities of U.S. imperialism in Indochina—above all the murder of the Vietnamese people—outrage the whole world. In the Middle East, the U.S. imperialists support Israeli aggression against the Arab peoples and encourage them to continue a policy of conquest which endangers world peace.

In Africa, Latin America, and Asia the American imperialists make every effort, in part overtly and in part covertly, to overthrow independent governments—bloodily quelling popular liberation movements—and to restore the old neocolonialist rule.

In the capitalist countries, the exploitation of the working people is intensifying. While a small group of multimillionaires become ever richer, the evils of capitalism—inflation, price hikes, unemployment, and social insecurity—burden the working people. . . . The United States itself, which is hailed by imperialist ideologists, represents a vivid illustration of the rottenness of the imperialist system. In the United States alone there are 5.7 million unemployed and racism is rampant. . . .

What good is such reality if the advocates of the imperialist system—be they from the camp of open reaction or from the rightist social democrats—speak about a change in capitalism in our world?

It is Lenin's appraisal of imperialism which is again confirmed today. Imperialism is parasitical and dying capitalism, trying to forestall its historic fate by increased aggression. What future can there be for a society in which everything is fiendishly and exclusively subordinated to the god of profit; for a society in which each day human beings are beaten down, thrown into jail or shot, merely because they want to live a decent life? What future could there possibly be for this imperialist society, compared with socialism, where citizens represent the future of mankind? Only within socialism is man able to breathe freely. [Applause.]

Experience has proved that imperialism cannot solve the problems of our times in a way which meets the interests of the peoples. It is the permanent enemy of peace, because monopoly capitalism is expansionist in nature. Peace is constantly in danger wherever armament and militarization are profitable business. . . . Imperialism is in no position to utilize scientific and technical progress for the benefit of man since it subordinates all the achievements of labor and intellect to the rules of profit.

. . . The struggle against imperialism is becoming stronger all over the world. The working class stands in the center of this fight, and is organizing powerful strike movements and political struggles in many capitalist countries. In 1970 some 64 million working people went on strike. In the first months of this year there were some 30 million strikers. Resistance against capitalist exploitation is growing, particularly among the young generations. The front against imperialist warmongers is expanding. More and more nations are taking the road to national independence, liberating themselves from imperialist domination.

Simultaneously the contradictions among the ruling circles of the imperialist countries are being aggravated. The most aggressive groups are willing to take such far-reaching measures as war to pursue their interest in profits. Other groups deem it more advisable, in view of the growing power of the socialist countries, to tackle international problems [in cooperation] with the socialist countries. We welcome this. If we prefer a solution in the sense of peaceful coexistence among states with different social orders, this certainly does not mean that they will serve socialism. For us, as Communists, it is clearly evident that it is correct and necessary to utilize all contradictions in the camp of the enemy in the interests of peace and progress.

The G.D.R. is directly confronted along the border between the two world systems with F.R.G. imperialism.

*   *   *

... During the past few years, the concentration of capital in the hands of a few supertrusts has shown a great upsurge in the F.R.G. This is seen in the existence of a military-industrial complex, an arms industry growing unchecked like cancer, an unprecedented degree of amalgamation between the monopolies and the state, and constant economic and military entwining with the United States. These processes provide the background for the persistent urge for a more influential position in NATO, for a predominant position in the EEC, and for increased neocolonialist activities.

* * *

The Central Committee of our party has always taken into consideration the entire range of various political processes in the F.R.G. We do not fail to note the differences between the approach of the conservative and the right-wing social democratic forces in the F.R.G. It is self-evident that our main attack is directed against the ultra-reactionary and openly revanchist forces in the F.R.G. But neither do we give any opportunity to those forces trying to work indirectly for imperialism against the G.D.R.

* * *

Comrades, the Central Committee of our party has clearly stated that the only relations possible between our socialist German Democratic Republic and the imperialist F.R.G. are those based on peaceful coexistence corresponding to the rules of international law. Relations of any other kind can never exist between states of different social orders. All talk in the West of the so-called unity of the German nation and of an allegedly special character of relations between the G.D.R. and the F.R.G. are obviously designed to strengthen those forces whose policy is now, as before, aimed at undermining the social and economic bases of our republic. The principal line of our party is that the overall course of the development and strengthening of our socialist state must and will inevitably lead to increased differences between ourselves and the capitalist F.R.G., and that therefore the process of delimitation between the two states in all spheres of social life will become increasingly deeper.
... If there are those in the West who [would like] to swallow the G.D.R. and liquidate our social system it is well to remind them that the G.D.R. is a stable socialist state and an inseparable part of the powerful socialist community and that it is backed by the whole force of the Soviet Union and the united socialist countries. [Long applause.]

* * *

3. The Struggle for Peace and Security and the Contribution of the G.D.R.

Comrade delegates, based on the vital interests of the citizens of our state and in conformity with our commitments in the alliance with the socialist countries, we have made an active contribution in the past to maintenance of peace and to progress toward security in Europe. As before our foreign policy is based on an effort to create the most favorable material conditions for building socialism [and] to contribute permanently to its strengthening. . . .

Our G.D.R. stands firmly by the side of the peoples of Indochina who have been attacked by American imperialism. We again demand the immediate cessation of U.S. aggression against the brave peoples of Vietnam, Laos, and Cambodia. [Applause.] . . . With equal determination we oppose the Israeli aggression against the Arab states which is inspired by American imperialism. We join the demand for the withdrawal of all Israeli troops from all territories they have occupied in violation of international law. [Applause.] We assess very favorably the conclusion of the important Treaty of Friendship and Cooperation between the Union of Soviet Socialist Republics and the U.A.R. It serves freedom and the progress of the U.A.R. and of all Arab peoples, the struggle for a just peace in the Middle East, and the alliance of all anti-imperialist forces of the world.

The commitment of our republic to peace and national independence strengthened the international reputation of our socialist state. This policy is increasingly being recognized and appreciated by the peoples and above all by the liberated national states. Following our Seventh Party Congress, this found expression in the establishment of diplomatic relations with an additional sixteen states, so that today the G.D.R. maintains diplomatic relations with twenty-nine states. Official contacts and many other relations have been established with other states. We value highly the fact that the Twenty-fourth CPSU Congress termed the strengthening of the international position of the G.D.R. as an important task in stabilizing the situation in Europe. . . .

Of course the Central Committee of our party has devoted special attention to questions concerning European security. As a member state of the Warsaw Pact, the G.D.R. actively cooperated in the preparation of the joint program of the socialist states for European security and the initiative for a European security conference. . . .

Great importance for European security must be attached to the treaties concluded by the U.S.S.R. with the F.R.G. and between the People's Republic of Poland and the F.R.G. To the benefit of all peoples, a significant step was thereby taken toward détente and an improvement in the climate in Europe. The treaties confirm the unshakeableness of the borders that have emerged in Europe, including the border along the Oder and Neisse rivers, as well as the border between the G.D.R. and the F.R.G. They affirm the renunciation of the use of force or threat of force. The special interest of the G.D.R. in these treaties goes without saying, because the territorial integrity of the G.D.R. has again been assured in this way.

What matters now, dear friends and comrades, is the ratification of the treaties so that they can take effect. This would be advantageous to all sides and favorably influence relations among European states. Still, ratification is meeting resistance among those well-known ultra-right F.R.G. circles which continue to openly advocate the old revanchist concept. It is also a disservice to the cause of détente to artifically construe an interrelationship between ratification of the treaties and the West Berlin negotiations.

We also have our demand that the F.R.G. unequivocally recognize as null and void from the very outset the notorious Munich agreement, which embodied the rapacious policy of Hitler, with all resulting consequences. [Applause]. This would undoubtedly reduce tensions on our continent.

Dear comrades, we wholeheartedly welcome the peace program of the Soviet Union promulgated by CPSU Central Committee General Secretary Comrade Leonid Ilyich Brezhnev at the Twenty-fourth CPSU Congress. We consider this impressive proof of the role of the main peace force played by the Soviet Union, which constantly produces powerful impulses for solving international problems in the interest of the peaceful life of the people. This also applies to the recent Soviet proposal to begin negotiations on troop and arms reductions in central Europe.

One must say, however, that there are influential forces in the West seriously hampering international détente, and particularly European security. This again became obvious a few days ago at the Lisbon meeting of the NATO Council and military committee. . . . The resistance of the enemies of peace and security will only prompt us to intensify our efforts in the fight for European security.

* * *

The G.D.R. has a clear-cut conception concerning its contribution to the safeguarding of peace in Europe:

First, the G.D.R. advocates the convocation of a European security conference as soon as possible and is willing to work toward the success of such a conference as an equal participant. However, the creation of obstacles to the preparation of such a conference in the form of preconditions, such as those raised time and again by the United States, NATO, and the F.R.G., do not serve the interest of peace in Europe. Just as all our allies, we put forward no preconditions whatsoever for the preparation and convening of a European security conference.

Second, we again state that we are willing to become a member of the United Nations and its specialized organizations. G.D.R. membership in the United Nations would fully correspond to the principle of universality of this world organization and would, by all means, contribute to détente in Europe.

Third, the G.D.R. is willing to establish normal diplomatic relations with all states, based on equality of all states and the principle of recognition of the G.D.R.'s sovereignty by every state and recognition of the sovereignty of other states by the G.D.R.

Fourth, the G.D.R., as before, advocates the establishment of normal relations under international law with the F.R.G. The F.R.G. government has known about our respective proposals in detail for some time. . . .

Fifth, the G.D.R., now as before, is willing to contribute to the normalization of relations with West Berlin and thus to détente in central Europe. Toward this end, the G.D.R. wishes success for the Four-Power talks on West Berlin. It would be in the interest of all parties to come to an understanding concerning this issue. This would also destroy the basis for disputes and conflicts regarding West Berlin. . . .

Comrades, the ruling circles in the F.R.G. try to support their revanchist line of the above mentioned inner-German relations with the spurious claim that a homogeneous German nation exists unchanged. Of course there can be no talk of that.

As far as the national issue is concerned, it must be said that history has already made its decision. . . . As a result of the predatory war of fascist German imperialism, the former German Reich perished in blood and fire. The German big bourgeoisie thus definitely lost the right to lead the German nation. Only the working class was competent to renew the nation on a democratic basis and guarantee its unity in an antifascist democratic German state. . . .

In dealing with the national problem, one must begin with its class significance. The socialist revolution, which leads to the renewal of all forms of human society, also basically renews the nation. As Marx and Engels pointed out in the Communist Manifesto, the proletariat, by taking over political power, becomes a national class constituting itself as a nation. Through the establishment of the worker-peasant power and the building of the socialist society a new type of nation was developed—the socialist nation.

In the F.R.G. the bourgeois nation continues to exist, and the national problem is characterized by an irreconcilable class contradiction between the bourgeoisie and the working masses, which—and we are convinced of this—will find solution within the world historical process of transition from capitalism to socialism. In contrast, in the G.D.R.—the socialist German state—the socialist nation is developing.

*　　*　　*

. . . Socialist society in the G.D.R. has a basically new class structure. Under the leadership of the working class in the G.D.R., different classes having socialist characteristics live in friendly coexistence. In the course of socialist development in our republic, a socialist ideology and a new socialist national culture, which embodies all humanist traditions of the German past, predominate. Our G.D.R. is forever and firmly rooted in the international socialist system, and its integration in the socialist community of states is constantly growing.

Dear comrades, the foreign political activities of the Central Committee of our party show that it has followed the decisions of the Seventh Party Congress. Concerning the future, we will do everything to continue to honestly fulfill our international obligations as before, and this we will do in firm alliance with the Soviet Union and the community of the socialist states. [Applause.]

POLAND

Document 9: Excerpts from the Program Report of the Political Bureau for the Sixth PUWP Congress, Delivered 6 December 1971 by Edward Gierek, General Secretary of the CC PUWP*

PARTY'S TASKS IN THE FURTHER SOCIALIST
DEVELOPMENT OF THE POLISH PEOPLE'S REPUBLIC

Comrade delegates, preparing for the Sixth Congress and formulating its political platform we had constantly in mind the bitter and painful experiences of the social conflict which shook our country a year ago. . . . Our party drew the essential lessons and conclusions from the December events.

First, the problems of the working people must always be kept in the center of the attention of the Marxist-Leninist party which exercises power in a socialist state. Social effort in the construction of socialism should always systematically result in a tangible improvement of the material and cultural conditions of the life of the masses.

Secondly, our whole activity must always be guided by the principle that the working class is the main social force of socialism and that constant ties with it are a condition of the successful development of our system.

Thirdly, construction of socialism necessitates systematic raising of the leading role of the party to constantly higher standards, consistent observance of the Leninist methods of party work and constant contact with reality.

Fourthly, in the contemporary conditions of the class struggle and rivalry between socialism and capitalism, developments and conflicts which delay progress and open the door to the activities of opponents of socialism, must be prevented.

The common denominator of everything we have achieved during the last year, of everything which has created a good atmosphere in our country and released social activeness and initiative, and which offers guarantees of correct development in the future, is Leninism, the inexhaustible source of the strength of our ideology; the unfailing guiding light of our actions.

The road to socialism and its principal characteristics are defined by general principles, typical for the development of all socialist countries. These general principles take concrete shape which cor-

*Source: *Program Report of the Political Bureau for the 6th PUWP* Congress (Warsaw: Polish Interpress Agency, 1971), pp. 3-5; 32-37.

responds to historical conditions and national characteristics. The experiences of our party fully confirm this dialectic truth. Lack of appreciation and understanding of this truth has always caused basic difficulties in the construction of socialism.

The errors of policy and distortions in the methods of leadership which we overcame . . . resulted primarily from violation of the general Leninist principles of socialist construction. By restoring Leninist principles . . . our party overcame serious difficulties, performed a tremendous task, and led the country back onto the correct road.

We are deeply grateful to the fraternal parties, and in particular to the Communist party of the Soviet Union for showing understanding of the essence of the difficulties which we encountered on the road of our development and for their fraternal assistance in overcoming them. In this we see a consistent implementation of the principles of proletarian internationalism.

Marxism-Leninism is the beacon of our party. Our party firmly opposes all trends and tendencies ideologically alien to Marxism-Leninism. In particular, our party is conducting an uncompromising struggle against revisionism, which attacks the fundamental principles of our ideology and undermines the achievements of our policy. We must ensure that the ideological standards of our party work are high enough to render all party organs capable of recognizing and combatting those opponents of socialism who use pseudo-socialist slogans and seek to politically confuse certain social environments and cultivate petite-bourgeoisie attitudes and opinions.

We are also overcoming dogmatic petrification and subjectivism marked by lack of faith in the strength of the working class, in the creative possibilities of the nation, and which ignores realities that will lead to the divorce of the masses from the party.

We are drawing the conclusions from our experiences in the recent difficult years and from the experiences of the years from 1956 and 1959 which have not yet been thought through with sufficient penetration. The party's basic weakness in this period was that the necessary elimination of specific dogmatic and sectarian errors as well as the restoration of respect for socialist law, was accompanied by compromises with revisionism and other tendencies alien to the ideology of our party.

The harmful effects of all this became apparent in later years and formed a soil for attacks on the fundamental ideological and sociopolitical principles of our socialist state. These attacks always met with the firm resistance of the working people, and above all of the working class.

We are drawing the conclusions from the whole multifarious and complex experience of our party in the consecutive stages of its activity. These experiences point to the need for full observance of Leninist principles, for Communist principledness, and for close unity between patriotism and internationalism in selfless service to our class and the whole Polish nation.

*   *   *

Comrade delegates, thanks to socialism our motherland has taken a place among other nations which guarantees her independence and security and provides all the conditions necessary for all-round development. This place is determined by our alliances—our ties of friendship and cooperation with the countries of the socialist community and solidarity with the international revolutionary movement. . . .

In our international policy the key role is played by the fraternal relations with the Soviet Union. They provided the historical chance of reconstructing the Polish state within just and advantageous frontiers and constitute lasting guarantees of independence and security for the Polish nation. . . . The prospects of Poland's further development, the possibility of meeting the basic aspirations of our nation, particularly of the young generation, can be fully implemented only within a framework of cooperation with the Soviet Union. . . . This is the supreme principle of our national policy. . . .

The Communist Party of the Soviet Union, the party of Lenin and of the first victorious socialist revolution, the most experienced party within the Communist movement, is bringing a particularly great contribution to our common cause. This role was fully confirmed by the Twenty-fourth Congress of the Communist Party of the Soviet Union. In the address given by Comrade Leonid Brezhnev were formulated the general regularities of socialist construction at the present stage of the development of our community. Our party has profited from the extremely rich creative achievements of the Twenty-fourth Congress of the CPSU in drawing up a program for the further socialist development of Poland for the present congress. . . .

. . . In the international cooperation of the countries of the socialist community, the strengthening of mutual economic ties, of which a higher form is socialist economic integration, is coming to the fore. A great step forward in this direction has been the comprehensive program for expanding scientific and technical cooperation, coproduction, and further deepening of the international socialist division of labor adopted at the recent twenty-fifth session of the Council for Mutual Economic Assistance. Poland will, for her part, do everything to implement this program in a consistent way.

Our country attaches great weight to strengthening bilateral relations with the fraternal socialist countries. We will strengthen economic bonds through joint investment projects and a wide program of specialization of production and industrial cooperation. We are determined to expand scientific and technical cooperation, and also cultural and social cooperation. We are of the opinion that we should jointly enrich the forms of cooperation in all fields and, among other things, promote the development of tourism. We also believe that conditions should be created for the development of cooperation among the youth of our countries. Let the younger generations of the socialist community get to know each other better, let them continue the ties of friendship which we—the older generations—have developed in the common struggle for socialism and the freedom of nations.

Comrades, a key problem is the strengthening of the unity of the socialist community. It can be furthered by the deepening of the ideological ties uniting our parties; by the development of cooperation in all domains. A very valuable form is the now more frequent meetings of leading representatives of the parties and governments of the fraternal countries. These make possible direct mutual information on the situation and the problems being tackled by our parties and governments. . . .

We set high store by the results of the several meetings and talks held this year with leaders of the Soviet Union, as well as the results of the meetings held not long ago with the party and government leadership of the German Democratic Republic and the Czechoslovak Socialist Republic—our neighbors to the west and south. We are developing and strengthening relations of friendship and cooperation with Hungary, Bulgaria, and Romania.

Our cooperation with the fraternal countries of the Warsaw Treaty is developing extremely well but there exist great possibilities for its further deepening to the benefit of each of our countries and the cementing of the unity of the socialist community.

We are satisfied with the favorable shape of friendly relations with socialist Yugoslavia. Our party also attaches great weight to the strengthening of cooperation with socialist countries outside Europe. Our relations with the Mongolian People's Republic are being constantly deepened.

Our party and the whole nation hold warm feelings of brotherhood and solidarity for the heroic, fighting nation of Vietnam. We consider full support for the Vietnamese patriots our basic internationalist duty. We also unwaveringly support the struggle of the other nations of Indochina against imperialist aggression. We crave a further development of relations of friendship with the Korean People's Democratic Republic. [Also], we are pleased with the friendly cooperation with socialist Cuba.

In all our relations with socialist countries in Europe, Asia and Latin America we are guided invariably by hopes of further cementing cooperation and strengthening the unity of the states of our system in the spirit of Marxism-Leninism and proletarian internationalism. . . .

Committed unflinchingly to the defense of the unity of the forces of socialism, our party maintains its opposition to all divisive tendencies, and especially to the particularly dangerous fomenting of anti-Soviet nationalism and chauvinism. Anti-Sovietism, irrespective of the vocabulary in which it is masked, cannot be reconciled with the genuine struggle against imperialism. Harm is being done to the cause of socialism by the divisive course of the Chinese leadership which is basically contrary to Marxism-Leninism and proletarian internationalism. . . . The vital interests of socialism require the abandonment of this course, and discontinuing all actions aimed against the Soviet Union and other socialist states.

In accordance with the line of our party, the Polish People's Republic is seeking all-round cooperation with the young states of Asia, Africa and Latin America which, struggling against the legacy of colonial policy and opposing neocolonialist pressures, are becoming an important factor in extending the anti-imperialist front. Many of these countries are confronted by fundamental decisions which will determine the character and prospects of their further development. . . . Yielding to the pressure of imperialism and anticommunism brings irreparable harm to the cause of independence and progress of the developing nations.

Because we entertain warm sympathies for both India and Pakistan, we are deeply disturbed by the new armed conflict on the Indian subcontinent. . . . We remain convinced that only a political settlement in East Pakistan which meets the aspirations and will of the population of this country and enables the refugees to return home, can put an end to the present tragic bloodshed and terminate a conflict which is causing a growth of international tension.

Poland supports the Arab countries in their striving to restore peace in the Middle East on the basis of the U.N. Security Council's resolution of November 1967. We maintain and will develop fraternal contacts with revolutionary democrats and other fighters for independence—for progress. We greet with pleasure the achievements of these forces, particularly the success of the left in Chile. The Sixth Congress of the Polish United Workers' Party wishes all the revolutionary democratic parties and national liberation movements success in their struggle for the independence and progress of their nations.

Peace and a sense of security lie in the deepest interests of the nations. This is the most important problem, particularly today when the threat to world peace is a nuclear threat. This is why the socialist countries and the whole international Communist movement consider it their most important historical mission to prevent a new world war, and are doing all that lies in their power to fulfill this mission. Thanks to the defensive might of the Soviet Union which is the basic guarantee of world peace; thanks to the joint coalition strength, and consistently peaceful policy of the fraternal socialist countries, it has been possible for more than a quarter of a century to prevent a new world war. Real conditions for a lasting peace have been created.

. . . In the international sphere the pillar of our security is alliance, fraternal friendship, and all-round cooperation with the Soviet Union and the other states of the socialist community, and active participation in the defensive Warsaw Treaty. On the internal plane we base the construction of defense forces on the dynamic development of the country's economic and scientific-technical potential, on the continually growing cohesion and moral and political unity of society, and on the strength and preparedness of the Polish army as a specialized arm in the defense of the country and an important link in the socialist defense community. . . .

Poland will continue to strive consistently toward strengthening the ties between fraternal countries, and toward the deepest possible coordination of foreign policy, which is the basic condition of the effectiveness of our common struggle for lasting security and peace in Europe.

The creation by the Soviet Union and the other socialist countries of defense capacities capable of countering the imperialist effort to deal with the socialist community from a "position of strength" . . . and the consistently peaceful policy of our community are bringing good results in international relations. Real conditions are arising for creating lasting security and peace, and for the development of peaceful cooperation between nations on a basis of equality. Peaceful coexistence is the only foundation for such a shaping of international relations.

This does not mean class peace; it is a form of ideological struggle and manifold confrontation between socialism and imperialism on a global scale. It is also, however, a form of struggle which makes it possible to settle the contradictions between socialism and capitalism without general armed conflict, and [at] the same time creates broad opportunities for peaceful cooperation between nations.

The entrenchment of peaceful coexistence lies in the most vital interest of all the nations of Europe. The new conformation of forces and the consistent policy of the socialist countries deprive the revisionist, revanchist, and militarist forces still active in the Federal Republic of Germany of the chance of undermining the territorial and political state of affairs which is the foundation of security in Europe. This was the basis of the treaties concluded last year between the Soviet Union and Poland with the F.R.G. which created conditions for a normalization of relations in this region of great importance to peace on our continent. To set the seal on this question, speedy ratification of these treaties by the Federal Republic of Germany is essential, a ratification which will also allow for effective implementation of the important Four-Power agreement on West Berlin. Also essential is the recognition, in accordance with international law, of the two sovereign German states—the G.D.R. and the F.R.G.—and their admission to the United Nations. Also necessary is the normalization by the F.R.G. of its relations with other European socialist countries.

This enormously important process of normalizing relations in Central Europe constitutes an integral part of the struggle for détente, for lasting peace, and the development of cooperation in the whole of Europe. Of critical importance at present to the entirety of European affairs is the preparation and early convocation—no later than 1972—of the conference on security and cooperation proposed by the socialist countries. This should open a chapter of joint efforts—by all the interested countries of Europe—to build a system of collective security and broad peaceful cooperation, particularly in the economic field, which forms the material basis for relations in all others. Poland, together with the other socialist countries, will continue to do everything in her power to advance the vista of such a Europe.

This goal is also served by our favorably developing bilateral relations with France and the Scandinavian countries. Our economic relations with Italy, Great Britain, Austria and other Western countries are also shaping up well. We wish to develop these relations further on a basis of peaceful coexistence and constructive cooperation.

We believe that the conclusion of bilateral agreements which would create a wider framework for economic, scientific, and technical relations, for cultural and tourist exchange, and also for political contacts over problems which are of mutual interest, would be of basic significance in this respect.

We also believe that the time is ripe for the Baltic countries to tackle in common the comprehensive regulation of the problems of shipping, fisheries, and conservation of the waters of the Baltic; and at the same time to do their utmost to ensure lasting peace in this region. The Baltic should fully earn the name of a sea of peaceful cooperation.

Poland is also in favor of framing principles of general economic cooperation in Europe, of tackling and solving in common such problems as the creation of a European infrastructure, and protection of the natural environment. Our country extends its full support to the important initiatives of the Soviet Union concerning the checking of the arms race, disarmament, and the strengthening of international security.

Foreign policy, like cooperation in the economic field and in all other areas, is carried out by people. . . . In the propagation of the most noble humanist ideal created by man—internationalist awareness—we see a great achievement and lasting goal for our party in the education of our society. Marxism has given this ideal a new and preeminent value, the class solidarity of the exploited. . . .

We shall continue to reinforce internationalist feelings in our society [and] to strengthen our sincere friendship with the first country of socialism—the Soviet Union. We shall always stand on the side of those who are destroying in a just struggle the old capitalist order, who are claiming their legitimate right to freedom and independence, and who refuse to accept imperialist coercion and violence.

In mapping out the directions of Poland's action in the international arena, our party attaches particular weight to the strengthening of the unity of the Communist movement and the whole anti-imperialist front. We are consistently carrying out the common program drawn up at the 1969 Moscow Conference of Communist and Workers' Parties.

The international Communist movement is now going through a period in which the struggle for the purity of the principles of Marxism-Leninism is acquiring ever greater significance for the cause of the unity and the successful solution of specific tasks in the confrontation with imperialism in the struggle for the progress of socialism. The cohesion and unity of the world socialist system and the international Communist movement is now, as in the past, a guarantee of success in the pursuit of common goals.

Our party, true to Marxism-Leninism and proletarian internationalism, will continue to contribute its share to the unity of the international Communist movement and all the anti-imperialist forces in the struggle for progress, the freedom of nations, and peace. We consider most useful the recent visits paid by leaders of the French Communist party and the Italian Communist party, and the talks conducted with us and with representatives of other fraternal parties.

We shall continue to strengthen in all forms, direct contacts and cooperation with fraternal Communist parties. Our party will continue to strengthen contacts with progressive anti-imperialist and national liberation forces. We also wish to extend our contacts with socialist and social-democratic parties particularly over the joint problem of building a lasting peace and developing friendly relations between nations.

In keeping with our best traditions, in keeping with the feelings of the working people in our country, and on the basis of the political line of the Sixth Congress, the Polish United Workers' Party is and always will be an unbreakable link in the international Communist movement.

HUNGARY

Document 10: Excerpts from the Report to the Tenth Hungarian Party Congress, Delivered 25 November 1970 by Zoltan Komocsin, Party Secretary in Charge of International Relations*

Dear comrades, according to the principles of Marxism-Leninism, the domestic and foreign policy of a country, whatever its social system, are connected with and interrelated to one another. Our foreign political interests and endeavors are determined by the objectives of socialist construction and service to the cause of the international working class. As the Central Committee report pointed out, the main task of our foreign policy is to assure favorable international conditions for the construction of a socialist Hungary.

On the subject of the connection between and interrelations of domestic and foreign policy, certain imperialist press organs are leveling charges against us. They are fond of attaching labels to the Hungarian party and state leadership, such as "the most courageous reformers" in domestic policy, and "conservative to the extreme" in foreign policy. It is clear to everyone that it would be impossible at one and the same time to be a courageous reformer and an extreme conservative.

* * *

Why are they then trying, nevertheless, to label us with "extreme conservatism"? Because we are faithful to our principles and to our commitment as an ally. We would not be regarded as conservative if we permitted anti-Soviet and chauvinistic actions that would loosen our alliance and unity—developments the imperialists would profit by. As far as we are concerned, we have pursued, are pursuing, and will in the future also pursue an international policy in accordance with our fundamental principles, the interests of our people and country, and our constructive socialist objectives. We are striving to do everything in our power to develop cooperation and friendship with the Soviet Union [and] the socialist countries, for the unity and the strengthening and cohesion of the international Communist movement and all the anti-imperialist forces, and for the triumph of our great common cause.

In our international policy, evolved on the basis of the principles of Marxism-Leninism and serving the interests and aims of the Hun-

*Source: *Foreign Broadcast Information Service Supplement, Eastern Europe*, no. 237, supp. 23 (8 December 1970), pp. 4-9.

garian People's Republic, proletarian internationalism is of cardinal importance. The significance of internationalism—the general definition of the concept—is no problem to the international Communist movement. Generally speaking, the fraternal parties, the Communists, profess identical beliefs. However, the situation is now such that everyone invokes internationalism: those who consistently profess the principles of Marxism-Leninism as well as the rightist or leftist opportunists.

*   *   *

The touchstone of internationalism is the relationship with the Soviet Union and its Communist party. The role and importance of the Soviet Union and its Communist party in the international Communist movement and the process of world development is constantly growing rather than declining with the passing of time.

In the international workers' movement and in the peoples' struggle in the liberated countries and countries striving for freedom, the Soviet Union represents an unshakable pillar of support and inexhaustible source of strength. . . . The fact that peace-loving mankind has thus far been successful in its struggle to avert a world war—and we can say with assurance that this will be the case in the future—is due primarily to the economic and military power, and the peace policy of the Soviet Union, which couples the justness of the global struggle for peace with strength, and multiplies its efficiency.

The importance of the Soviet Union and its Communist party is rooted in the historically evolved reality of our time and is not dependent either on the subjective opinion of the imperialist class enemy or the nationalism of rightist or leftist opportunists existing within our international movement. On the basis of all this, it is with a principled conviction that our party declares that the yardstick of our internationalism is our relationship with the Soviet Union and its Communist party.

The motivating factor behind our international policy and its primary objective is fostering and strengthening the unbreakable and everlasting Hungarian-Soviet friendship. Our strivings for the enhancement of the strength and unity of the socialist world system are closely linked with this constant endeavor.

Our point of departure in our international policy is that only that which is good for our friends and allies can be good for us, because we are strengthening ourselves and our community alike. If life produces situations—and this does happen, to be sure—in which our specific interests clash with joint interests, we subordinate them to joint interests in the conviction that only this can lead to success in the long run. Our national interests and the common objectives of our world system cannot be lastingly antithetical. However, we subordinate our particular interests to the totality of interests when this divergence prevails because we are convinced that thus we are acting in the true interests of our people as well. Our country's bilateral and multilateral relations with the other socialist countries also bear out the fact that this is fundamentally decisive, binding us and rallying us to unity. . . .

A beautiful example of the assertion and force of internationalist principles is the solidarity shown toward our heroically fighting Vietnamese brethren. . . . In their self-sacrificing war, by their achievements of historic importance, [they] have proven to the entire world that even the strongest imperialist great power, the United States, is unable to conquer a numerically smaller and economically weaker people who are ready for every sacrifice for the freedom and independence of their fatherland.

The solidarity of our party and people with the people of Vietnam obliges us to continue to work with all our strength and utilize all our international opportunities for the greater effective unity of the international Communist movement, for the benefit of the heroically fighting Vietnamese brethren, the people of Laos and Cambodia, and all anti-imperialist forces. Our party, government, and people are vigilantly watching the struggle of our Korean and Cuban brethren, who are holding their own before the constant harassment of American imperialism. . . .

*   *   *

In the midst of our efforts for unity, the change which has taken place in the P.R.C. foreign policy has given rise to hope. Opportunities are ripening for improving interstate relations between China and the other socialist countries. After a decade we have now reached a position in which we can again look forward with great expectation and readiness to action, not to the prospect of estrangement, but to that of rapprochement.

Of course, one must not lose sight of the fact that the Chinese leadership is now prepared only to undertake the normalization of interstate relations, not the restoration of party relations. Our regret that they and the Albanian party leaders have not accepted our invitation to the congress is connected with this. As far as we are concerned, we would like to go forward along the road initiated, and we want to normalize and develop Chinese-Hungarian interstate relations.

We are realizing our international policy on the basis of our Marxist-Leninist principles regarding the people fighting to eliminate the vestiges of colonial exploitation and oppression, and regarding the liberated countries. We express our solidarity by political, financial, and every other means in our power, with the people fighting against the fascist regimes in the Portuguese colonies and in racist South Africa. Our economic, political, and diplomatic relations with the developing countries are prompted by unselfish readiness to help.

Our policy of eliminating the hotbed of war in the Middle East proves with particular clarity the principles which are guiding us. We are in solidarity with the just struggle of the Arab people and condemn the Israeli aggressors and their imperialist supporters. . . . For us, naturally, Israel does not present a religious or Jewish question. On the basis of our conviction of principle, we oppose the reactionary ideology of anti-Semitism as well as Zionism. The Jewish worker or peasant, whether he lives in Israel or anywhere else in the world, is our class brother in the same way as an Arab worker and peasant is or as the worker or peasant of any country is. It is not the Israeli workers with whom we are in conflict, but the ruling class which, on the basis of the Zionist ideology and its unbridled hatred of Communists and its anti-Arab attitude, not only proclaims the policy of racism, but has also embarked on its implementation, and which is the servant of imperialist policy in the Middle East.

*   *   *

In the realization of our party's international policy we believe like the other socialist countries, that the Hungarian People's Republic should maintain manifold relations with countries whose social system is opposite to ours. Even when, on the basis of the principle of peaceful coexistence, we develop our relations with the capitalist countries, we always bear in mind our alliance commitments.

Evidence of the great strength and possibilities inherent in the socialist countries' united and coordinated stand can be seen in the results we have achieved by our initiative in the organization of the European security conference. The European people, and the governments in most countries, agree on the need for a European security conference. . . .

Conditions for the European security conference have been improved by the U.S.S.R.-F.R.G. treaty, and the Polish-West German treaty will also have a positive effect. An early ratification of these treaties would greatly promote progress along the path already begun. However, the interests of European peace and security call for a further step forward by the West German government: it should recognize the G.D.R. under international law. It would also help if steps were taken to halt the activities of propaganda machinery and émigré organizations set up in West Germany and enjoying official support there, which are organizing incitement and diversion against all the socialist countries.

*   *   *

Dear comrades, as a result of the honorable trust placed in us by the fraternal parties, a long and important period of preparations for the 1969 international Moscow conference rested with us. We have entered into direct and regular relations with the great majority of Communist and workers' parties. We see in the Budapest preparations for the Moscow conference evidence of the fraternal parties' confidence in, and appreciation of, our party. We are grateful for this confidence and shall also strive in the future to live up to the expectations of the fraternal parties.

*   *   *

At this point we are entitled to say that trust among the fraternal parties has become greater. The Moscow meeting's prolonged preparation, and particularly the conference itself, have removed many obstacles. . . .

Our party, and I am sure the same applies to our congress, will also be ready to do everything in the future to accomplish the common goals, to develop further cohesion in the international Communist movement, and to achieve unity of action of all the anti-imperialist forces. Being mindful of these objectives of imperative significance in our time, we are continuing to foster our bilateral relations with all fraternal parties which are prompted by similar intentions.

Our party will also participate in multilateral gatherings of Communist and workers' parties in the future. There is no greater or more honorable task for our party than to serve the aspirations and the realization of the objectives of our working class, of our people, and at the same time of the international Communist movement. . . .

3
GROUP TWO

YUGOSLAVIA

Document 11: Excerpts from the Report of the CC LCY to the Eighth Party Congress, Delivered 7 December 1964 by Josip Broz Tito, General Secretary of the LCY*

GENERAL CHARACTERISTICS OF THE INTERNATIONAL SITUATION AND STATE IN THE INTERNATIONAL WORKERS' MOVEMENT

International development between the Seventh and Eighth Congresses (1958–1964) of the League of Communists of Yugoslavia moved in the direction of major changes in favor of the forces of peace and a peaceful constructive policy—the policy of active and peaceful coexistence.

The policy of force which the most reactionary imperialist circles have still not renounced is steadily losing support even among some of those who until recently considered such a policy the most effective and indeed the only means by which they could achieve their aims—domination in the world by force. A major role in preventing wars has been played by the United Nations, by what are known as the nonaligned countries, by the majority of socialist countries together with the Soviet Union, and by the other forces of peace. The world found itself on the brink of a new war of worldwide proportions several times in the period between the Seventh and Eighth Congresses.

* Source: *Review of International Affairs*, vol. 15, no. 353 (Belgrade, 20 December 1964), pp. 15-23.

It is not difficult to imagine the consequences of such a war in view of the tremendous destructive power of the atomic weapons that some big powers possess today. The Berlin crisis, and especially the Cuban emergency could have led mankind into the greatest tragedy the world has ever seen. Thanks, however, to the common sense of those who were in the most responsible positions, a catastrophe was avoided.

We are still uncertain as to what the future may bring, although the past two years have been marked by a certain relaxation of tension in the world. The agreement between the Soviet Union, the United States of America and Great Britain to ban nuclear tests in the atmosphere, in outer space, and under water is one of the chief proofs of relaxation in international tension. It is a very modest agreement, but we may nevertheless state that East-West relations are developing for the better toward relaxation, toward a gradual surmounting of the cold war and affirmation of the policy of negotiation and agreement. Simultaneously, we may observe that a process of general polarization is taking place in the world—with the forces of peace and progress and new relations among nations on the one side, and the forces of reaction, cold war and solution of controversial international problems by force on the other. Major political problems remain unsolved and the process of solving them will be a long one. . . .

No visible progress has been made in the province of disarmament—general and complete disarmament remaining our fundamental goal—although it is our firm opinion that conditions do exist for a rapprochement of views and for the achievement of realistic, if initially only partial, solutions. The big western powers have still not demonstrated a sufficient measure of readiness for substantial agreements along these lines. The process of evolution in the West toward renunciation of cold war targets set up earlier is still unfolding slowly, attended by powerful resistance from the forces of reaction. After France, the People's Republic of China began nuclear tests; she continues to oppose the Moscow Treaty and is making preparations for new experiments, the purpose of which is to improve this destructive weapon. It is therefore becoming increasingly necessary for all the progressive forces in the world, primarily the nonaligned countries and the countries of socialism, to make their contribution in broader, more determined, and increasingly unified actions, to the discovery of realistic solutions in the spirit of the positions and proposals of the Belgrade and Cairo conferences. . . .

*   *   *

The problem of the arms race is closely associated with the problem of liquidation of underdevelopment in the world. Instead of spending huge sums on continuing the arms race, it would be of tremendous benefit if even one small part of the resources involved were utilized for assistance to developing countries. This would simultaneously eradicate all kinds of elements that cause conflicts and tension in the world.

The existence of foreign military bases is one of the chief obstacles to a constructive approach to the solution of problems like disarmament. . . . The setting up of denuclearized zones would also have a favorable effect on disarmament and foster the atmosphere of relaxing tension. It is a certainty that the establishment of an atom-free zone in Central Europe would have a broad and favorable influence on the entire international situation. It is also time that Africa, Southeast Asia and other parts of Asia and Latin America be proclaimed atom-free zones.

Contemporary development as a whole, and against that background the gradual relaxation of tension, have offered nations and states an opportunity to consolidate their sovereignty and act more independently in international affairs. The world, now in the initial phase of a process in which international relations are being democratized, is striving to an increasing degree for the affirmation of equality between large and small nations; between more developed and less developed countries. A place of importance in this process belongs to the newly liberated countries which have become a real moral-political force capable of bringing considerable influence to bear on the development of world events.

. . . Reactionary forces in various countries, helped by reactionary circles from outside, are trying with all their might to prevent certain nations from achieving their desire to emancipate themselves from all forms of colonial oppression and to attain full-fledged independence and national integration. These are focal points of danger not only to the freedom and independence of nations in certain regions, such as is the case, for instance, with Laos, South Vietnam and Cambodia in Southeast Asia, with Cuba in Latin America, with Cyprus, the Congo, Angola, and other countries which are still struggling for their independence. These are simultaneously focal points which may lead to the great danger of a new war, as reactionary and colonial powers interfere in the international affairs of such countries from outside. It is obvious that there is a tendency—especially where the influence of big monopoly circles is still strong—to confine the policy of coexistence to direct relations between East and West and still to treat certain other areas, particularly the insufficiently developed ones, as spheres of influence and control of the big colonial powers. It must therefore be perfectly clear even to these reactionary circles that the question of active and peaceful coexistence is very much the concern of all countries—both large and small—with differing social systems. . . .

All of this jeopardizes the further consolidation of peace and democratic relations among nations. Postwar development as a whole has demonstrated that the methods of cold-war pressure, local military undertakings, and demonstrations of power have not been able to offer a permanent solution to a single international dispute, but rather that new and even graver problems have arisen as a result.

No matter how tenaciously certain colonial powers still hang on, the era of colonialism is drawing to a close. National liberation movements are recording fresh successes and the number of newly freed countries is growing. Now in the offing is a bitter and determined struggle for emancipation of the peoples in South and Southwest Africa, in Southern Rhodesia, Angola, Mozambique and the so-called Portuguese Guinea, in the south of the Arabian Peninsula, in British Guiana and other dependent territories, for the liquidation of apartheid, and for the granting of rights to the African majority in South Africa. In the Congo, the people are waging a hard and fierce battle against the anti-people's regime of Tshombe and against aggression by certain Western countries which support that regime by all possible means. . . . The remaining strongholds of colonialism seriously obstruct the stabilization of conditions in broad regions and represent a total anachronism from the political and the humanitarian standpoint.

Having emerged as a substitute for classic colonialism, neocolonialism has become a dominant form in the relations of certain imperialist powers and monopoly capital with insufficiently developed countries that were formerly colonies. In the first place, neocolonialism endeavors to keep these countries in a state of economic dependence, thereby restricting their political independence and putting limits on their equality in international relations.

Neocolonialism is no less a threat to peace in the world than classic colonialism. It is fraught with elements of internal and external conflict. . . .

An extremely important role in the liquidation of classic colonialism and in the struggle against neocolonialism should continue to be played by the United Nations, with undeferable implementation of the Declaration on the Granting of Independence to Colonial Countries and Peoples. In this connection, all progressive forces in the world must foil attempts at foreign intervention. . . .

The policy of nonalignment is experiencing continued affirmation and evolution now that the process of surmounting the cold war and strict division of the world has been launched. Year in and year out, the number of those choosing such a policy grows. . . . This was demonstrated by the broad attendance of nonaligned countries at the Cairo conference [1964] where the number of participants and observers rose from twenty-eight to fifty-seven in comparison with the Belgrade conference [1961] thereby covering about one-half of the membership of the United Nations. . . .

The policy of nonalignment has greatly extended its scope of action. The essence of this policy is realistic and principled action along the lines of active and peaceful coexistence which makes broad cooperation and unity possible, not on the basis of artificial and formal alignment, but in keeping with common interests and independent and free choice. The Belgrade and Cairo conferences are replete with proof of the wide opportunities for, and advantages of, such cooperation.

The policy which has from the very beginning resisted alignment of any sort has not only indicated to many countries, and particularly the newly liberated ones, the right road and way to preserve and strengthen independence and secure conditions for social-economic progress, but has become a factor to be reckoned with in the maintenance of peace and advancement of international cooperation. New forms of increasingly universal active international cooperation and friendship among nations are being developed on this basis. Regional groupings along these lines, like the Organization of African Unity and the Arab League, represent a significant contribution to the development of international cooperation.

The fundamental substance of the nonalignment policy is the struggle for peace and consistent removal from international relations of all causes of instability. Today this means primarily struggle against all aspects of subjugation and inequality, the eradication of the remnants of colonialism, and for the democratization of international relations. This is at one and the same time the struggle of underdeveloped countries for independent social transformation and rapid economic growth, not only in words but in deed.

* * *

War and its consequences caused many countries to ponder the question of how mankind could organize to avoid similar disasters in the future and create better and more equitable relations among nations. The Atlantic Charter was the first effort in that direction while the United Nations Charter laid down some of the principal bases, or foundations, upon which relations among states and peoples should be built further. Unfortunately, soon after the war was over, attempts were made to divide up the world and a long period of cold war was ushered in which is still going on, though in a somewhat abated form. Many countries could not accept this state of affairs. [This was] especially [so for] developing countries, some of which had only recently won their liberation and desired to progress in peace. Therefore, the entire foreign policy of what are known as the nonaligned countries was directed toward the struggle to preserve peace and create new equitable relations among states and peoples. Therein lies the essence of the policy pursued by the countries that adopted declarations outlining their policy at Belgrade and Cairo. The substance and principles of these relations are contained in the declarations of the Belgrade and Cairo conferences.

*   *   *

The role of the policy of nonalignment and its influence on international trends have grown constantly even during the peak period of the cold war when it was in the center of world events and prevented the complete division of the world, and also in recent years when the cold war began to wane. Moreover, as the cold war relaxes, a much larger number of states opt for the policy of new relations among states as demonstrated by the recent conference in Cairo. The policy of nonalignment wins recognition even from those forces that do not count themselves in its ranks. Therefore, the existence and functioning of this policy must be linked up primarily with social political trends in the world. . . .

For all these reasons, the policy of nonalignment is not merely a factor of peace in the world; it also signifies the kind of democratic international relations that helps countries whose peoples wish to bring about social changes that suit their needs without interference from the outside. Regarded from both its aspects, the internal and the external, the policy of nonalignment is a progressive one and consequently has a lasting and profound international and national significance. Through its progressive activities in the common struggle with socialist and other progressive forces, it has become one of the major factors in the present international ratio of forces, and equally so in changing the present state of affairs in the world by accelerating progressive social processes.

Grasping from the very beginning that its real and elementary interests lay in such a policy and in association with all socialist and progressive forces in the world, Yugoslavia, as a socialist country, has been a constituent and active part of these progressive trends which we call the policy of nonalignment. . . . The tremendous interest evinced in the Cairo conference also reaffirmed the general recognition of the policy pursued by the nonaligned countries and was an expression of confidence in its effectiveness. . . .

During the period under consideration, our country was again among the most active participants in the work of the United Nations Organization. . . . It is of prime importance to consolidate the United Nations further, and particularly, to apply [fully and more consistently] the principles of universality and democracy.

*   *   *

As it implements the foregoing principles, Yugoslavia endeavors in practice to establish mutually advantageous relations of cooperation and friendship with all countries. . . .

Progress was especially registered during this period in relations with all socialist countries, excepting China, Albania, North Korea and North Vietnam, along the lines of long-range, common interests in the building of socialism and world peace, for which the positive processes inspired by the positions adopted at the Twentieth (1956) and Twenty-second (1961) Congresses of the Soviet Communist party were of particular importance. The achievements of the past year or two in the province of economic, political, and cultural cooperation with the Soviet Union and the majority of other socialist countries by far surpasses everything that had been done earlier over a much greater number of years. Our relations are based on the sound foundations of equality of mutual interests and friendship which correspond fully to the aspirations of our peoples. It is our conviction that joint efforts must continue to be made along these lines, without hesitation or temporizing which could only harm the interests of our countries and our common aspirations.

Our relations with the capitalist countries in the West, if we except certain measures of economic discrimination deriving from the European Common Market, have been developing successfully on the principles of active and peaceful coexistence between countries with differing social-economic systems. This country wants such a development of mutual relations and considers that both sides would enjoy multiple benefits from cooperation along these lines. . . .

This country has developed particularly fruitful bilateral cooperation with a number of newly liberated countries in Asia and Africa, and in recent years with those in Latin America as well. We have found a common language with these countries, achieved close cooperation and developed sincere friendship within the scope of the policy of nonalignment and common general interest in the eradication of colonialism and the economic backwardness of developing countries.

Developing Countries

* * *

At the Seventh congress [1958] and earlier, we constantly emphasized that the problem of the differences in the rates of growth between developed and developing countries, primarily in the economic sphere, was one of the fundamental issues of contemporary relations in the world. . . .

* * *

What is actually involved here? Far-reaching political and social changes have taken place in the developing countries with the breakdown of the colonial system. This impressive process actually means social transformation in enormous areas that were formerly part of colonial empires. Its essential characteristics are the establishment of new national states and their struggle for independence and equality in interational relations. As there can be no national independence without social-economic equality, the problems of economic development in these countries have inevitably assumed prime importance. These problems have, as I said, appeared since the decline of colonialism, which failed precisely because of the economic relations it has imposed on the colonies during the period of colonial rule.

As each new nation emerges, there emerges with it a new and justified demand for a new international division of labor without which the nation in question cannot create a material base for better living conditions. As a large number of countries have been emancipated from colonial rule, over a billion and a half people have posed the problem of changing the imperialist international division of labor as imposed by colonialism with the concomitant merciless appropriation of surplus value. It is not only this that is involved. This entire process has another aspect as well. The present degree of development of productive forces, and the advances made by science and technology, particularly in the developed countries, offer undreamed of opportunities for progress under the condition that a new international division of labor is carried out. This will depend primarily on the accelerated economic development of the developing countries. Therefore, the struggle for a new international division of labor need not be considered an obstacle in international cooperation, but rather a condition for the consolidation of economic cooperation and social progress in all countries on new foundations.

Under the present circumstances, many of these countries have reached the conclusion that they can achieve economic development swiftly and successfully only on new foundations, which inevitably means the socialization of key economic positions and a socialist orientation in economic development. . . .

In the meantime, certain tendencies have been manifested more forcefully and certain problems of the economic growth of under-developed countries have become more evident. What has been characteristic in this respect over the past few years?

In the first place, difficulties in the economic development of developing countries are much more obvious today than they were previously. There is no longer any disputing the fact that the widening gap between the developed and the developing countries is the most acute problem of the day and simultaneously a very serious political issue.

In the second place, recent years have shown that the obstacles and difficulties in the way of accelerated progress of developing countries—deriving from international economic relations which are not by the nature of things under the control of the developing countries—are greater and more serious than was previously supposed. . . .

*   *   *

In the third place, all these difficulties facing the developing countries derive essentially from the obsolete and inadequate principles and institutions upon which foreign trade and economic relations rest in the present-day world. Having been established in the past, these principles and institutions in world trade and in international financial and monetary relationships favor the economically developed countries. . . .

*   *   *

Owing to this indisputably very difficult economic position of the underdeveloped countries, it was imperative to convene a world economic conference speedily, which we urged at the Belgrade conference in 1961. A beginning had to be made in solving, along new lines, the grave problems of the trade and economic development of the developing countries.

As we know, the conference in Geneva was held in spring this year [1964] at the insistence of the underdeveloped countries. We feel that the historic significance of the Geneva conference lies in its having described international economic problems in detail and having stressed their decisive importance for developing countries; it indicated the ways and means of solving these problems and made important recommendations for action to be taken on certain problems. . . .

In our opinion, the Geneva conference, resulting from the recommendation made at the Belgrade conference of nonaligned countries, took the first determined step toward solving the problems of trade and development of the developing countries. But no substantial solutions benefitting these countries have yet been adopted. Such solutions still have to be fought for and won. . . .

This country has laid stress on, and firmly supported the demands of, the developing countries on all occasions. . . . It is easy to comprehend such activity on our part for, as a socialist country and as a country emerging from inherited backwardness, we had to support actively the endeavors of the underdeveloped countries to win better conditions and their struggle against neocolonialism for that struggle is also of essential importance for us.

Parallel to such political stands aimed at stimulating the accelerated economic development of developing countries, we endeavored to promote our economic relations with the developing countries. Naturally, our activities along these lines are limited in scope. Our resources are much too insufficient to enable us to aid these countries decisively. Yugoslavia accounts for less than one percent of world trade. . . . However, regardless of Yugoslavia's restricted possibilities as an economic partner, the important thing is that we have, in our economic relations with developing countries, been consistent in our political actions and our policy of developing economic cooperation with these countries. Within the limits of her possibilities, Yugoslavia has contributed, and shall continue to contribute to the development of these countries. Such a policy benefits our country, too, if the prospect of further economic relations with these countries is kept in mind.

Yugoslavia's foreign trade with the developing countries in Asia, Africa and Latin America is worth over $300 million at present. These countries account for almost 18 percent of Yugoslavia's foreign trade, which is higher than their share in the trade of a large number of other European states. Since 1957, when the process of more intensive economic association with these countries was launched, our trade with them has virtually tripled. . . .

. . . Judging from the volume of our commitment, we shall not in any case become a decisive factor in extending assistance to the developing countries, but we can become an example of participation on a sound and equal footing to a better and even greater extent than we have hitherto been. This is imperative also from the standpoint of the interests of our own development. Association with the developing countries through foreign trade, capital construction projects, and specialized technical assistance is not only a political obligation on our part, but also a real long-range economic need for our own country.

Relations in the International Workers' Movement

During the last few years extremely important changes have taken place in the international workers' movement towards further democratization, both within individual movements and parties and in their mutual relations, and towards gradual elimination of those dogmatic Stalinistic impediments which prevented the international revolutionary workers' movement from independently performing, in its respective countries, the function of rallying and mobilizing the working and progressive masses in the struggle for new, more equitable social relations. . . . Today, socialism is becoming a form of development of contemporary society and of social progress in general.

Having become aware of this altered reality, the larger part of the international workers' movement is adopting new methods of struggle, and abandoning those which suited the period of the Third International and the times of "capitalist encirclement." On the one hand, the predominant part of the international workers' movement is increasingly accepting socialism as a worldwide process, and is developing its activity on the basis of the broad cooperation of all the progressive forces and movements which are taking shape in a vast variety and wealth of forms; and on the other hand, in its internal struggle as well, it is availing itself of new forms, acknowledging the specific features of every country with the aim of establishing connections with the masses—with progressive forces—on a growing scale.

[The international workers' movement has been] gradually ridding itself of the undemocratic methods in achieving unity of action which were typical of the period of Stalin and the Cominform. . . . This re-orientation in the international workers' movement deserves to be termed historical. . . .

It would be a mistake to consider the conflict now taking place in the international workers' movement merely as an internal affair, since it did not arise only from the internal changes in the movement or only from the conflict between the Soviet Union and China, but arises primarily from differing perceptions of the profound changes that are taking place in the world today [and] from differing approaches to the solution of the ever sharper contradictions that are shaking the world, and threatening general conflict. The different and opposing views in the international workers' movement have emerged also as a result of the different positions which individual parties have adopted in regard to the most crucial questions of the present epoch, such as the question of war and peace, and the question of coexistence between states with different social systems which is becoming a necessity if the world wants to avert a new disaster. As an expression of this disharmony, antagonisms have developed which can neither be concealed nor reconciled by means of formal compromise. A new polarization has taken place in the international workers' movement, which is primarily an expression of the following basic contradictions:

—between the new trends towards socialism in many newly liberated countries, and the narrow-minded dogmatic bureaucratic criteria of these trends;

—between the view on the objective possibilities for the further expansion of socialism under conditions of peace and coexistence, and the view that it is possible only by force—by war with the capitalist forces—to achieve the complete victory of socialism in the world;

—between the views on the need for a greater autonomy and independence of the Communist parties and socialist movements, and the attempts to conserve the old forms of unity and cooperation that are encumbered with hegemony and inequality.

Through the confrontation of different positions and policies in the international workers' movement and through the squaring of accounts with the pseudo-revolutionary and sectarian positions of the leadership of the Communist Party of China, the conviction is growing that there exist illusions as to the possibility of overcoming the conflict by compromise and by an artificial reconciliation of the antagonistic tendencies that have found expression.

The causes of the present Chinese policy in world affairs and of its behavior in the international workers' movement are indeed extremely complex and numerous and as such deserve patient consideration and study. Many factors have been in action here: economic backwardness, the earlier state of relations in the international workers' movement, the policy of isolation and blockade of the People's Republic of China by the United States. But we shall dwell here only on an appraisal of the most marked immediate causes and effects which this policy has in the field of international events and especially in the international workers' movement.

. . . Leaving aside the adverse attitude of the Chinese leadership towards our country, we have always maintained that China should be helped to develop at a stepped up rate and without hindrance and to take its right place in the international political community and in the United Nations Organization. But, like most of the international workers' movement, we are entirely in the right when we make a distinction between these objective rights and justified aspirations of the Chinese people, and the greater state objectives and hegemonic methods to which the Chinese leadership has taken recourse.

It is clear that the Chinese leadership is not even trying to conceal its dogmatic conceptions and reversion to Stalinist methods, and it is, moreover, evident that the present activity of the leadership of the Communist Party of China is in essence inspired with the desire to impose power politics upon the world, with the prospect of ultimately assuming a decisive role in the international workers' movement and in the world. . . .

The recent explosion of the first Chinese atom bomb has alarmed the world, not only because China is thus also joining in the nuclear arms race, but primarily because it is not prepared to cooperate constructively in the efforts to reject arms in general, as a means of bringing influence to bear on international politics.

The endeavors of the Chinese leadership to present the conflict with the international workers' movement merely as an ideological disagreement can hardly conceal the essence of the motives of this policy. That the ideological disagreement which attends this conflict is actually only a screen for the real Chinese aims is best borne out by the fact that, notwithstanding the continual invoking of respect for the principles of Marxism-Leninism, the leadership of the Chinese Communist party is prepared, in disregard of all principles, to resort to any step that accords with its needs and ambitions—to the extent of offering to set up a "third force" together with some capitalist countries, and to the extent of provoking frontier conflicts and voicing territorial pretensions of vast proportions. It is also important to emphasize that the Chinese ideologists do not deny the need of the existence of a leading country and party in the international workers' movement. They only deny the Communist Party of the Soviet Union the right and ability to perform such a role; they claim this role for themselves.

. . . They [also] persistently slander our foreign policy and deny our socialist reality. Over the past few years they have also been directing attacks at many Communist parties and their leaders and primarily at the Communist Party of the Soviet Union and its leading men. I think it would be wrong if no answer were given to all this. . . .

Evidently overestimating their role in the world, the Chinese leaders expected that their long and intensive campaign, to which the atom bomb test has now been added, and their persistent efforts to discredit the policy of peaceful and active coexistence, would now influence the Soviet government and party to change the whole of their internal and foreign policy and to revert to that of the Stalinist period. When this expectation was not fulfilled, the Chinese leaders, through their press, reinforced their attacks on the present leaders of the Soviet Communist party and government as well. Though these attacks are now indirect, they are sufficiently clear to show to whom they are directed. Even now, the former first secretary of the Central Committee of the Communist Party of the Soviet Union, and President of the Ministerial Council, Comrade Nikita Sergeivitch Khrushchev, who has since handed in his resignation, continues to be the main target of these attacks.

The Chinese magazine *Hung Ch'i* has put out a well-known pamphlet against Khrushchev teeming with the most abusive language, insulting not only to Khrushchev—who for more than ten years headed the government and party of the Soviet Union—but also to the Central Committee of the Communist Party of the U.S.S.R. and to the whole of the Soviet people. Although in the last few years Comrade Khrushchev did have certain failures and mistakes while heading the party and government, he played a great role in regard to de-Stalinization and in promoting freedom of expression, and also had great merits in safeguarding world peace, as well as in restraining various imperialist undertakings—during the Suez crisis, for example, or during the crisis over Cuba. I feel I must emphasize on this occasion that he deserves much credit for the normalization and improvement of relations between Yugoslavia and the Soviet Union. . . .

In that case what is the tendency of the *Hung Ch'i* pamphlet which contains a number of extremely offensive expressions? Actually, it simply demonstrates the moral and political features of those who aspire to the leadership of the international workers' movement.

*   *   *

The more consistently the antidogmatic platform of foreign policy and relations among the socialist countries and Communist parties—which still contains elements of the Stalinist period—is established and pursued in practice, the sooner will the present conflict definitely discard the appearance of an ordinary dispute in the international workers' movement and of a narrow antagonism between China and the Soviet Union, and reveal far more clearly and broadly the real essence of this conflict and the consequences this state of affairs can have for the international workers' movement and for the progressive forces in the world generally. Only in this way can a new basis for unity of action in the international workers' movement be formed on lasting and realistic foundations.

What, in our opinion, should be the relations between Communist parties? . . . Stalin's old conception and Mao Tse-tung's "new" conception of leadership of the world revolutionary movement have conflicted sharply with the increased political and moral responsibility of every party before its own people and with its specific strivings and needs. As a result of this, the present-day demands for the autonomy and independence of parties and countries in their actions do not stem merely from adherence to a principled view, but primarily reflect the real present-day need for independent and responsible action, in keeping with the conditions of each country. There is no contradiction between internationalism and the differences which arise from specific internal conditions, on the basis of which each party should in fact act; internationalism does not start where autonomy and independence end. Real revolutionary unity and socialist solidarity must be based on such a community of interests and views as arise from the full independence and responsibility of each party. Today more than ever before, the international workers' movement needs such unity as does not conceal differences, but on the contrary, recognizes them. After all, total unity in the international workers' movements has never existed. This is corroborated by the entire history of the international workers' movement, and especially by the present state of affairs in the movement.

Discussion, and even constructive polemics, between parties, as well as different views will bring no harm to the international workers' movement. On the contrary, discussion and criticism within the movement are necessary; if these are objective and loyal, if they contain no elements of interference in the internal affairs of others, if they are not incited by the intention of imposing one's own views upon others, and above all, if they are based on full equality, they can only be useful and fruitful for the cause of unity and cooperation. . . .

The principle of equality and autonomy is not an ideal for which the Communist parties and socialist countries alone are striving. The whole of progressive mankind is fighting for it today, including many new states which have broken free from dependent positions and foreign hegemony. We need only call to mind the Algerian revolution and the present efforts of the Algerian leaders, who are steadfastly creating the foundations for socialist social development in their country. . . . Another example is the United Arab Republic: aggression against the Suez and various other external pressures could not turn the leaders of that country away from their course of progressive socialist achievements. This is also the case of many other countries in Asia and Africa.

The international workers' movement would lose prestige if it were not to offer the best examples of its respect for this principle, through the entire practice of its relations. In this sense, much of the credit goes to the Twentieth Congress of the Communist Party of the Soviet Union for having declared an accounting with the Stalinist forms of relations between socialist countries and Communist parties, which, as is known, have caused the international workers' movement severe political and moral damage.

The League of Communists of Yugoslavia, on its part, has covered the difficult road of struggle for socialism in its country, and has stood for relations of equality in the international workers' movement. The League of Communists of Yugoslavia has objectively always been an organic part of that movement, regardless of the harsh attempts made in the past to isolate it, "evict" it and set it against the international revolutionary movement.

The struggle of the League of Communists of Yugoslavia for widest international cooperation and relations of equality in the international workers' movement is precisely the reason why the Chinese leadership judged it as an obstacle to their actions. The Chinese leadership was especially annoyed by the fact that the policy of the League of Communists of Yugoslavia in relation to many developing countries, primarily in Asia, Africa and Latin America, strengthened those very conceptions of international relations which objectively exposed the ambitions of the Chinese leaders. This, in the first place, explains why the Communist Party of China has for years unrestrainedly been attacking the policy of Yugoslavia even though it is a comparatively small country and thousands of kilometers away from China.

*   *   *

The League of Communists of Yugoslavia will further endeavor not to give cause to the Chinese leaders for unprincipled attacks on the League of Communists and on Yugoslavia itself, and will always be prepared to answer and discuss the Chinese attacks or criticism with the Chinese leaders in a principled manner.

Yugoslavia will continue to strive most actively for close cooperation with the Soviet Union and other socialist countries, aware that the growth of mutual understanding, on a basis of equality and mutual respect, is an essential component of the struggle for solidarity among all the progressive forces in the present-day world.

Finally, the League of Communists of Yugoslavia will do everything for the further advancement of socialist thought and practice in its country, conscious of the fact that this is an essential condition for the fulfillment of its revolutionary and international obligations.

The League of Communists of Yugoslavia will remain consistent in this respect to the responsibility it has undertaken before its people, who have untold times thus far declared themselves in favor of this policy and upheld it in practice.

Document 12: Excerpts from the Report of the CC LCY to the Ninth Party Congress, Delivered 11 March 1969 by Josip Broz Tito, General Secretary of the CC LCY*

FOREIGN POLICY AND INTERNATIONAL RELATIONS

The world situation has not changed much since the Eighth Congress of the League of Communists of Yugoslavia, although tremendous efforts have been made towards relaxation and peaceful solution of controversial problems. However, up to this day not a single major problem depressing international relations and imperiling world peace, has been solved. On the contrary, new problems are stockpiling, making the situation in the world even more complicated and dangerous, especially for the small nations. Rather than breaking down, bloc divisions are being exacerbated at the expense of the small and medium-sized countries, thereby acquiring a new quality. The attempts at direct negotiation between the big powers particularly cause the small and medium-sized states growing anxiety because of the possibility that their vital interests may be threatened. In pursuing such a policy, some of the big powers are not bringing us any closer to peace or stability, or to guarantees for the security of the small countries. Only struggle for consistent and universal implementation of peaceful coexistence between states can secure lasting and stable foundations for the consolidation of peace and more rapid progress in the world. Of course, we are not thinking of the kind of coexistence that would conserve the status quo, but rather of active engagement by all countries and progressive social forces for the purpose of solving outstanding international problems and surmounting all forms of inequality and subordination.

On the other hand, it would be mistaken not to perceive that the period between the Eighth and Ninth Congresses has seen important progressive trends and successes in the struggles of peoples to consolidate their independence, to secure free internal development, and to achieve participation on a footing of equality in the international community. The irrepressible emancipation of peoples that has swept all parts of the world is attended by growing demands for the development of such international cooperation and more rapid progress. These endeavors have found expression particularly in the struggle of countries and peoples in Asia, Africa, and Latin America for emancipation from all forms of dependence. These countries are

* Source: *Ninth Congress of the League of Communists of Yugoslavia* (Belgrade: Aktuelna Pitanja Socijalizma, 1969), pp. 52-68.

becoming an increasingly important factor positively influencing trends in the contemporary world. . . .

In the policies of a number of European countries, there has also been an important evolution towards a more independent approach to world problems. There is a growing awareness that equitable cooperation among all countries on this continent is the only possible basis for reducing tension and transcending bloc divisions.

During this period, too, the conviction has grown that the independence, sovereignty, economic development and equality of all countries is the basic precondition for preservation of world peace. The policy of nonalignment is the most adequate expression of this aspiration. Developments have confirmed the worth of this policy, as a genuine alternative to the policy of force, pressure, domination and discrimination. In addition to the nonbloc countries, certain countries that do belong to blocs are increasingly adopting the basic principles of this policy and engaging in the effort to democratize international relations.

However, at the same time, the world is faced with the intensified use of force in international relations. This dangerous practice has manifested itself in the form of various kinds of pressure, direct interference in the internal affairs of other countries, armed interventions, and so-called local wars. Imperialistic and hegemonistic forces are trying to frustrate the achievement of the legitimate aspirations of peoples for independence and free development; to preserve their positions and expand the sphere of their domination. The newly liberated countries are subjected to constant pressure from the imperialistic and neocolonialistic forces which, taking advantage of the internal difficulties of those countries, endeavor to retain the old and impose new relationships of dependence and exploitation. To that end, they incite and exacerbate regional and boundary disputes and antagonisms, meddle in the internal affairs of others, and provoke coups d'etat and putschs.

Under these circumstances, it is more difficult to solve crucial international problems like the economic advancement of the underdeveloped countries, the abolition of colonialism and racial discrimination, and the consolidation of the U.N.'s role. Instead, the existing unsolved problems are compounded by new ones.

The orientation of the biggest powers to avoiding a nuclear conflagration is undoubtedly positive. However, the avoidance of dangerous conflicts between the biggest powers and the reduction of the direct danger of a nuclear war does not at the same time guarantee peace and security for all peoples. The policy of peace and progress cannot be grounded in division of the world or exclusion of the majority of countries from solution of international problems that concern their vital interests. The tendency of certain countries in the military-political groupings to become more independent testifies to the crisis of bloc policy which has become an obstacle to the achievement of their national aspirations and interests. Bloc policy also prevents the big powers from playing a different role in the world. The stuggle for peace must also encompass efforts to transcend these divisions and constantly to expand the area of equitable international cooperation.

The use of force in international relations aggravates the problem of security, above all of the small and medium-sized countries. Their lasting security cannot be assured by a balance of power between the big powers, or by affirmation with blocs or by guarantees from the big powers. . . .

*　　*　　*

In spite of the endeavors of a large number of countries, the U.N. has not become a decisive factor in the preservation of peace, security and solution of world problems. The changes that have taken place in the world, particularly with the appearance of many new states and with independent action by them, have not yet found full expression within it. If the U.N. is to fulfill its mission, it will be indispensable for it to consider and solve the most important world problems, and to become universal. The absence of the People's Republic of China not only represents an anachronism but seriously obstructs the normal activity of this world organization and the solution of the most crucial international problems. It is in the interests of the entire international community, and particularly the small and medium-sized countries, for the United Nations to become capable of contributing to the solution of long-term world problems, such as security, economic development, disarmament, decolonization, and racial discrimination, as well as the solution of acute international conflicts and controversies.

*　　*　　*

It is well known that our country supports all initiatives for the definitive liquidation of colonialism. It is absurd and untenable today, in the second half of the twentieth century, for peoples to live in colonial enslavement, which is still being maintained, particularly in Africa, by methods of the most brutal violence and terror. Such a situation directly imperils the independence and territorial integrity of many African countries and represents a source of aggravation and instability in international relations. This focal point of colonialism is being utilized to strangulate the social and national emancipation of the African peoples and to enable imperialists and neocolonialists to exert pressures of various sorts. It is the duty of the international community to offer support to the peoples of Angola, Mozambique, the South African Republic, Rhodesia, Guinea-Bissau, and other territories in their struggle for full liberation, and to take the most urgent measures to liquidate all the remnants of colonialism. Yugoslavia has extended direct political support and material assistance to the liberation movements and developed the broadest possible cooperation with all anticolonialist forces.

The arms race continues, and threatens peace and security. According to certain assessments, about $200 billion a year are spent on armaments. . . .

We have signed the nonproliferation treaty in the conviction that, despite its shortcomings, it is an initial step toward the solution of the problem of disarmament. The goal of that treaty will be achieved if it is followed by other measures leading to general and complete disarmament. Our country has also supported the taking of partial measures in this sphere, considering that they are useful steps toward general and complete disarmament. The nuclear powers certainly have a special responsibility and should take urgent measures to stop the arms race and to start their own disarmament. This does not, however, diminish the need for engagement by all countries, nor the significance of their contribution to the solution of this problem. The Conference of Non-nuclear Countries in Geneva reaffirmed the need for participation by all countries in the solution of this problem, and continuity in these efforts.

As concerns international economic relations, our country has continued to engage intensively in all activities designed to lead to a new international policy for development. We have also made our contribution to formulation of the program of work of the U.N. Conference on Trade and Development, and to the elaboration of the Charter of Algeria, which represents the platform and action program of the developing countries.

Further, we have frequently, and on various occasions, pointed out the harmful consequences of the low economic growth rate of the developing countries. The per capita gross national income is rising in the developing countries by only two dollars per year, and in the developed countries by sixty dollars. At the same time, the share of economic assistance to the developing countries in the GNP of the developed countries is declining from year to year.

*   *   *

The grave economic situation in the developing countries makes it necessary for all developed countries to reexamine critically their attitude toward the problems of economic development. . . . In view of the material and technical advancement that has been made in the world, objective possibilities exist today for helping the developing countries to advance and for closing the gap between the rich and the poor countries. However, the developed countries are engaged, in dangerous proportions, in building up systems of economic exclusivity and bloc autarky. . . . The question of development is one of the most acute world problems, and not solving it results in the further deterioration not only of the economic, but also the political position of the developing countries, and inevitably leads to aggravation of international relations and threatens world peace.

The development of international relations has reaffirmed the significance of the policy of nonalignment, which has played an exceedingly important role in easing tension, removing the danger of a world conflict, and solving major international problems.

* * *

The results of the Belgrade and Cairo conferences had a powerful influence on international relations. The Belgrade conference contributed to promoting the course of negotiation and reducing tension in international relations. The U.N. General Assembly passed proposals submitted by the conference, relating to disarmament, decolonization, and economic development. [Also at the urging of the Belgrade conference] the U.N. Conference on Trade and Development was convened, a decision was passed to convene a world disarmament conference; and work was launched on the codification of the principles of coexistence. Both conferences gave impetus to the emancipation of peoples and countries, and to efforts to transcend bloc divisions as well as to contribute to the general improvement of relations and cooperation between many states.

* * *

The United States of America has imposed upon the peoples of Vietnam a most cruel war that has been waged for a number of years now. The struggle of the Vietnamese people for independence and freedom has become an example and a symbol of triumphant resistance to aggressive imperialist policy. . . . A lasting solution will, however, be made possible only by recognizing the full independence of the people of Vietnam and their right to decide their own future without any interference from the outside.

* * *

Yugoslavia very decisively condemned the Israeli aggression against the Arab countries and consistently supported the removal of its consequences. At meetings in Moscow, Budapest, Warsaw, and Belgrade, we have come out for extending comprehensive material and political assistance as well as other kinds of support to the U.A.R. and other Arab countries. Simultaneously, we undertook a number of concrete measures to assist, to the limits of our possibilities, the victims of aggression.

At a special session of the U.N. General Assembly, together with a number of other countries, we initiated a resolution on the withdrawal of Israeli troops from occupied Arab territories. In August 1967, we visited the U.A.R., Syria, and Iraq and considered possibilities for starting action to find a platform for a political solution to the crisis. Later we formulated the well-known five points, with which we acquainted the governments of virtually all countries. This initiative of ours was favorably received in the world, as a constructive contribution to the effort to find a political settlement to the crisis. . . .

The Israeli aggression, postponement of solution of the Middle East crisis, and the growing military potential of the big powers seriously aggravates the situation in the Mediterranean region. The Soviet fleet, which sailed into the area after a long presence by the American Sixth Fleet and after the eruption of the Middle East crisis, is one of the aspects of assistance to the Arab countries in the situation created by the Israeli aggression.

However, the increasingly powerful armed presence of the big powers and their competition with each other in this respect, aggravates the problems and controversies in this area, and has a negative influence on the situation not only in the Mediterranean but elsewhere. It is in the vital interests of the Mediterranean countries to act together to make this area a zone of peace and security rather than a region of bloc conflicts. . . .

Identical or similar attitudes toward the fundamental international problems have come to the fore in our relations with most countries of Asia and Africa. Yugoslavia has collaborated closely with these countries, within the U.N. and in other international organizations, both in the sphere of bilateral relations and in implementation of the principles of nonaligned policy which are common to us. Yugoslavia extends full support to the efforts of the peoples of Asia and Africa in their fight to consolidate their independence and to achieve more rapid economic development. Our relations with those countries have been promoted through various forms of cooperation, by meetings between heads of state and government, by the practice of exchanging views on the most important international problems, and by cooperation between sociopolitical organizations. Furthermore, in recent years Yugoslavia has established diplomatic relations with a number of African and Asian countries with which she had not maintained relations before.

Although visible results have been attained in the advancement of our economic relations with Asian and African countries, these results still lag behind possibilities and mutual interests. They are developing, by and large, within bilateral frameworks and on the foundations of classic commodity exchange. Tripartite cooperation between India, the U.A.R. and Yugoslavia gave impulse to new forms of cooperation which are only in the initial stage. Important impetus to the development of economic relations with the countries of those regions was represented by the relatively large credit amounting to some $850 million granted by this country on the basis of which over 120 industrial projects have been constructed or are in the process of being constructed. However, trade with the countries of Asia and Africa represents only about 10 percent of total Yugoslav foreign trade and demonstrates a tendency to decline and stagnate. . . .

It may be observed with satisfaction that scientific and technical collaboration with Africa and Middle East countries has developed successfully. Roughly 1,200 Yugoslav experts are now working there and there are possibilities for raising that number. There are about 3,500 students from African and Arab countries regularly studying or specializing at our universities. Of that number, about 1,000 have Yugoslav government scholarships.

In the preceding period, we have intensified contacts with a number of Latin American countries. Very fruitful cooperation has been established with these countries within the framework of the United Nations Conference on Trade and Development and the Group of Seventy-seven. . . . However, in the sphere of economic cooperation, the existing possibilities have not been plumbed sufficiently. It is in our interests to intensify efforts to expand and develop our relations with the countries of Latin America in this sphere.

Similarities in political views and the common economic interest make it incumbent on us to continue to accord full attention to our relations with the countries of Asia, Africa and Latin America.

Yugoslavia attaches particular significance to political developments in Europe and to relations with European countries, particularly the neighboring ones. Positive development was already under way in Europe, freer forms of cooperation were being practiced, and a climate had been created for transcendence of divisions. A cold war atmosphere gradually replaced the policy of relaxation of tension, which had opened up the vista of more comprehensive cooperation between the European states. This development intensified the conviction of the majority of countries in Europe that the policy of relaxation of tension and mutual cooperation has no alternative. Although the armed intervention in the Czechoslovak Socialist Republic dealt a serious blow to such favorable development, we may observe that the European countries are profoundly concerned to prevent a relapse into the cold war and to make it possible to continue the processes that had been launched, naturally with strict respect for independence, sovereignty, territorial integrity, and the principle of nonintervention.

Positive evolution in Europe intimates the possibility of a change in approaches to solving outstanding European problems. There is a growing conviction that the questions of European security and Germany can be solved only by further rapprochement and promotion of cooperation between European countries. In this respect, it would be indispensable to take as a point of departure the fact that there are two German states and that the present borders are immutable.

Our relations with European countries are acquiring ever more substantive and richer forms of economic, cultural, and political cooperation. This also comes to the fore in increasing exchanges of views and in meetings both at the state and at the sociopolitical level. Yugoslavia's relations with Western European countries are a case in point of successful collaboration between countries with differing social systems. . . .

In 1968, our trade with Western European countries achieved the sum of over $1,500 million. . . . It should also be mentioned that the abolition of visas with most of these countries has given impetus to the tourist trade. This complex of positive development is, however, at odds with the discriminatory policy of the European Economic Community which is, in the present phase, a grave obstacle to the further promotion of our economic relations with the countries of this group. . . .

We are devoting special attention to development of relations with neighboring countries. The relations we are promoting with Italy and Austria represent, in our conviction, an example of fruitful and mutually useful cooperation. The openness of the boundaries with these two countries is eloquent testimony to the high level of good neighborly relations. Relations with Greece, despite well-known difficulties, are gradually improving.

There are differences between the kind of relations we have with the neighboring socialist countries. With Romania, for instance, we are developing highly fruitful and comprehensive friendly collaboration reflecting similarity in positions and the endeavors of the two socialist countries to promote relations on the grounds of equality and the mutual interest. Relations with Hungary, too, are developing under the aegis of a wish on both sides for good neighborly relations. We should like to normalize relations with Albania but that naturally does not depend on us alone. In spite of their attitude toward our country, we stand on the position that the independence, full sovereignty, and integrity of Albania are essential elements for stability and peace in the Balkans.

Our efforts to develop cooperation with Bulgaria are coming up against increasing difficulties. Bulgaria's recent policy directly violates the interests of the Socialist Federal Republic of Yugoslavia and the peoples of Yugoslavia. In Bulgaria, Macedonian national individuality is being denied openly, and territorial aspirations towards this country are simultaneously being revived and incited. The campaign even goes so far as to claim that the occupation of parts of Yugoslavia by Czarist Bulgaria, an ally of Hitler's Germany during the Second World War, was an act of liberation. Cooperation with Bulgaria, which we should like, cannot be developed if Bulgaria persists in such a policy.

Yugoslavia, as a socialist country, has always attached great importance to cooperation with other socialist countries, regarding this as being in the common interest in terms of the consolidation of peace, international cooperation, and development of socialism in the world. Special stress should be laid on the fact that the tangible achievements and results of cooperation were possible thanks to its being founded on the principles of respect for sovereignty, independence, equality, and noninterference in the internal affairs of others; on the principles contained in the Belgrade and Moscow Declarations of 1955 and 1956, as well as in other documents which we signed with the socialist countries.

The military intervention by five socialist countries in Czechoslovakia had, however, a negative influence on the development of cooperation. Owing to our stand of principle toward this intervention, stagnation developed in the sphere of political and party relations. Our position on the events in Czechoslovakia was taken by the U.S.S.R. and certain other socialist countries as the motive for a broad anti-Yugoslav campaign, involving "criticism" and attacks on our socialist system of self-government, and our independent foreign policy. Such activity is continually a negative factor in our relations.

On a number of occasions, and especially at the Tenth Session of the Central Committee of the LCY, we submitted our position on the intervention in Czechoslovakia. This action, which violated the independence of a sovereign state, and which is completely at odds with the generally accepted principles of international law and the U.N. Charter, dealt a grave blow to the interests of progress, peace, and freedom—all the more so as it was undertaken by socialist countries in the name of protecting socialism.

Simultaneously, there appeared in certain East European socialist countries the unacceptable doctrine of "collective," "integrated" sovereignty—[essentially a restricted sovereignty]. This doctrine, propounded in the name of an allegedly higher level of relationships between the socialist countries, negates the sovereignty of those countries and endeavors to legalize the right of one country or a number of countries, upon their own assessment, and even by resorting to military intervention, to impose their will on other socialist countries. Of course, we adamantly reject such a conception as running counter to the basic right of all peoples to independence, and counter to the principles of international law. Moreover, such a conception is incompatible with the interests of the struggle for socialism.

However, on this occasion, too, we wish to underscore that Yugoslavia, regardless of the existing differences in views, supports the surmounting of the resulting difficulties and seeks the further development of relations with all socialist countries, since this is in the common interest of our peoples, of peace and of socialism. Time and practice will be the best judge of the correctness of any specific policy.

As a socialist and nonaligned country, Yugoslavia will develop comprehensive cooperation with all countries on principles of equality, independence, sovereignty, and respect for the territorial integrity of all countries. In line with these principles, Yugoslavia will continue to fight consistently against the policy of force, domination, and interference in the internal affairs of other countries, in the conviction that by pursuing such an orientation, it is also defending its own independence. We accept no restrictions on independence and sovereignty, regardless of the motives and arguments by which attempts are made to justify it.

Yugoslavia will participate actively in all actions by nonaligned countries. Our lasting orientation to the policy of nonalignment reflects the conception that it is a policy of independence, of transcendence of division in the world, and of democratization of international relations, which creates the best possible conditions for progressive social transformation. It is also the fullest possible expression of the interests of Yugoslavia's self-managing and socialist society, and provides the most adequate basis for equitable cooperation with all countries.

During this period, the international position and prestige of our country were enhanced. This is the result of revolutionary and stable internal development, grounded in the unity of our peoples and their determination to defend uncompromisingly their independence and the right to their own road of development. All the steps we have undertaken in internal development have inevitably led us to open up to a greater extent and to cooperate comprehensively with countries and peoples throughout the world. Experience has confirmed that the genuine respect, understanding, and support of the international community can be won only by those countries whose international activity is based on defense of their own independence and respect for the independence of others. We may observe with satisfaction that the world demonstrates an intensified interest in the independent position of our country as a factor of peace and stability.

In the preceding period we have witnessed exceptional new achievements in science and technology, the tumultuous development of productive forces, and the increasing socialization of production on the one hand and, connected with this, profound social upheavals in all parts of the world on the other. Unrest, mass strikes, demonstrations, and frequently bloody conflicts in many countries reflect various aspects and degrees of dissatisfaction on the part of the broad working masses with their position in society. . . . The ideas of socialism and their positive achievements are becoming ever more attractive to various progressive, social, political, cultural, and scientific strivings and movements.

*   *   *

It is becoming increasingly clear that revolutionary forces can contribute more to the more rapid advancement of socialism as a worldwide process and to its further affirmation if, under the complex contemporary social and international conditions, they succeed in uniting all democratic progressive and socialist aspirations in the struggle for peace, freedom, independence, equality, and an independent road of development for each people. Those who shut themselves up into closed systems of various sorts show a lack of confidence in the creative capacities of the working people, obstruct the full affirmation of the democratic and human values of socialism and frequently lose perspective in terms of the socialist solution of contradictions and antagonisms in the present-day world.

In this connection, in recent years broad discussions and polemics have developed, and clashing viewpoints have become deeper. Such a state of affairs reflects the objective need for political organization of working class, liberation, and other democratic movements and parties; to find new replies to problems imposed by contemporary realities. This can be attained only through free and equal discussion, attended by courageous analysis of experience—both achievements and failures—and further development of the basic values of Marxism, thinking in line with new manifestations and trends in the world.

The League of Communists of Yugoslavia has always devoted special attention to relations between socialist countries, between Communist and working-class parties, and to cooperation with socialist people's liberation and other progressive democratic parties and movements.

The development of the socialist countries and their mutual relations hold exceptional significance because they wield a growing influence over all trends in the world. It is a well-known fact that in relations between various socialist countries, certain problems emerge from their differing or contradicting interests. As a result, major differences and even conflicts arise from time to time. We consider that socialism, as the most progressive form of social order, must demonstrate its advantages by accepting the inevitability of various roads of socialist development in various countries and by solving, in democratic fashion, those problems that arise in relations between socialist states. The ideas and achievements of socialism act as a tremendous mobilizing force, precisely because they open up for enslaved and suppressed peoples the prospect of freedom and equality. Consequently, relations between socialist countries should serve as an example of respect for, and application of, the principles of independence, noninterference, and equitable cooperation. These and similar problems of relations crop up also between Communist and working-class parties, and their resolution must be pursued through the same principles. We have always stood staunchly for the strict implementation of those principles, and against practices which lead to the opposite results.

During this period, forces have strengthened in the revolutionary and progressive movement that support and fight for equal relations. Turbulent social trends in a large number of countries, and the mounting desire for independence and equality make it necessary for political organizations of the working class to solve those questions which the situation in their own country imposes upon them. This found strong expression recently, for instance, during the congresses and other meetings of leading bodies of Communist parties, particularly in certain West European countries. This creates more favorable conditions for gradually surmounting divisions and antagonistic relations in the working-class movement, and between progressive forces in various countries, and for bringing them together, on a basis of equality, in the struggle for social progress. The necessity for parties and movements to establish their own programs and policies and to develop their organization independently, in line with the interests of the working class and people of their country, also makes it incumbent on them to cooperate in the international sphere on a footing of equality; to find common interests in the fight for freedom, peace, progress, and socialism. So far, experience has demonstrated that the conception that one state or party has a leading role—that is, that there is an international center or forum discharging the role of arbiter—exacerbates differences and aggravates conflicts in the ranks of the international revolutionary and progressive movement and disunites the front of the struggle against imperialism. At the same time, such practices engender great internal difficulties in the life of individual parties. This has been thrown into sharp relief especially during recent times.

In international relations, the link between the struggle for national independence and socialist internationalism is one of the questions about which there has been comprehensive discussion. From our own practice, both in internal and international relations, we know how important it is for the revolutionary forces to adopt, and to implement in practice, the right attitudes on the national question. As a rule, those forces have always won when they succeeded in dovetailing class interest with properly conceived national interest. We energetically reject the artificial dilemma represented by pitting the interests of socialism in the world against authentic national interest. It is known that in its struggle against socialism, the reactionary class pits the national interest against the class and international interest. On the other hand, we find that such attempts of departure are weak in that the position of the class and international interest is presented as known and determined in advance, and that hence there can be no discussion about it. It is all the stranger for these and similar views to be proclaimed socialist principles, as this leads to particularly grave and harmful consequences when they are translated into corresponding political action by various socialist countries.

The strength of socialism lies in its respecting and, by democratic resolution, linking the different and contradicting interests deriving from different conditions with the wealth of national roads and forms of socialist practice in various countries and regions of the world.

On this basis is built a socialist internationalism that assumes both mutual support and assistance by revolutionary, socialist, and progressive forces in the world, as well as mutual solidarity and unity of action in the fight for further development, progress, and socialism. Any interference in the internal affairs of other countries and parties, any imposition of solutions or "models" from abroad can only delay the socialist transformation of the world and therefore runs counter to the goals of socialist internationalism.

Taking as a point of departure the principles of independence, noninterference and equality, the LCY and our sociopolitical organizations have, in the intervening period, developed fruitful cooperation with a large number of Communist, working-class, socialist, anti-imperialist and other democratic parties and movements. The basis of that cooperation is provided by bilateral forms of cooperation. Thus, for instance at various meetings in 1968, the LCY and the Socialist Alliance of the Working People of Yugoslavia exchanged views and experiences with the representatives of 113 parties and movements. . . . The experience of our practice confirms us in the conviction that the best results of cooperation between Communists, working-class, socialist, anti-imperialist and other democratic parties and movements, and the further development of their international solidarity can be achieved if all forms of imposing narrow interests and views are eliminated; if respect is accorded to different opinions and a common interest is found in the struggle against imperialism and for peace and progress in the world. . . .

Our working people have always demonstrated great interest in trends in international relations. As our country opens up to the outside and incorporates into the international division of labor, the people inevitably become an active factor in the construction and implementation of foreign policy. Our foreign policy is based on principles; it is open, public, and known to each and every citizen. For this precise reason, it is not susceptible to wavering and surprise turnabouts. Its essence is determined by the character of internal sociopolitical and economic relations. A consistent orientation toward having our working people, and our sociopolitical communities and organizations, take an active part in managing all spheres of social life, makes it incumbent on us to ensure that the development and implementation of policy in international relations and international cooperation become a component part of our socialist self-managing society.

Document 13: Excerpts from the Report of the CC LCY to the Tenth Party Congress, Delivered 27 May 1974 by Josip Broz Tito, General Secretary of the CC LCY*

CHANGES IN THE WORLD TODAY AND YUGOSLAVIA'S FOREIGN POLICY

Progressive trends in this country have been paralleled by complex and turbulent events in international life. The depth of social transformations—with their numerous and intricate contradictions—is a feature of the contemporary world, and bears out that mankind is without doubt at one of the most important junctures in its history. . . .

Behind the radical changes occurring in the world we find, on one hand, a powerful awakening of the political consciousness and self-confidence of numerous peoples and social movements who can no longer live under the old political and economic conditions; and on the other, the unprecedented upsurge of productive forces associated with the present scientific and technological revolution.

Earlier social structures and obsolete social relations are incompatible with the dynamic growth of productive forces and social consciousness. New, basically socialist social relationships, appearing in many of the world's countries, are irrepressibly breaking through, in various forms and different ways. All of this demonstrates, as we have frequently stressed, that socialism is penetrating through various pores of human society, even at less advanced levels of social and state life. Any dogmatism in the approach to different forms and roads of socialism would therefore completely miss the mark and could only do harm to such processes.

Another side of this process is a growing objective interdependence and integration, attended, however, also by mounting disproportions in the development of individual countries and regions. The result is exacerbation of existing tensions and emergence of new social antagonisms on a worldwide scale. . . .

There has been a tremendous growth in the number of active international factors—independent states, political movements, and other factors of international life. Apart from the rising number of socialist, progressive states and their ever more decisive role in world trends, the most distinctive feature of present world processes has been the rapid collapse of the colonial system, developed for cen-

* Source: *The Struggle for the Further Development of Socialist Self-Management in our Country and the Role of the League of Communists of Yugoslavia* (Belgrade: 1974), pp. 4-17.

turies and maintained in a variety of ways. Many new independent states have come into being. Anticolonial, national liberation, and other progressive movements in many parts of the world, with special reference to Asia, Africa, and Latin America, have intensified their activities.

The readiness of many of the world's peoples to make their own decisions on the social forms and modes of their internal life, and to act as equal partners in the international community, is decisive in its significance for the present-day world and far-reaching in its implications for further development. This is the basis on which emerged the policy and the world movements of nonalignment—an increasingly powerful force of mankind along its road towards more equitable international relations, general social progress and durable peace.

The contemporary anticolonial and revolutionary national liberation struggle is being conducted at different tempos and in various ways. I have in mind, above all, the victory of the Chinese Revolution, the achievement of independence by the peoples of Southeast Asia, the triumph of the armed revolution conducted by the Cuban and Algerian peoples, the struggle of the Arab nations for self-determination and independent statehood, the fight of the peoples of Africa, and the strengthening of political consciousness and struggle on the part of the peoples of Latin America for economic and political emancipation. Let us not forget that mankind has paid for these major changes with dozens of so-called local wars waged in the course of this quarter of a century. . . . An example of such a war was that in Vietnam.

The international community today differs radically in appearance from the post-World War II community. The momentous changes that have occurred in the past twenty-five years in international relations and in many areas of society are such in nature and significance as to warrant the assertion that mankind has embarked on a new era in its history.

The sources of these major changes are traceable to the Second World War—to its preponderantly liberating nature and its positive repercussions on the further development of relations in the world. In contrast to the First World War, dominated by the conflict between the imperialist powers over a new division of the world, and above all the colonies, the Second World War was invested with its basic characteristic—that of a war of liberation—by the struggle of peoples for national emancipation and social progress. The First World War did not solve a single one of the fundamental international antagonisms, and not only did it fail to bring nations a secure peace, but gave rise to new conflicts. Having erupted from the general crisis of capitalism as a system, the First World War simply aggravated that crisis which was in turn deepened further by the October Socialist Revolution in Russia. Its victory, launching the epoch of socialism, signified the first breakthrough into the imperialist system.

... The world depression of the thirties shook capitalism to its very foundations and set the scene for the emergence of its most reactionary outgrowth—fascism. Hardly twenty years after the First World War, mankind was propelled into an even greater catastrophe, the Second World War, prompted by the aggressive fascist powers in their desire to rule the world.

But this time the policy of war and the plans for world mastery were opposed by the socialist revolution, that is the first land of socialism, and by the burgeoning forces of liberation and revolutionary movements around the world. This fact acted to work a basic change in the character of the Second World War and wielded a decisive influence on its entire course.

*   *   *

The entry of the U.S.S.R. into the war was decisively instrumental in endowing the Second World War with its liberating character. The enslaved peoples of Europe saw this as a guarantee that their struggle against fascism would not be in vain.

*   *   *

Against the background of the powerful national liberation movements, grown from the resistance to fascism and imperialist aggression, many popular, basically socialist, revolutions developed and triumphed in the course of World War II.

The results and consequences of the Second World War for the further course of world history therefore differed radically from those produced by the First World War. In addition to the formation of new socialist states and of socialism as a world process, these consequences were manifest also in the liberation of a large number of colonial peoples and thereby in the collapse of the world colonial system.

*   *   *

All this indicated that the forces of imperialism had weakened considerably. The positive goals of the Second World War, intimated in the Atlantic Charter, found particularly strong expression in the Charter of the United Nations as well as in the founding of this world organization, which plays an increasingly significant role in the solution of international problems and in the struggle for international relations based on democratic principles.

Understandably, reactionary imperialist forces did not reconcile themselves to the loss of monopolies and privileged positions. Rather, they endeavored to reverse social progress and stop the advance of the anticolonial revolution; to impose on the world the policy of dividing the globe into spheres of interest among the great powers. The upshot of this effort was the cold war, which escalated into shooting wars on a local scale. The cold war also brought bloc divisions and military-political confrontation. . . .

Thanks to the growth of the forces of peace and progress around the world, the dangers of nuclear war have been reduced and the great powers have had to start regulating their relations by negotiation and the achievement of understanding. Since the Belgrade conference [1961], the nonaligned countries have been active in their support of détente and transcendence of the cold war, making a notable contribution to this process and to affirmation of active peaceful coexistence.

Far-reaching changes in international relations and in the internal development of many countries are altering the ratio of forces in favor of peace and progress. Imperialism and inequitable international relations are so deeply in crisis that there can be no reversal to one-time world domination. . . .

*   *   *

Exceptional significance attaches to the socialist countries, and to all other socialist forces throughout the world, in the continuing world movement towards progressive changes in international relations. The responsibility of the socialist countries is all the greater and more serious for the fact that socialism as a social system has so far been established largely in relatively underdeveloped countries, which have therefore been compelled, while discharging the tasks of the socialist revolution—that is, the building of new social and economic relations—to perform also many of the important tasks of preceding epochs.

The combination of these historical circumstances is compounded by the fact that disproportions in the development of the modern world are manifest also in the development of the socialist countries. That is, socialism, also, is developing unevenly . . . [Thus,] contradictions have regrettably led to aggravation of relations and conflicts between individual socialist countries. And this has repercussions on international relations as a whole, and on the role and positions of these countries in such relations.

Socialist countries cannot strengthen their position in the world—they cannot promote the cause of peace and socialism—unless their own mutual relations are based on the principles of equality, independence, mutual respect, and noninterference in the internal affairs of others.

Socialist countries guided by Marxist science—according to which the same laws that should prevail among men should also govern relations among countries and nations—must strive to eliminate mutual controversies to the maximum, and thus assure the smoothest possible movement toward common socialist goals.

Now that the scientific and technical revolution with its epochal achievements specifically offers socialism the chance of a lifetime, the socialist countries must not absolutize or glorify only their own roads and the specific features of their own development, nor should they impose their system on others. Differences in specific features are inevitable and must be respected. This does not, of course, preclude the need for dialogue and mutually constructive criticism. . . .

Along a broad front, the progressive forces of the working class, which has grown enormously, are strengthening their alliance with other sections of society in the fight for progressive transformations. . . .

Throughout the world today possibilities are widening for the international workers' movements to play a greater role and wield more influence. The conviction is increasing that independence and noninterference are the basic premise for development of relations, based on equality and solidarity, among the socialist countries, Communist and workers' parties, and other progressive forces and progressive movements. . . .

The League of Communists of Yugoslavia has steadily developed cooperation with Communist and workers' parties and progressive movements, proceeding from the principle of the full autonomy of every party and movement and its responsibility to its own working class and people. We have always advocated the view that differences in positions, reflecting the diverse conditions under which individual parties and progressive movements function, need not present an obstacle to cooperation. On the contrary, genuine unity can be forged only if the interests and views of each party and movement are respected.

National liberation movements are a constituent part of progressive forces. By fighting for national liberation, they contribute importantly to the anti-imperialist and anticolonial struggle. It is the internationalist obligation of all socialist and democratic forces to extend comprehensive support and assistance to these movements.

Nonaligned policy, having emerged from struggle for liberation and opposition to imperialism and foreign domination—from the most profound aspirations of nations and countries for independence, equality and development in freedom—is playing a more meaningful role in international relations. By its consistent advocacy of the principles of active peaceful coexistence, it has asserted itself as a world policy and an international factor with widening influence. Nonaligned policy has continued to strengthen and expand the directions of its activity. From the Belgrade conference [in 1961], through the conferences in Cairo, Lusaka and Algiers [in 1964, 1970, and 1973 respectively], the nonaligned countries have shown mounting determination in their resistance to all forms of foreign domination and their support for the democratization of international relations, the independent development of countries, and the preservation of world peace. At present, over two-thirds of the members of the United Nations are nonaligned and developing countries. Acting in unity, they bring substantial influence to bear on the character and substance of decisions and directions in which the world organization engages its forces.

In terms of its social-historical essence, nonaligned policy is anti-imperialist and anti-hegemonic; consequently it is not and cannot be the instrument of anyone, nor can it be something that is held in reserve by any one, or by any other policy. As I have already said, this derives from the very fact that it emerged as a reflection of the struggle for the independence and equality of peoples. Its anti-imperialist character is grounded in the objective situation and does not depend on whether this is or is not recognized. The orientation of nonaligned countries to such a policy is not the product of passing tactical expediencies, but is in their vital interest. We have always maintained that in no case does nonalignment mean neutrality. Nonaligned policy's attitude to the great powers and other states depends on their actual behavior and activities in international life.

The fight for national and social emancipation is unfolding in uninterrupted conflict with forces that would retain obsolete relations of inequality and exploitation. Imperialism endeavors to preserve its privileged positions and to protect them with all the means at its disposal—interference, pressures of various kinds, and even the use of force, military interventions and armed aggression. . . . Imperialism relies particularly on the so-called military-industrial complex and techno-bureaucratic structures which are in growing degree becoming a force above society and an instrument for the maintenance of inequitable relations in the world.

Multinational companies, as an explicit form of monopoly capitalism and neocolonialism, are endeavoring to impose themselves as a dominant factor, even in many developed countries. . . . The activities of such companies are particularly negative in the developing countries: on the economic plane in their extraction of excessive profits, and on the political plane in their interference in the internal affairs of those countries. . . .

Antagonisms in international relations are worsening in the area of world economy. Obviously, the attempt to conserve the present system of international economic relations is not the way out of the situation. Spiraling prices for oil and other raw materials has brought home in a drastic manner the full depth of these antagonisms and the degree to which the developed world has been waxing rich for decades on the basis of low prices for the energy and raw materials of the developing countries. The industrially advanced countries have grown prosperous while the developing countries stagnated; the upshot being a growing gap between the developed and underdeveloped. Today, too, the developed countries have an incomparably greater part of world income at their disposal, while the large majority of mankind is encumbered by problems of economic underdevelopment, want, and even mass hunger in some parts of Asia and Africa.

Political decolonization has not therefore been attended by economic decolonization. Today, however, this process has finally been inaugurated and there is no stopping it. The orientation of the nonaligned and the developing countries, supported by the decisions of the Fourth Nonaligned Summit Conference [1973], toward asserting their sovereignty over natural resources and their right to carry out nationalization is gaining in import. Relying in growing degree on their wealth in energy and raw materials, they will fight for and win an equitable position in international trade, and thus accelerate their own economic and social advancement.

The recent special session of the United Nations General Assembly, devoted to raw materials and development, represents a major stride forward in this respect. And it is the nonaligned countries which have, by their joint action, made the greatest contribution to this.

*   *   *

Much importance attaches to the earliest possible implementation of the Fourth Nonaligned Conference decisions relevant to setting up the fund for the economic and social development of nonaligned countries. This will signify the establishment of the first independent financial institution devised to serve all nonaligned and developing countries. It will therefore be necessary to collect the greatest possible financial resources for this fund. In line with its possibilities, Yugoslavia will make its contribution to the fund.

Relaxation of tension, through negotiation and peaceful settlement of international problems, is undoubtedly a positive process although still very limited and unstable. The achieved power balance on a global scale, resting on military might, cannot provide a lasting and firm basis for world peace and security. Nuclear parity has reduced the danger of a worldwide conflict. However, local and limited wars continue to be fought as the outgrowth of the scramble for positions and influence. We also cannot preclude the possibility of strikes by imperialist and reactionary forces against the freedom and independent development of countries, such as the putsch perpetrated by the military-fascist clique in Chile which has instituted unprecedented terror against the population, savagely suppressing the basic human rights. Not only has the arms race not been brought under control but it has recently intensified and spread to new areas. Over $200 billion a year are expended on armament.

Détente cannot progress unless it encompasses and solves international economic problems. It is not only world peace and security that are indivisible, for closely linked with them are the economic development and prosperity of countries. No country no matter how developed it may be, can live in isolation.

I have stressed on several occasions that the international situation is pregnant with many dangers. Crises and focuses of war in many parts of the world seriously encumber international relations. The October War in the Middle East has changed the earlier situation in many ways. But even today there is no guarantee that developments will really move in the direction of seeking and finding a just and lasting peace. Apparently Israel has not yet grasped the fact that aggression and expansion at the expense of adjacent Arab countries cannot form the basis of its security. For neither there, nor anywhere else, can peace and good relations be built on force and dictates. Every country has the legitimate right to use all means for defending its rights and independent existence.

We continue to believe that a just and durable solution to the Middle East problem can be found only on condition of Israel's complete withdrawal from all Arab territories occupied from June 1967 onwards, of restoration of the legitimate national rights of the Arab people of Palestine, and recognition of the right of all countries and peoples in the Middle East to sovereignty and integrity; to a life in peace. . . .

Although the war in Vietnam was formally terminated after the Paris Agreements, it has not yet ceased. . . . Counter to the will and true interests of the peoples of Vietnam and Cambodia, every attempt is being made to prop up the puppet regimes in Saigon and Phnom Penh at all costs. It must be obvious that the cessation of all interference by the U.S.A., and recognition of the legitimate right of those peoples to decide their own destiny, are essential preconditions for a stable and lasting peace in Vietnam. . . .

In Africa, as in some other areas of the world, colonialist strongholds still exist and the peoples of the countries concerned are not permitted to achieve freedom and independence. This is flagrantly at odds with the general course of contemporary trends in the world. The racist regimes in Africa, which flout world public opinion, could not remain in power were it not for the support of international capital and some reactionary circles in the West. We hope that the changes in Portugal will facilitate the process of liquidating colonialism and accelerate the emancipation of the peoples of Angola, Mozambique, and Guinea-Bissau from colonial domination. . . .

Widening and ever more determined action by the Latin American countries for full political and economic emancipation is tremendously important for progressive development in the world. The nonaligned countries of this region, by linking their activities with those of nonaligned countries in other continents, are making a valuable contribution to the common struggle for equitable international economic and political relations. . . .

As far as Europe is concerned, it needs to be underlined that considerable progress has been made in relations and cooperation among European countries on the principles of peaceful and active coexistence. The earlier exclusivity is gradually disappearing and cooperation transcending divisions is intensifying and expanding. . . . In the present work of the Conference on European Security and Cooperation which is drawing to a close, great importance attaches to agreement on the principle of inviolability of boundaries and to the establishment of other principles which are to provide the foundation for relations among the countries participating in this conference. All of this is, of course, extremely positive from the standpoint of consolidating peace. But these processes have not yet stabilized. Moreover, in certain aspects, the point of departure is still the bloc structures.

*   *   *

If it is thought possible, for instance, to accept the principle of territorial integrity and inviolability of boundaries while at the same time raising territorial pretensions vis-à-vis a neighboring country, then such behavior most certainly does nothing to help settle conditions in Europe.

In contradiction to the spirit and practice of neighborly relations and long years of cooperation during which enviable results were achieved, the Italian government recently voiced open territorial pretensions towards Yugoslavia. This is a direct attack on the sovereignty and territorial integrity of this country. We consider the border question nonexistent. We can no longer negotiate on this matter. . . .

Yugoslavia has always attributed great importance to friendly cooperation and good relations with all adjacent countries on the principles of equality, sovereignty, territorial integrity, and non-interference in internal affairs. Such cooperation has been beneficial to both sides. . . .

National minorities play an extremely significant role in this sense. . . . We have always proceeded from the position that national minorities are bridges which should bring peoples closer together, contribute to friendship and cooperation between the countries of their national affiliation and those which are now their homeland. We have also always proceeded from recognition of the right of every people to its national identity and self-assertion. Assuring full equality and free comprehensive development to each one of our nations and nationalities, and the reciprocal enrichment of national cultures, we have strengthened the unity of our country and the fraternity of its peoples, thereby also contributing to cooperation with neighboring countries. We cannot therefore fail to show an interest in the life and position of those sections of the Yugoslav peoples who are living as national minorities in adjacent countries or to endeavor to see to it that they enjoy all the rights belonging to them on the grounds of the United Nations Charter and interstate treaties.

The entire postwar period shows that the struggle for fairer international relations includes the struggle for the emancipation of the working man and of all nations from all forms of exploitation and inequality. If mankind is to progress, there can be no alternative to consistent application of active peaceful coexistence in relations among all countries. This assumes the complete exclusion not only of wars but of all kinds of domination and of the rule that might makes right. There can be no stable world peace or security until détente encompasses all the world's regions and until all countries take part on terms of equality in settling the basic international problems. . . .

As an active participant in international affairs, our socialist and nonaligned country has endured in adhering to the principles we opted for during the National Liberation War. Yugoslavia's foreign policy rests on the same foundations as its socialist system of self-management. It is a unified policy, reflecting the interests of all our nations and nationalities—of all our working people. Every one of the republics and provinces of this country, and all other factors in society, participate in the making and implementation of this policy.

We have on more than one occasion been exposed to pressure to renounce our policy or to change it. We have always been able to withstand such pressures because we were united and ready to defend our independence. And this shall be so in the future as well. Let no one harbor vain hopes that Yugoslavia might change. Independent, socialist, and nonaligned Yugoslavia best serves, just as it is, the interests of peace and progress in the world.

Yugoslavia will continue, in line with the principles of active peaceful coexistence, to promote relations and cooperation with all countries, with special reference to nonaligned and socialist countries, as with all forces fighting for peace, equality, and general progress in the world.

ROMANIA

Document 14: Excerpts from the Report of the CC RCP to the Tenth Party Congress, Delivered August 1969 by Nicolae Ceausescu, General Secretary of the CC RCP*

ROMANIA—AN ACTIVE FACTOR IN THE STRUGGLE FOR THE TRIUMPH OF SOCIALISM AND PEACE IN THE WORLD

1. The World Balance of Forces

Dear comrades, the international developments in the last four years have fully confirmed the appreciations and general lines of our foreign policy as established by the Ninth Party Congress. A Marxist-Leninist analysis of the changes which have occurred in the world spotlights the growing influence of the forces of socialism, of the anti-imperialist front, [and] the fact that they are to an ever greater extent determining the social life on our planet.

*   *   *

In characterizing the international situation, we start from the fact that, in spite of the contradictory development of events, the balance of forces is continuously changing in favor of socialism and peace. How do we assess imperialism? It is known that imperialism has been manifesting itself by the tendency of economic and political domination over other peoples; by the violation of their rights to freedom, independence, and national sovereignty, by the promotion of colonialism and neocolonialism. . . .

The creation and development of the world socialist system have deepened the general crisis of capitalism in the postwar period, have narrowed down the basis of action of imperialism, and have considerably weakened its positions. The collapse of colonialism has also dealt a hard blow to imperialism; it has exercised, and is exercising, a special influence on the capitalist countries. The great class battles which have taken place in recent years in the capitalist countries demonstrate the huge revolutionary force of the working class, and its important role in the fight of the masses for liberty and social justice, against the capitalist order. At the same time, the rapid development

---

* Source: Nicolae Ceausescu, *Romania on the Way of Building up the Multilaterally Developed Socialist Society, April 1969-June 1970* (Bucharest: Meridiane Publishing House, 1970), pp. 314-333.

of the productive forces in the capitalist countries, as a result of the technical-scientific revolution, has produced profound changes in the life of society and in men's thinking; it creates new objective promises for doing away with the capitalist system and for the victory of socialism throughout the world.

Nor can we overlook the increasingly accentuated sharpening of inter-imperialist contradictions. As a result of the unequal development of the capitalist countries, the fight for markets and bases of raw materials—for the conquering of economic and political positions —is being intensified. . . .

. . . Imperialism—especially American imperialism—continues to hold strong positions both economically and militarily. The whole analysis of reality shows that imperialism preserves its aggressive character, that it remains the principal enemy of progress and civilization, and that as long as there exists imperialism the danger of a new world war continues.

Starting from these considerations, one cannot, however, reach the conclusion that a world war is impending or inevitable. . . . The socialist countries, the working class, the Communist and working-class movement, the peasantry, the intellectuals, the younger generation, the women's organizations, and the peoples fighting for the final liquidation of colonialism and neocolonialism, for free and independent development—these democratic forces are capable of thwarting the aggressive plans of imperialism, and preventing the unleashing of a new world war.

The Romanian Communist party and the government of our country have carried out, and are carrying out, an active foreign policy; militating for the consolidation of the anti-imperialist forces, for the development of international collaboration, and for peaceful cooperation with all the states of the world regardless of social system. . . .

*   *   *

2. Our Foreign Policy Focuses on Friendship and Cooperation with the Socialist Countries

*   *   *

Comrades, [as always,] we shall place the development of relations of friendship and collaboration with the socialist countries in the center of our external policy. We start from the fact that the world socialist system—which has developed continuously since World War II—today includes fourteen states. It has obtained and is obtaining remarkable successes in the growth of industrial production of goods, in the development of science and culture. It is increasingly becoming the decisive factor of the fight against imperialism, for peace. By the world socialist system we understand not a bloc in which the states are fused into a whole, giving up their national sovereignty, but the assertion of socialism as an international force through its victory in several independent states, which develop independently and organize the relations between themselves on the new principles of Marxism-Leninism and proletarian internationalism. . . .

. . . Naturally, in the spirit of proletarian internationalism, the peoples of the socialist countries must aid each other, in case of imperialist attack, fighting shoulder to shoulder for the defeat of the aggressor. The establishment of plans for mutual aid in such cases must be the result of agreement between the leading party bodies, and between the constitutional leading bodies of each country. The solidarity and mutual aid of the socialist countries presupposes relations of equality between all the socialist nations. It must not lead to interference in the internal affairs of any people, as this would cause great prejudices to the cause of socialism. In this we see a decisive condition for the further consolidation of proletarian internationalism; of the world socialist system's force and influence in the world.

It is known that between the socialist countries there are a series of different opinions and divergences on a number of problems connected with socialist construction and international life. We consider that many of them originate in [objective] differences existing in their historical-social development, and in the differences of the level reached by their productive forces. Partly, however, these divergences, especially their sharpening, have subjective causes; they are determined by the failure to understand or heed the [objective] differences existing between countries, and by the inconsistent observance of the Marxist-Leninist principles on which relations between them are based. That is why our party considers that the increase in the tension could have been avoided, and that there are no insurmountable obstacles for developing bonds of close cooperation between all the socialist countries. We consider that if one puts first what is common in uniting the socialist countries, the supreme interests of the cause of socialism and of the anti-imperialist fight; and that if relations between them are based on the observance of the principles of socialist internationalism—national independence and sovereignty, equal rights, noninterference in internal affairs; and mutual and comradely reciprocal assistance—then, the present divergences and animosities can be surpassed successfully.

The fact is well known that in the period which has elapsed since the Ninth Congress, Romania's relations of friendship and cooperation with the other socialist countries have been developing continually. ... Our party declares solemnly that in the future, too, it will actively pursue the development of multilateral relations with all socialist countries; that it will make its contribution to constantly strengthen the unity of the world socialist system.

I want to underline here, before this congress, that in the spirit of our party's traditional policy, we shall continue in the future to act for developing the relations of friendship and multilateral cooperation with the Communist Party of the Soviet Union, and with the Union of Soviet Socialist Republics; this being one of the cornerstones of our country's foreign policy. We also attach particular importance to the development of relations with the Communist parties and the peoples of the European socialist countries: Bulgaria, Yugoslavia, Hungary, Poland, the German Democratic Republic, Czechoslovakia, and Albania.

*   *   *

The Romanian Communist party and the government of the Socialist Republic of Romania give a special appreciation to the relations with the Chinese Communist Party and the People's Republic of China; we shall in the future, too, act for the multilateral development of collaboration and friendship between our parties and peoples. We shall also develop the relations of collaboration and friendship with the Democratic Republic of Vietnam, the Korean People's Democratic Republic, the Mongolian People's Republic, and the fraternal parties of these countries. An important place in our international activity will be further held by the development of relations with the Communist party and the people of Cuba, the first socialist state on the American continent.

Our party attaches great importance to the exchange of views, information, and experience with the other fraternal parties of the socialist countries, both on problems related to the process of socialist construction and to international policies and activity. ...

The fact that there are differences of views between our party and the parties of certain socialist countries cannot, in our view, be an obstacle in constantly expanding the fruitful, mutually advantageous collaboration and cooperation. We hold that there are no essential problems that may hinder the good relations between our parties and peoples! We are convinced that the ever more powerful development of each of our countries, the intensification of their multilateral collaboration, will secure the steady strengthening of the whole world socialist system.

3. A Large International Activity in the Spirit of Peaceful Coexistence

Dear comrades, translating into life the general direction given by the Ninth Congress and by the Central Committee of the party, the government of our country, acting in the spirit of the principles of peaceful coexistence of states with different social systems, has carried on an active foreign policy of expanding economic, political, technical-scientific, and cultural cooperation with all the states of the world. The results of this policy are also mirrored in the fact that Romania has at present diplomatic relations with ninety-four countries, and economic and technical-scientific relations with more than 100 states. . . . In the years that have elapsed since the Ninth Congress, Romania has played host to government delegations from forty-eight countries, and government delegations of our country have visited fifty-two states. We can say that never in her history has Romania carried on so active an international policy and had so many friends as today.

Underlying Romania's relations with other states are the principles of sovereignty and national independence, of equal rights, of noninterference in internal affairs, and the observance of each people's right to decide by itself its own fate, in keeping with its own vital interests and aspirations. These principles assert themselves ever more widely in international life, and are recognized by more and more states as a sure basis of collaboration, security, and peace.

Developments ever more obviously confirm the fact that in the contemporary world, international issues cannot be solved without the active participation of all states, big and small. In shaping the line of our foreign policy we must bear in mind the fact that the world is in full transformation, that the technical-scientific revolution exerts a strong influence on the rapid development of states, and that the time is not too far off when new countries on different continents will experience a powerful economic, scientific, and technical upsurge, giving them an increasingly important place in the international concert of peoples.

*   *   *

One of the most important problems of the world today is the final elimination of colonialism and neocolonialism . . . which will ensure the independent economic and social development of the young states. Our party has relations with the national liberation and democratic movements with numerous organizations in countries fighting to shake off the imperialist yoke and for the defense and consolidation of their national independence. . . . We deem it necessary to intensify these relations even more [and grant them our full support]. . . .

The war which has been waged by the United States of America in Vietnam for almost five years has preoccupied the broad peoples' masses and political circles throughout the world. Through its political and military implications, and through the influence which it exerts on international life this war may be said to mark a new stage in the evolution of the world balance of forces. The characteristic feature of this stage is the ever more evident demonstration of the failure of the policy of strength—the fact that however strong, the aggressor cannot subdue a people determined to fight and to defend its liberty and national independence at any cost. The Vietnamese people, by the heroic fight which they have led against the intervention of the United States of America, has defended its independence, and at the same time has shown to all the peoples of the world the sure way for defeating any imperialist aggression. . . .

Romania hailed the starting of the American-Vietnamese negotiations in Paris. However, we cannot fail to note that these negotiations have for a long time scored no progress. We consider that the proposals of the National Liberation Front of South Vietnam provide a positive basis for a speedy solution of the conflict. To this end it is necessary for the United States to stop the military actions and withdraw its troops from Vietnam, allowing the Vietnamese people to solve [their] internal affairs, . . . in accordance with their own will, and without any interference from the outside. . . .

The events which led to the Middle East War in 1967 are well known, but this conflict has not been settled even today. . . . Romania's opinion is that the Security Council resolution of November 1967 offers a reasonable basis for solving the situation in the Middle East. In concord with this resolution, we consider it necessary that Israel should withdraw its troops without delay from the occupied territories, and renounce any territorial claims. Concurrently, it is imperative to ensure the integrity of the frontiers and the security of all the states in that area of the world. . . .

As a European country, Romania pays particular attention to the problem of European security. Twenty-four years have elapsed since the end of World War II but nevertheless there are still controversial issues in Europe. There are still revenge-seeking militarist neo-Nazi forces acting in the Federal Republic of Germany which would like to reconsider the situation created after the war, thus menacing peace on our continent and in the world. There are reactionary circles in other countries as well which oppose the policy of détente and cooperation between states. However, these circles and forces are ever more isolated. . . . The manifold contacts and talks which the representatives of the Romanian government had with the representatives of various European states made us reach the conclusion that there are favorable conditions for advancing on the path of European security. Conclusive in this respect is the strong response which both the 1966 Bucharest statement of the Warsaw Treaty member states and the Budapest appeal of April 1969 of the same states have aroused with respect to European security, and to the organization of a conference of all the European states. . . . Romania considers that in achieving European security, one should start from the realities created after World War II, first of all recognizing the two German states and the existing borders, including the Oder-Neisse frontier.

Romania also declares itself in favor of regional agreements, including those establishing areas free of nuclear weapons. In this respect our country holds the view that the establishment of relationships of good understanding between the Balkan states, and the development of economic and technical-scientific collaboration and cooperation between them would be valuable contributions to the cause of European security.

The problem of general disarmament, particularly the achievement of nuclear disarmament, holds an important place in our country's foreign policy as also in the concern of the whole of mankind. . . . We therefore consider it imperative to intensify the struggle for disarmament, and to make firm strides towards banning nuclear weapons and liquidating the existing stockpiles.

We also consider that doing away with the foreign military bases on the territory of other states, the withdrawal of non-European troops from the continent and, generally speaking, the withdrawal of all foreign troops to within their national frontiers would be particularly important. . . . The abolition of military blocs—the aggressive North Atlantic bloc and, simultaneously, the military Warsaw Treaty —would also bring a positive influence to bear on security and all-round peace.

Convinced as it is that all the avenues toward peacefully settling the disputes between states should be used, our country makes a constructive contribution to the activities of the United Nations Organization. Because of the significance of the U.N. in extending the collaboration between states, in observing international law, and in promoting efforts for securing peace, Romania considers that it is absolutely necessary that all the countries should be represented in this forum. It is imperative that the legitimate rights of the People's Republic of China—the only representative of the Chinese people—should be reestablished in the U.N., that the German Democratic Republic and other states should be admitted to this organization, that the principle of U.N. universality should be carried out.

The Romanian Communist Party and the government of the Socialist Republic of Romania consider that new concrete actions should be undertaken towards European security, disarmament and the safeguarding of peace; no matter how small progress might be in the beginning, we have to persevere, because it is in this way alone that we can safeguard peace and the peoples' security. . . .

4. Strengthening the Internationalist Solidarity of the Communist and Workers' Parties, with All the Anti-Imperialist Forces

Comrades, as an active detachment of the international Communist movement, the Romanian Communist party has developed relations of fraternal cooperation with all the Communist and workers' parties. In the years which have elapsed since the Ninth Congress, our party had meetings and exchanged delegations with fifty-eight Communist and workers' parties on all the continents. We regard these meetings and exchanges of opinions as having an especially important role in developing the international solidarity of the Communist and workers' parties, and in finding the most adequate avenues to strengthening cooperation and unity of the Communist and working-class movement.

We start from the fact that the Communist and workers' parties carry on their activities in different historical, social, and national conditions; that the different levels of development of the productive forces and of social relations themselves cause the tasks of the immediate struggle to differ from one country to another. To understand this reality means to consider it absolutely natural that the Communist and workers' parties, guided by the universal truths of Marxism-Leninism, should independently work out their policy, strategy, and tactics.

. . . Unfortunately, when differences of opinion crop up in one problem or another, the labeling of certain parties is resorted to. The taking of a different stand by one party can by no means be interpreted as an attitude against another party. We consider that the friendly, frank character of the relationships that should exist between fraternal Communist parties calls for the discussion of the differences of opinion in a comradely way.

. . . To strengthen internationalist solidarity presupposes fully equal relationships, and unflinching concern for strengthening unity, and developing cooperation between all the socialist countries and between all the Communist parties, without any exception whatever. This is an essential prerequisite of the full expression of proletarian internationalism in the conditions of an ever stronger assertion of socialism as a main factor of present-day social development.

Our party considers that bilateral meetings and exchanges of views between parties have a prime role in developing the solidarity and unity of the Communist movement. Concurrently, we consider that an important role is also played by multilateral meetings, including international meetings of the Communist and workers' parties. Appreciating the importance of such meetings, our party attended the international meeting which took place early in June in Moscow. As has already been shown, this meeting was not convened under the best conditions, first of all because of the absence of a great number of parties—five of them from the socialist countries. The existence of sharp divergencies, as well as criticism leveled against other Communist parties have, in our opinion, diminished the efficiency of the meeting. However, the Central Committee of the party considers that the Moscow meeting had a series of positive characteristics. First of all, the fact must be appreciated that the meeting occasioned a free exchange of views on various aspects of international life, a comprehensive discussion of the problems of the relations between the Communist and workers' parties, and of the unity of struggle of all anti-imperialist forces—thus making it possible for public opinion to know the stand of each and every party. In spite of the fact that the main document contains certain unclear and confused formulations in connection with which our party expressed its reservations at the respective time, it also embodies a broad platform of action—of objectives which can mobilize the Communist and workers' parties and the revolutionary and progressive forces everywhere in the struggle against imperialism—for the cause of liberty and independence and of socialism and peace. At the same time, we attach special importance to the fact that this document contains the Marxist-Leninist norms and principles, as well as those of proletarian internationalism underlying the relations between the Communist and workers' parties; the development of their cooperation as independent parties, not only equal in rights, but also in the independent way they work out their policy, tactics, and revolutionary strategy. We have positively appreciated the fact that the main document of the meeting contained no criticism and no condemnation of any fraternal party; that it emphasized the will of the participating parties to develop relations of cooperation with all Communist parties, both with those taking part in the meeting and with those not attending it. [The main document also] started from the premise that participation or non-participation in international gatherings is a privilege of each and every party and that this, as well as the decision to sign or not to sign a document, should not in any way affect the relations between parties. By its final results, the Moscow meeting can have a positive role both in rallying the anti-imperialist forces and in paving the way for the liquidation of divergencies between the Communist and workers' parties and the rebuilding and strengthening of their cooperation and unity. This of course depends, in the last analysis, on the way in which each and every party will act. . . .

* * *

As is known, many years ago our party considered it a mistake that in the past it too followed the line of condemning and blaming some fraternal parties, and that is why it took the decision not to proceed in such a way any longer, considering that this does not correspond to the Marxist-Leninist principles of the relations among parties, or to the interests of the Communist and working-class movement. In our opinion, when certain problems or different opinions crop up between some Communist parties, these must not be tackled at international meetings or at the congresses of other parties by attitudes of blame and condemnation. In this respect, we propose that the congress give mandate to the Central Committee that, in solving the differences of political or ideological views, it should not take the line of blaming or condemning another fraternal party, but should militate for their solution by means of discussion from party to party, from leadership to leadership. . . .

Furthermore, our party maintains, and will continue to develop, links with socialist and social-democratic parties, some of which have their representatives at our congress. This corresponds to the need of strengthening the unity of the working class. . . .

The Romanian Communist party will most firmly militate also in the future in favor of developing relations of cooperation with all Communist and workers' parties, with all revolutionary, democratic, and anti-imperialist forces, making its contribution to the cause of the unity of the Communist and working-class movement, and to the struggle for the triumph of socialism throughout the world.

* * *

Dear comrades, a review of the quarter of a century which has elapsed since our country's liberation, as well as of the activity carried on after the Ninth Congress, boldly emphasizes the capacity of our party, of its Central Committee, to lead with success the destinies of Romania, to ensure the continuous advance of the people along the bright road of socialism. No doubt our congress will approve the vast political and organizational activity carried on by the Central Committee, which creditably fulfilled the task entrusted to it by the Ninth Congress of conducting the whole activity of our party and people and for implementing the program of Romania's multifaceted flourishing.

*　　*　　*

We consider that we have at our disposal everything that is necessary for the materialization of this inspiring program: we have a developed technical-material base as a starting point; we have a powerful and united party, armed with the Marxist-Leninist teaching and closely linked to the masses; we are a diligent and staunch people endowed with special qualities, devoted body and soul to the cause of socialism.

*　　*　　*

We wish the Communists, the workers, peasants, and intellectuals, and all working people irrespective of nationality, full success in their struggle waged under the banner of the party for the building of a well-rounded, fully developed socialist society; for the flourishing of Romania and the welfare and happiness of the entire people.

Long live the Romanian Communist party—the tested leader of our socialist nation!

Long live the Socialist Republic of Romania, our heroic people, the builder of the new world!

May the friendship and solidarity of the socialist countries, of the Communist and workers' parties, of the revolutionary, anti-imperialist forces throughout the world strengthen!

May the invincible ideas of Marxism-Leninism and the cause of socialism and peace triumph!

Document 15: Excerpts from the Report of the CC RCP to the Eleventh Party Congress, Delivered 25 November 1974 by Nicolae Ceausescu, General Secretary of the CC RCP*

Esteemed comrades, the situation in the modern world is characterized by a deep sharpening of world economic, social, national and political contradictions. One can state that we are on the brink of a new phase in the crisis of the capitalist system, a crisis that embraces all spheres of social life and affects all continents to various degrees. This very complex situation is hastening the revolutionary process of change in the international balance of forces in the favor of social progress and of the forces which speak out for a better and more just world. [Applause.]

We are now at a stage of reestablishing relations between states and groups of states. This process stresses international instability, creates dangers for the security of certain states, zones and continents of the planet and for the peace of the entire world. At the same time, the changes that are occurring at the world level are opening up new prospects for the revolutionary change of society; they are leading toward the intensification of the struggle of the masses to safeguard economic, social, national interests and democracy; they amplify the struggle against the imperialist policy of force and diktat, against colonialism and neocolonialism, for national and social liberation, for a world of international peace and cooperation among peoples. [Applause.]

The current international crisis, which embraces all the facets of socioeconomic life, strongly demonstrates that the obsolete internal and international relations created by the capitalist system no longer suit the new forces of production, the impetuous development of the scientific-technical revolution can no longer offer adequate solutions to the complex problems which are concerning contemporary mankind. Mankind is being increasingly confronted with the contradictions created by the capitalist system, by the imperialist, colonialist, and neocolonialist policy. These contradictions are expanding with the deepening of the gaps between developed and backward countries and with the world division into rich and poor countries which results from colonialist and neocolonialist oppression.

The objective laws, social dialectics, and requirements of social progress require the crushing of the old fetters which endanger

* Source: *Foreign Broadcast Information Service, Eastern Europe*, vol. 2, no. 230 (27 November 1974), pp. H5-H20.

human civilization itself; they require the creation of a world of social and national justice, both within each state and throughout the world, a world capable of insuring a new upsurge of the forces of production, science and culture, and general progress. [Applause.]

From many points of view contemporary international life can be compared with the situation prevailing before World Wars I [and] II. But current problems are more complex and serious in view of the unprecedented growth of the crisis of the capitalist system, a crisis deepened particularly by the energy, raw materials and financial crises. At the same time, contemporary international life radically differs from the period which preceded the two world wars. This difference lies primarily in the existence of the world socialist system, which makes up almost 40 percent of the world economy, and which, in view of the successes it has reaped in the construction of the new social system and its policy of international peace and cooperation, opens up new prospects for solving the complex problems in the interests of the masses and of all the peoples, in the interest of progress and peace. [Applause.]

As a result of the crumbling of the colonial system, scores of independent states have emerged in the world. These states have overthrown foreign domination and are struggling for their independent socioeconomic and national development and are playing an ever more important role in international life. Powerful, unprecedented social forces are acting on all the continents. The workers, peasantry, intelligentsia, the middle classes, the broad masses of women and youth, and various other social strata are increasingly speaking out for a new policy of social progress, for a new path in solving problems, for the establishment of a new international economic and political order. [Applause.]

This is why, despite the seriousness of the situation prevailing in international relations, one may state that the modern world also features forces capable of precluding a new world conflagration, of insuring the solving of complex problems through peaceful means, in the interests of all the peoples. To turn these possibilities into realities, the masses struggle in all the countries and the struggle of all the peoples against the imperialist policy of force and diktat, for disarmament, and primarily for nuclear disarmament, for avoiding a war which could inflict unprecedented losses on mankind and for achieving new international relations—based on full equality of rights among all the peoples and on their right to develop in keeping with their own will and on democratic world cooperation—must be intensified. One may state that now more than ever in peoples' history, the peoples have it in their power to build their own future, to pave the way for a new era of blossoming of human civilization. [Applause.]

Dear comrades, the fundamental and revolutionary changes which have occurred in international life since the Tenth RCP Congress [1969] fully confirm the assessments and guidelines established by the congress: they strongly demonstrate the correctness of the foreign policy consistently promoted by the RCP and the Socialist Republic of Romania. Throughout this period, the Central Committee and the government have carried on intensive international activity to expand our country's relations of cooperation, to promote Romania's active participation in solving the great problems confronting mankind. They unabatedly militated for a policy of cooperation, security and peace in the world. We may assert that Romania has participated in every important problem of world affairs, and in one form or another, it has contributed to the solving of these problems in the interests of all the peoples and of international cooperation. [Applause.]

The changes which have occurred in the international balance of forces during this period, the fact that certain international problems have been solved through negotiations, the beginning of negotiations and the improving of relations between various world states with different social systems, the organization and the positive proceeding of the all-European conference, and the growth of the upsurge of the masses' struggle everywhere have brought about a transition from the policy of cold war to a policy of cooperation. This led to the dawning of a new trend in international relations and to an incipient détente. An important role along these lines was played by the socialist countries, by the activity carried on by the Soviet Union, which is playing a very significant role in international life, and by the participation of all the socialist countries in solving mankind's problems. The role of the P.R.C. in international relations and in solving the complex problems that concern the modern world has also grown.

True, the trend toward détente which has emerged in the past years is only at its beginnings. It is still rather fragile. There still remain many problems to be solved in the world. There still exist zones of tension and conflict, which can lead to military confrontations and to wars with grave consequences for all mankind. There are still imperialist and reactionary forces which have not given up their old policy. We must, therefore, frankly admit that as long as the imperialist, colonialist, and neocolonialist policy exists, and as long as reactionary forces exist in the world, the danger of wars, including the danger of a new world war, will remain.

Proceeding from these considerations, we believe that highly responsible steps must be taken to consolidate the trend of détente, to find negotiated solutions to contentious and complex current problems, to promote a policy of peaceful cooperation and equality among all the peoples, to insure peace in the world. Life has demonstrated and continues to demonstrate that the policy of force and wars does not and cannot lead to solutions to problems. On the contrary, any war creates new complications, sharpens relations among states, deepens mistrust, and opens new sources of tension. At the same time, the events of the past years strongly confirm the real possibility of finding peaceful solutions even for the most complicated problems and situations. This can have particularly positive effects on strengthening interstate trust and cooperation on the establishment of a lasting peace among all the peoples in the world. [Applause.]

All Romania's international activities during this period were aimed at consistently promoting the policy of international cooperation and peace, of developing relations with all the states in the world, regardless of social system; they were aimed at increasing our country's contribution to consolidating the new trend toward détente. As a result of this policy, Romania currently has diplomatic relations with 119 states; it is developing economic, trade, and cooperation relations with almost 130 states. Due to this policy, Romania has won friends throughout the world, and its policy enjoys the esteem and appreciation of peoples on all the continents. [Applause.]

Esteemed comrades, our country has consistently focused its international policy on developing relations of cooperation with all the socialist countries, as we believe this to be in keeping with both the interests of the Romanian people and with the interests of the other peoples who are building the new system and with the general cause of socialism and peace.

I want to take this opportunity to stress with great satisfaction the developing relations with the Soviet Union, which is our major partner in international exchanges and economic cooperation. We want to reassert at this congress the determination of the RCP and of socialist Romania to continue to act with all resolution to develop relations with the CPSU [and] with the Soviet Union, since we believe that this is in keeping with the interests of both parties and peoples and with the general cause of world socialism and peace. [Applause.]

During this period, treaties of friendship, cooperation and mutual assistance with the U.S.S.R., with the Bulgarian People's Republic, with the Hungarian People's Republic, and with the Polish People's Republic have been renewed. All these treaties have supplied a lasting long-term base for our alliance, friendship, and cooperation with those socialist states. We have also concluded the first treaty of friendship, cooperation and mutual assistance with the G.D.R., and this has opened up a new stage for our bilateral relations. . . . The relations of cooperation between Romania and the C.S.S.R. have also broadly developed. We believe that great opportunities are available to further intensify these relations, and will do everything to turn them into reality. [Applause.]

*   *   *

During this period, the relations of friendship and cooperation between Romania and Yugoslavia, between the RCP and the LCY have greatly progressed. The commissioning of the Iron Gates hydropower system constituted an important point in our bilateral relations and offers a model of cooperation based on fully equal rights between two socialist, neighborly, and friendly countries. We are determined to continue to do everything to develop the relations of multilateral cooperation between our parties and countries. [Applause.]

I want to stress with satisfaction that during this period, Romania's relations of cooperation with Albania have also significantly developed. We believe that all necessary conditions exist for developing them even more in the coming years. We will do everything along these lines. [Applause.]

An important point within the development of our relations with the Asian socialist countries was the visit to these countries by a party-government delegation in the summer of 1971. This visit paved the way for intensifying cooperation with all countries in that part of the world. I want to mention with great joy the ascending trend of cooperation relations between the RCP and the CCP, between the Socialist Republic of Romania and the P.R.C., and the yearly growth of our economic exchanges and all-round Romanian-Chinese cooperation.

We believe that real opportunities exist to expand our relations of cooperation in the coming years. We shall do everything to develop these relations which are in keeping with the interests of our parties and peoples and of the cause of social progress and peace in the world. [Applause.]

Our cooperation with the D.P.R.K. has also greatly developed during these years, as have the relations between the RCP and the Korean Workers' party. Even greater opportunities are emerging for expanding this cooperation. We shall consistently act toward this goal. [Applause.]

Relations of friendship and cooperation have also developed . . . with the D.R.V. The Romanian people granted all-round aid to the

Vietnamese people in their struggle against foreign domination for independence. We are firmly determined to broadly develop the relations between our parties and peoples in the future, too. [Applause.]

Relations have developed intensively between the Socialist Republic of Romania and the Mongolian People's Republic and between our parties. We shall continue to do everything to make these relations register ever greater progress. [Applause.]

As a result of the exchange of summit visits, the relations between Romania and Cuba have also greatly developed. We want to take further steps to expand the relations between our parties and peoples, in the interests of the socialist development of each of our countries and of the cause of progress and peace. [Applause.]

Comrades, in view of the contemporary international situation, we believe that relations of cooperation must be developed among the socialist member states of the Warsaw Pact and between the armies of these states, proceeding from the need to develop and strengthen each national army and the defense and combat potential of each people. At the same time, the struggle to dissolve military blocs must be intensified; the political aspect of the Warsaw Pact must be strengthened even more, with a view to consolidating the trend of détente and cooperation in Europe and throughout the world.

At the same time, Romania has acted and will continue to act to expand cooperation between our army and those of all the socialist countries, as well as with the armies of other friendly states, since we believe this to be an internationalist obligation made necessary by the continuation of the state of tension and of the danger of new aggressions and wars.

The development of our relations of cooperation with the socialist countries during this period is part and parcel of the general policy of strengthening the solidarity and unity of the socialist countries. We proceed from the fact that the greater the results obtained by each socialist country along the road of socioeconomic development, the greater the development of their international cooperation, the greater is the force of socialism and its prestige in the world. [Applause.]

Understandably, the diversity of historic, national, and social conditions is directly reflected in the forms of socialist construction adopted by each country. But this is precisely the source of the superiority of socialism and, implicitly, the superiority of the new relations between the countries which are bulding a new social system. The existence or emergence of certain differing opinions or assessments should not, in our opinion, interfere with the cooperation of the socialist countries. Proceeding from what we have in common— from the socialist principles, from the general interests of socialism and peace—we must do everything to develop active cooperation and to overcome divergencies of any nature. It is in this spirit, in accordance with the mandate of the Tenth Congress, that the RCP and socialist Romania have been acting. We shall continue to do everything to actively contribute to the cause of cooperation among all the socialist countries, as we believe this to be fully in keeping with the interests of our people and with the interests of all the peoples of the socialist countries, for the cause of socialism and peace in the world. [Applause.]

Esteemed comrades, since the Tenth Party Congress, Romania has carried on intensive activity to expand all-round cooperation with the developing countries, with all the states which are speaking out for independent socioeconomic development. As a result of our policy, our country currently maintains diplomatic relations at embassy level with eighty-five states of the third world. I want to mention with great satisfaction the intensification of relations of friendship and all-round cooperation between Romania and the Arab countries. We are firmly determined to expand our economic, scientific-technical and cultural cooperation with these countries, and to best fulfill all the agreements and conventions established with them.

We hope that the peoples of our countries—linked together by old relations of friendship and by traditions of common struggle—will cooperate ever more closely in all spheres. [Applause.]

We are happy to note the powerful development of our relations of cooperation with African countries during the period between party congresses. The agreements of all-round cooperation between Romania and a large number of African countries open up great prospects for intensifying economic, scientific-technical and cultural cooperation between our countries. . . . Our country's relations with a large number of Latin American countries have also powerfully developed. We are linked to those countries by standing historical traditions and strong affinities of Latin origin and culture . . . I think I should also mention the establishment of relations with additional states in Asia . . . [Applause.]

All these provide a sound base for the economic, political, scientific-technical cooperation between the Romanian people and the peoples who are independently developing. They reflect the new, democratic international relations and insure lasting prospects for Romania's cooperation with the states of the third world. At the same time, they constitute a valuable contribution to the struggle to generalize new interstate relations in the world and to establish a new international political and economic order. [Applause.]

Consistently acting in the spirit of peaceful coexistence, we have continued to expand our cooperation with all states, regardless of social system, including the developed capitalist countries. I want to emphasize with great satisfaction the great development of relations with the European countries, which, after the socialist countries, occupy the most important place in Romania's economic, scientific, technical, and cultural relations. In the spirit of the old traditions of friendship between the Romanian people and the European peoples, we shall resolutely act to expand mutually advantageous cooperation in all fields in the future, too. [Applause.]

Romania's relations with the United States of America have also greatly developed. These relations, have been particularly enhanced by summit visits, and have as their basis the joint declaration of 1973. We believe that conditions exist for the all-round development of economic, scientific-technical, and cultural cooperation between the two countries. [Applause.]

Our country's relations with other developed capitalist countries have also powerfully developed, and we are determined to continue to expand our economic, cultural, and other exchanges with all these countries. [Applause.]

We are inspired by the firm resolution to continue to act in the coming stage in the spirit of the principles of peaceful coexistence, to intensify all-round cooperation with all states, regardless of social system, since we believe that this is in keeping with our mutual interests and with the cause of general progress and peace in the world. We are resolutely basing our relations with all states on the principle of full equality of rights, respect for national independence and sovereignty, noninterference in internal affairs, mutual advantage, renunciation of the use and threat of force, respect for each people's right to decide its socioeconomic development in accordance with its will, without any foreign interference, [and] on the right to build a free and independent life. [Applause.]

All these principles, which have been almost unanimously recognized in the past years, increasingly assert themselves as the only ones capable of insuring new relations of cooperation among peoples and peace in the world. Since the Tenth Congress, Romania has intensively participated in UN activities; it has sponsored various proposals for solving international problems, including those pertaining to the improvement and democratization of UN activities and the growth of its role in solving the great problems of contemporary life. Our country has also actively participated in the activity of the other international bodies and contributed to promoting the principles of cooperation.

Currently, Romania is a member of over fifty international governmental organizations and of hundreds of other nongovernmental organizations. This reflects the consistency with which our country's party and government participate in international life and contribute to solving mankind's problems. . . . I propose that the congress empower the new Central Committee to further resolutely act to expand Romania's all-round cooperation with all the states, to promote its intensive participation in the activity of international bodies, thus actively contributing to solving mankind's current problems and the cause of creating a world of justice, cooperation and peace. [Applause.]

Dear comrades, I will now speak of our country's activity and stands on certain important problems of current international life. As a European country, Romania attaches particular importance to the achievement of new relations on our continent, relations capable of insuring for each country the possibility of concentrating its forces on socioeconomic development and progress and allowing broad cooperation among all states. This is precisely why Romania has been resolutely acting—together with the socialist countries and other European states—for achieving European security. We believe that the beginning of the all-European conference and the proceedings of its two phases to date have yielded positive results. For the first time the European peoples have been given the opportunity to discuss— on an equal footing—the major problems which decide the continent's peace and security.

In our opinion, sustained efforts are further required to successfully conclude the second phase and to compile as complete as possible documents to provide a lasting basis and broad prospects for relations of all-round cooperation among all the European states, to insure a full guarantee against any aggression or interference in the affairs of a European state. We attach particular importance to the establishment of a permanent consultative body to insure the continuation of contacts to implement the principles established within the all-European conference. We speak out for the holding of the third phase of the conference at the highest level. We believe that the successful conclusion of the all-European conference will open up new historic prospects not only for the European continent, but for the entire world. [Applause.]

While mentioning with satisfaction the steps registered in solving some European problems and the progress achieved by the all-European conference, we cannot overlook the complex situation that still prevails on our continent. The sad reality is that the most powerful military, human, and material forces of our times are currently concentrated in Europe—actually historically unprecedented forces. This fact alone creates grave threats to peace and must seriously concern all peoples on the continent and all mankind. This is precisely why we believe that political and diplomatic activities must be intensified, that peoples must actively participate in the general struggle to find negotiated solutions, through peaceful means, to contentious problems, to expand multilateral cooperation among all European peoples.

We pay particular attention to Balkan problems. We believe that within European security the achievement of regional agreements, including the Balkans, constitutes a highly important factor. Proceeding from this principle, we believe that everything must be done to develop cooperation and understanding among all the Balkan countries, to find various and complex forms of expanding cooperation, to turn the Balkans into a zone free of foreign troops and military bases, free of nuclear arms, into a zone of peace and cooperation. [Applause.]

We are deeply worried by the situation created in Cyprus. We resolutely speak out for finding a political solution to this situation, for the sovereignty and integrity of Cyprus, for peaceful cooperation between the two communities. . . .

As for the situation in the Middle East, we believe it is still complicated and that the danger of resumed clashes and a new war with unforeseeable consequences still exists. Romania has consistently spoken out and continues to speak out for a political, peaceful solution of the Middle East conflict. We believe that Israel must withdraw its troops from the Arab territories occupied in the 1967 war and that settlements must be found to insure the integrity and sovereignty of each state in that area and to pave the way for peaceful cooperation. At the same time, the problems of the Palestinian people must be satisfactorily solved, proceeding from recognition of their right to independently organize their life in accordance with their national interests, including their right to establish an independent state.

The assertion of the Palestinian people as a distinct national entity and broad recognition of this entity at the international level, including the United Nations, constitutes a fundamental change in the Middle East situation and opens up new prospects for a just and equitable peace in that area. In the future, this reality will have to be taken into consideration in any decision on the Middle East.

Romania recognizes the Palestine Liberation Organization as the only representative of the Palestinian people. We maintain relations of broad cooperation and actively support the Palestinian people in their just struggle for a new, free, and independent life. The solution of the Palestinian problem—a primary factor for the establishment of just and lasting peace in the Middle East—requires the achievement of new relations, one may say of a historical reconcilation between Palestinians and Jews, on the basis of recognition of each people's right to free and independent development, of peaceful and democratic coexistence. [Applause.]

We believe it is necessary to resume as soon as possible the Geneva conference with the participation of all interested states, including representatives of the Palestine Liberation Organization and of other states, especially from Europe and the Mediterranean area, which can contribute to solving this conflict as quickly as possible. . . .

We are happy to note the important successes obtained over this period by the people of Indochina. The conclusion of the 1973 Paris peace agreement marked an important victory in the struggle of the Vietnamese people. Nevertheless, the provisions of the agreement are not yet being resolutely implemented, with the result that tension and grave dangers still exist for the situation in Vietnam. We resolutely speak out for the consistent and real implementation of these agreements, for respect for the Vietnamese people's right to independently decide and solve their problems, without any foreign interference.

We hailed the agreements arrived at in Laos on the end of hostilities and the formation of a provisional government of national union and of a national coalition council. We express our hope that this will consolidate the national independence of Laos and will lead to its independent socioeconomic development. We believe that all foreign aid to the reactionary forces of Cambodia and all foreign interference must cease. The Cambodian people must be allowed to independently solve all their internal problems. As in the past, we will continue to grant our full support to the government of national union of Cambodia in its just struggle, up to the final victory. [Applause.]

We hailed the initiative of the D.P.R.K. on the peaceful reunification of the north and south of Korea. We believe that this initiative is fully in keeping with the interests of the Korean people and with the cause of peace in that part of the world. We will continue to support the struggle for the peaceful reunification of Korea, which will pave the way for the free and independent development of the entire country. [Applause.]

Recently, the national liberation movements of Africa have been achieving important success in winning their independence. The victories won are the result of the long struggle waged by these movements, to which Romania granted political, material, and moral support all along. The victory was made possible also due to the overthrow of the fascist dictatorship in Portugal and to the formation of a democratic government in that country, a government which proceeded toward the final solution of the colonial problem.

From the forum of this congress we want to convey our greetings to the people of Guinea-Bissau who won their independence, to the people of Mozambique, who have established a provisional government and are acting to fully consolidate their independence, to liberation movements in Angola, and the Angolan people who are making efforts to win their full independence. We wish them full success. [Applause.]

Romania will develop broad relations of cooperation with Portugal and with the newly independent African states; it will continue to grant full support to liberation movements in Namibia and to liberation movements in Rhodesia and South Africa, against the racist policy of apartheid. We believe that efforts must be intensified to finally eliminate colonialism and all forms of exploitation of one people by another, to finally liquidate the policy of racial discrimination, to establish democratic relations among all peoples, regardless of race or color. [Applause.]

Esteemed comrades, one of the most topical problems of current life is the gaps that have deepened between developed and developing countries. The liquidation of underdevelopment, the insuring of the more rapid socioeconomic progress of the backward countries are major requirements for the development of all mankind and for the achievement of lasting cooperation and peace in the world. The fact that some countries are lagging behind is caused—as I said before—by the imperialist, colonialist, and neocolonialist policy, by the unequal relations of the past. Therefore, to liquidate the existing gaps, a new policy in international economic and political relations is required.

Needless to say, the phenomena of the current economic-financial crisis with all its consequences are the result of the development of certain states at the expense of others, of reduced opportunities for economic development resulting from the gap between the advanced and the developing countries, or irrational consumption and waste of raw material and energy resources in some countries. This state of affairs strongly emphasizes the need to solve problems on the basis of the principles of equality with the participation of all states, the need to establish a new international economic and political order and to democratize international relations, to establish new norms of international law in accordance with the changes that have occurred in the world.

One must proceed from the fact that the new order does not mean replacing the old wrapping by a new one, even if it were a golden one. Changing the wrapping alone will not solve any problem. On the contrary, the current state of affairs, as well as the economic crisis, instability, and the general crisis of capitalism, will further deteriorate with all their consequences for international peace and cooperation.

In our opinion, to establish a new order, the following points should be considered:

1. The new international economic and political order requires the resolute elimination of the old relations of inequality. It requires the liquidation of the imperialist, colonialist, and neocolonialist policy.

2. It requires the achievement of relations based on full equality of rights among all nations, on respect for each people's right to master its national wealth and to sovereignly decide how it will be utilized.

3. It also requires respect for each people's right to elect the social system it favors, without any outside interference, for each nation's right to independent socioeconomic development.

4. The new order requires resolute steps to rapidly liquidate the gap between developed and underdeveloped countries, to bring the level of socioeconomic development of all the countries closer together, taking into account, of course, the specific historical, geographic, and climatic features of each state and the peoples' material needs in relation to the conditions in which they are living.

5. It also requires the establishment of an equitable relationship between the prices of raw materials and manufactured products, prices set on the basis of economic laws and accounting for both the utility value of the items and for the value devolving from the amount of work invested in their production.

6. The prices of raw materials and of manufactured products must proceed from the need to enhance the productive activity of all the problems. Under the current conditions, these prices must benefit the more rapid progress of the underdeveloped countries.

7. At the same time, it must be insured that all countries have access to raw materials and energy resources, and that all states have access to modern scientific-technical achievements, in view of the fact that the liquidation of underdevelopment and the rapid progress of all nations can only be achieved on the basis of the most recent scientific-technical achievements.

8. Along these lines, we believe that special programs must be compiled under the sponsorship of the United Nations and other international bodies, programs designed to concentrate the states' efforts on achieving vitally important projects for the development of mankind.

9. Within the new international economic and political order, special attention must be given to the food problem. Resolute measures are required to increase agricultural output more rapidly, to utilize additional resources, particularly in the developing countries, to achieve vast irrigation projects and land and soil melioration projects, to rapidly develop the production of fertilizers and other chemical substances required for agriculture. At the same time, scientists must make sustained efforts to produce new species of highly productive seeds and new animal breeds suitable for the developing countries. In this respect, we believe it is necessary that the FAO draw up a complex program to rapidly solve the food problem—a problem of vital importance for the existence and progress of all mankind.

10. Resolute measures are also required to insure technical assistance in both the industrial and the agricultural fields, to intensify aid in training national cadres for the achievement of these programs. Naturally, the speeding up of socioeconomic progress must be based primarily on the work and efforts of each people and nation. At the same time, the more developed peoples and states, particularly those which have developed by oppressing underdeveloped peoples, must grant greater and more substantial aid for the socioeconomic progress of those states. This is the only way to achieve programs of rapid socioeconomic development which will yield results in liquidating the gaps separating the advanced from the underdeveloped countries.

In our opinion, in the fulfillment of the above-mentioned goals, an important role is incumbent on bilateral cooperation based on principles of equality, in concert with the multilateral activity of the various international bodies—cooperation which can contribute to asserting the new international economic order. Romania resolutely develops its cooperation with the developing countries in all fields of activity on the basis of mutually advantageous foundations. . . .

Esteemed comrades, we believe that in the fulfillment of these measures an important role is incumbent on the United Nations and on other international bodies. One must consistently proceed from the fact that all the current economic and political problems cannot be solved by only a few states. Their imperative solution requires the active participation of all states on an equal footing. In this context we believe that the small and medium-sized countries are called upon to play an ever more active role in asserting the new principles of interstate relations and a new international economic and political order. An important role is incumbent on the nonaligned countries— most of which are small and medium-sized countries—which can make a particularly valuable contribution to the achievement of these goals.

Another important problem of current life is general disarmament and primarily nuclear disarmament. The Communists have always considered the struggle for disarmament, and for saving mankind from a new destructive war, and the struggle for insuring world peace a goal of honor. Proceeding from this fact, the RCP and the Socialist Republic of Romania have acted consistently and continue to act to implement a program of real disarmament, especially for achieving nuclear disarmament. In this spirit, our country put forward concrete proposals both in Geneva and within other international bodies. Unfortunately, while discussions are being conducted on disarmament, military expenditures grow year by year. There is no doubt that the intensification of the arms race, the stockpiling of ever new destructive weapons and the growth of military expenditures create grave dangers for the security of all peoples, for international peace and at the same time constitute a heavy burden for all peoples.

In fact, the staggering growth of inflation and the economic crisis which is deepening in the capitalist countries are to a large extent caused by the arms race, by the enormous military expenditures which, according to the most recent U.N. data, have totaled approximately $270 billion yearly. Romania believes that in the field of disarmament, it is time to pass from words to deeds, to adopt concrete measures to halt the arms race. In our opinion, [the following requirements are necessary]:

1. The first requirement is to take measures to freeze and gradually reduce war budgets, to ban the use of thermonuclear arms and other mass destruction weapons.

2. Second, each state which has nuclear arms must solemnly assume the obligation to halt the production of new arms and to begin destroying the existing ones under appropriate agreements. Only thus will it be possible to prevent the proliferation of nuclear weapons and really preclude the danger of a destructive thermonuclear war.

3. Third, at the same time, denuclearized zones must be created, foreign military bases must be dismantled, national troops must be gradually reduced, and troops must be withdrawn from the territory of other states.

4. Fourth, as for the reduction of troops, arms and military expenditures, this must not be of a symbolic nature only; we believe that as a first stage, a reduction of 10–15 percent and a more sub-

stantial reduction in the large, powerfully armed countries is necessary.

5. Fifth, consistent steps are required along these lines to develop interstate trust and cooperation, so that antagonistic military blocs can be dissolved and all war propaganda can be finally ended.

6. Sixth, the problem of general and primarily nuclear disarmament, the establishment of concrete measures in this field, must be carried out on a broad democratic basis, with the participation of all interested states. For this purpose, the activity of the Geneva disarmament committee must improve, and the proceedings of all conferences and bodies devoted to disarmament must be organized on democratic bases.

7. Seventh, more than in any other domain, international public opinion must be kept permanently informed, through periodical, at least biannual accounts, on the activity being carried on in this respect.

These problems are of great importance and topicality. They concern all peoples equally, whether large or small, and the broad masses everywhere and, therefore, they cannot be solved behind sound-proof doors. Disarmament is the problem of the peoples themselves, and the peoples have the right and must know what steps are being taken toward this goal, so that they can have their say on the measures which must be taken. [Applause.]

The problem of disarmament, which is decisive for the fate of mankind's civilization itself cannot be solved without the united struggle of the masses and of all peoples on our planet. [Applause.]

This, esteemed comrades, is the stand of our party and of Romania on certain important problems of current international life. . . .

We are highly responsible before our peoples and all mankind for doing everything to pave the way for an era of cooperation and peace, in a world of justice and social and national freedom. [Applause.]

*   *   *

Esteemed comrades, acting in the spirit of the rich internationalist traditions of our workers' revolutionary movement, since the Tenth Congress the RCP has been carrying on a broad international activity of multilateral cooperation with all the Communist and workers' parties. As a result, our party is maintaining relations with eighty-nine Communist and workers' parties. Over these years, we have intensified our relations of cooperation with the socialist and social-democrat parties, so that today we have relations with twenty-seven socialist parties. I want also to stress the development of an extensive cooperation with sixty-eight government parties and other democratic parties in friendly developing countries, and with other revolutionary and democratic parties.

At the same time, the RCP is maintaining relations of cooperation with eleven national liberation movements. To this we must add the broad contacts between our trade unions, youth, women's and other mass and civic organizations with similar organizations in other countries.

We may therefore state that from this point of view, too, the period since the Tenth Congress has been the most fruitful, and that it has marked a powerful development in our party's relations of internationalist cooperation and solidarity. As a result of the fact that the Communist parties have taken more into consideration the concrete problems prevailing in each country, proceeding from the specific conditions under which they are active, they have been able to attain ever more remarkable successes and have become powerful national political forces and are playing an active role in the unfolding of events both in their countries and in the international arena.

There are still countries in which the Communist parties still have to carry on their activity under difficult conditions, underground and in terror. Life demonstrates, however, that neither persecution nor terror can break the combat determination of revolutionaries. The crumbling of the reactionary dictatorships in Portugal and Greece are additional proof of the fact that the future belongs to social progress.

*   *   *

We assure the Spanish Communist party—to which we are linked by relations of long-standing solidarity . . . of our complete solidarity with their struggle for democracy, freedom, independence and welfare of the Spanish people. [Applause.] We [also] convey our greetings of solidarity to all the victims of terror in Chile. . . . We express our solidarity with the revolutionary and progressive forces everywhere, forces which despite difficult conditions are carrying aloft the banner of the struggle for social and national freedom. [Applause.]

Proceeding from the important role of the Communist and workers' parties and of other socialist, progressive and democratic forces in the revolutionary change of society, the RCP believes that efforts to continuously strengthen their unity and cooperation must be intensified. Account must be taken of the fact that the parties are carrying on their activity under specific historical, social, national conditions and at different stages of social development and revolutionary struggle; therefore, in drawing up their strategy and revolutionary tactics, as well as their political line, they must proceed from given realities and must creatively apply general truths to create conditions.

This urgently requires the achievement of a new type of unity, based on each party's independence and right to independently decide its own political line. At the same time, the new unity must be conducive to the more intensive development of cooperation and international solidarity among the revolutionary, anti-imperialist parties and forces everywhere. [Applause.]

We must keep in mind that to be powerful the Communist parties must permanently strengthen their ranks, must increase their influence on the masses in each country and strengthen their own unity. These are the indispensable factors of broad cooperation and of developing international solidarity and a new type of unity. This is why we believe that nothing, absolutely nothing must be undertaken to weaken the unity of any Communist party, that no interference by any party in the affairs of another party can be tolerated.

* * *

We are in favor of developing broad cooperation, exchanges of opinions and delegations with all parties, for participating in the democratic debates of mankind's current problems. We regard the conference of European Communist and workers' parties in this spirit. We proceed from the need that this conference, and any other international meeting, be held in a democratic spirit, that they insure the full equal participation of all interested parties in preparations and in discussing problems. We believe that there should be no trends toward the compilation of obligatory documents, that other parties should not be discussed, criticized or condemned. The conference's aim must be to strengthen the unity of all the Communist and workers' parties. It is in this spirit that our party will participate and act at the preparatory proceedings and at the conference of European Communist parties. [Applause.]

As for the problem of a world conference, we believe that it is not of topical interest. We therefore believe it is necessary that the future Central Committee tackle this problem at the right time and then inform the party of its conclusions, but proceeding from the same considerations and factors to which I have referred.

On the basis of the above-mentioned considerations, I propose that the congress empower the Central Committee to continue to carry on an extensive international activity of developing cooperation with all the Communist and workers' parties. Our party must continue to participate actively in strengthening international solidarity and the new type of unity among the Communist and workers' parties. At the same time, the party should not let itself be involved in any censuring of other parties in the future either, as such acts harm the unity and cooperation of the Communist parties. On the contrary, it must do everything to promote the unity and cooperation of international Communist unity and cooperation. [Applause.]

The RCP will intensify its cooperation with the socialist and social-democratic parties in the struggle for a more just world and for peace. Now more than ever current social development and international events urgently require the strengthening of the unity of the workers' class and of all progressive, revolutionary forces on new bases. Of primary importance along these lines is the cooperation and unity between Communists and socialists. . . .

. . . We will also continue to act to develop our relations with governing, democratic parties in developing countries, and in all countries. We will expand and strengthen our solidarity with the national liberation movements in the struggle for winning full independence and for the free socioeconomic development of each people. [Applause.]

In this huge struggle, the progressive forces and all those who want to see the establishment of a new type of relations based on equality and cooperation among states and peoples, regardless of their political and philosophical concepts and religious faith, must unify their efforts to insure the democratic and progressive development of human society.

As a revolutionary detachment of the great front of progress, socialism and peace, in view of the trends of social development and of the fact that an increasing number of people are adopting the road of socialist-democratic development, the RCP will continue to do its national duty—insuring the unfaltering fulfillment of the program of the construction of the comprehensively developed socialist society and of Romania's advancement toward communism—and its international duty, by contributing to all peoples' struggle for a free and independent life, for peace and progress throughout the world. [Applause.]

4

GROUP THREE

PEOPLE'S REPUBLIC OF CHINA

Document 16: Excerpts from the Report of the CC CCP to the Ninth Party Congress, Delivered 1 April 1969 by Lin Piao*

ON CHINA'S RELATIONS WITH FOREIGN COUNTRIES

Now we shall proceed specifically to discuss China's relations with foreign countries. The revolutionary struggles of the proletariat and the oppressed people and nations of the world always support each other. The Albanian Workers' party and all other genuine fraternal Marxist-Leninist parties and organizations, the broad masses of the proletariat and revolutionary people throughout the world, as well as many friendly countries, organizations and personages, have all warmly acclaimed and supported the Great Proletarian Cultural Revolution of our country. On behalf of the great leader Chairman Mao and the Ninth National Congress of the Party, I hereby express our heartfelt thanks to them. We firmly pledge that we, the Communist Party of China and the Chinese people, are determined to fulfill our proletarian internationalist duty and, together with them, carry through to the end the great struggle against imperialism, modern revisionism, and all reaction.

The general trend of the world today is still as Chairman Mao described it: *"The enemy rots with every passing day, while for us things are getting better daily."* On the one hand, the revolutionary

---

* Source: *Peking Review*, no. 18 (30 April 1969), (Peking: Pai Wa Chuang, 1969), pp. 30-34.

movement of the proletariat of the world and of the people of various countries is vigorously surging forward. The armed struggles of the people of southern Vietnam, Laos, Thailand, Burma, Malaya, Indonesia, India, Palestine, and other countries and regions in Asia, Africa, and Latin America are steadily growing in strength. The truth that: *"Political power grows out of the barrel of a gun,"* is being grasped by ever broader masses of the oppressed people and nations. An unprecedentedly gigantic revolutionary mass movement has broken out in Japan, Western Europe and North America, the "heartlands" of capitalism. More and more people are awakening. The genuine fraternal Marxist-Leninist parties and organizations are growing steadily in the course of integrating Marxism-Leninism with the concrete practice of revolution in their own countries. On the other hand, U.S. imperialist and Soviet revisionist social-imperialism are bogged down in political and economic crises, beset with difficulties both at home and abroad and find themselves in an impasse. They collude and at the same time contend with each other in a vain attempt to redivide the world. They act in coordination and work hand in glove in opposing China, opposing communism and opposing the people, in suppressing the national liberation movement and in launching wars of aggression. They scheme against each other and get locked in strife for raw materials, markets, dependencies, important strategic points, and spheres of influence. They are stepping up both arms expansion and war preparations, each trying to realize his own ambitions.

Lenin pointed out: Imperialism means war. *". . . imperialist wars are absolutely inevitable under such an economic system, as long as private property in the means of production exists."* (Lenin, *Selected Works*, Chinese ed., vol. 22, p. 182.) Lenin further pointed out: *"Imperalist war is the eve of socialist revolution."* Lenin, *Collected Works*, Chinese ed., vol. 25, p. 349.) These scientific theses of Lenin's are by no means out of date.

Chairman Mao has recently pointed out, *"With regard to the question of world war, there are but two possibilities: One is that the war will give rise to revolution and the other is that revolution will prevent the war."* This is because there are four major contradictions in the world today: The contradiction between the oppressed nations on the one hand and imperialism and social-imperialism on the other; the contradiction between the proletariat and the bourgeoisie in the capitalist and revisionist countries; the contradiction between imperialist and social-imperialist countries; and the contradiction between socialist countries on the one hand and imperialism and social-imperialism on the other. The existence and development of these contradictions are bound to give rise to revolution. According to the historical experience of World War I and World War II, it can be said with certainty that if the imperialists, revisionists and reactionaries should impose a third world war on the people of the world, it would only greatly accelerate the development of these contradictions and help arouse the people of the world to rise in revolution and send the whole pack of imperialists, revisionists and reactionaries to their graves.

Chairman Mao teaches us: *"All reactionaries are paper tigers."* *"Strategically we should despise all our enemies, but tactically we should take them all seriously."* This great truth enunciated by Chairman Mao heightens the revolutionary militancy of the people of the whole world and guides us from victory to victory in the struggle against imperialism, revisionism, and all reaction.

The nature of U.S. imperialism as a paper tiger has long since been laid bare by the people throughout the world. U.S. imperialism, the most ferocious enemy of the people of the whole world, is going downhill more and more. Since he took office, Nixon has been confronted with a hopeless mess and an insoluble economic crisis, with the strong resistance of the masses of the people at home and throughout the world, and with a predicament in which the imperialist countries are disintegrating and the baton of U.S. imperialism is getting less and less effective. Unable to produce any solution to these problems, Nixon, like his predecessors, cannot but continue to play the counterrevolutionary dual tactics, ostensibly assuming a "peace-loving" appearance while in fact engaging in arms expansion and war preparations on a still larger scale. The military expenditures of the United States have been increasing year by year. To date the U.S. imperialists still occupy our territory of Taiwan. They have dispatched aggressor troops to many countries and have also set up hundreds upon hundreds of military bases and military installations in different parts of the world. They have made countless airplanes and guns, countless nuclear bombs and guided missiles. What is all this for? To frighten, suppress, and slaughter the people and dominate the world. By doing so they make themselves the enemy of the people everywhere, and find themselves besieged and battered by the broad masses of the proletariat and the people all over the world. This will definitely lead to revolutions throughout the world on a still larger scale.

The Soviet revisionist renegade clique is a paper tiger too. It has revealed its social-imperialist features more and more clearly. When Khrushchev revisionism was just beginning to emerge, our great leader Chairman Mao foresaw what serious harm modern revisionism would do to the cause of world revolution. Chairman Mao led the whole party in waging resolute struggles in the ideological, theoretical, and political spheres, together with the Albanian Workers' Party headed by the great Marxist-Leninist Comrade Enver Hoxha, and the genuine Marxist-Leninists of the world. They struggle against modern revisionism with Soviet revisionism as its center. This has enabled the people all over the world to learn gradually, in struggle, how to distinguish genuine Marxism-Leninism from sham Marxism-Leninism, and genuine socialism from sham socialism, and brought about the bankruptcy of Khrushchev revisionism. At the same time, Chairman Mao led our party in resolutely criticizing Liu Shao-chi's revisionist line of capitulation to imperialism, revisionism and reaction, and suppression of revolutionary movements in various countries; and destroying Liu Shao-chi's counterrevolutionary revisionist clique. All this has been done in the fulfillment of our party's proletarian internationalist duty.

With its baton becoming less and less effective and its difficulties at home and abroad growing more and more serious since Brezhnev came to power, the Soviet revisionist renegade clique has been practicing social-imperialism and social-fascism more frantically than ever. Internally, it has intensified its suppression of the Soviet people and speeded up the all-round restoration of capitalism. Externally, it has stepped up its collusion with U.S. imperialism and its suppression of the revolutionary struggles of the people of various countries, intensified its control over, and its exploitation of, various East European countries and the People's Republic of Mongolia, intensified its contention with U.S. imperialism over the Middle East and other regions, and intensified its threat of aggression against China. Its dispatch of hundreds of thousands of troops to occupy Czechoslovakia and its armed provocations against China on our territory of Chenpao Island are two foul performances staged recently by Soviet revisionism. In order to justify its aggression and plunder, the Soviet revisionist renegade clique trumpets the so-called theory of "limited sovereignty," the theory of "international dictatorship," and the theory of "socialist community." What does all this stuff mean? It means that your sovereignty is "limited," while his is unlimited. You won't obey him? He will exercise "international dictatorship" over you—dictatorship over the people of other countries, in order to form the "socialist community" ruled by the new tsars; that is, colonies of social-imperialism, just like the "New Order of Europe" of Hitler, the "Greater East Asia Coprosperity Sphere" of Japanese militarism, and the "Free World Community" of the United States. Lenin denounced the renegades of the Second International. *"Socialism in words, imperialism in deeds, the growth of opportunism into imperialism."* (Lenin, *Collected Works,* Chinese ed., vol. 29, p. 458.) This applies perfectly to the Soviet revisionist renegade clique of today which is composed of a handful of capitalist-roaders in power. We firmly believe that the proletariat and the broad masses of the people in the Soviet Union, with their glorious revolutionary tradition, will surely rise and overthrow this clique consisting of a handful of renegades. Chairman Mao points out:

> *The Soviet Union was the first socialist state and the Communist Party of the Soviet Union was created by Lenin. Although the leadership of the Soviet party and state has now been usurped by revisionists, I would advise comrades to remain firm in the conviction that the masses of the Soviet people and of party members and cadres are good, that they desire revolution and that revisionist rule will not last long.*

Now that the Soviet government has created the incident of armed encroachment on the Chinese territory of Chenpao Island, the Sino-Soviet boundary question has caught the attention of the whole world. Like boundary questions between China and some of her other neighboring countries, the Sino-Soviet boundary question is also one left over by history. As regards these questions, our party and government have consistently stood for negotiations through diplomatic channels to reach a fair and reasonable settlement. Pending a settlement, the status quo of the boundary should be maintained and conflicts avoided. Proceeding from this stand, China has satisfactorily and successively settled boundary questions with neighboring countries such as Burma, Nepal, Pakistan, the People's Republic of Mongolia, and Afghanistan. Only the boundary questions between the Soviet Union and China, and between India and China remain unsettled to this day.

The Chinese government held repeated negotiations with the Indian government on the Sino-Indian boundary question. As the reactionary Indian government had taken over the British imperialist policy of aggression, it insisted that we recognize the illegal McMahon line which even the reactionary governments of different periods in old China had not recognized. Moreover, it went a step further and vainly attempted to occupy the Aksai Chin area, which has always been under Chinese jurisdiction, thereby disrupting the Sino-Indian boundary negotiations. This is known to all.

The Sino-Soviet boundary question is the product of tsarist Russian imperialist aggression against China. In the latter half of the nineteenth century, when power was not in the hands of the Chinese and Russian people, the tsarist government took imperialist acts of aggression to carve up China, imposed a series of unequal treaties on her, annexed vast expanses of her territory, and moreover, crossed the boundary line stipulated by the unequal treaties in many places, and occupied still more Chinese territory. This gangster behavior was indignantly condemned by Marx, Engels, and Lenin. On 27 September 1920, the government of Soviets, led by the great Lenin, solemnly proclaimed:

> It "declares null and void all the treaties concluded with China by the former Governments of Russia, renounces all seizure of Chinese territory and all Russian concessions in China and restores to China, without any compensation and forever, all that had been predatorily seized from her by the Tsar's government and the Russian bourgeoisie."

(See *Declaration of the Government of the Russian Socialist Federated Soviet Republic to the Chinese Government.*) Owing to the historical conditions of the time, this proletarian policy of Lenin's was not realized.

As early as 22 August and 21 September 1960, the Chinese government, proceeding from its consistent stand on boundary questions, twice took the initiative in proposing to the Soviet government that negotiations be held to settle the Sino-Soviet boundary question. In 1964, negotiations between the two sides started in Peking. The treaties relating to the present Sino-Soviet boundary are unequal treaties imposed on the Chinese people by the tsars. But out of the desire to safeguard the revolutionary friendship between the Chinese and Soviet people, we still maintained that these treaties be taken as the basis for the settlement of the boundary question. However, betraying Lenin's proletarian policy and clinging to its new tsarist social-imperialist stand, the Soviet revisionist renegade clique refused to recognize these treaties as unequal, and moreover, it insisted that China recognize as belonging to the Soviet Union all the Chinese territory which they had occupied or attempted to occupy in violation of the treaties. This great-power chauvinist and social-imperialist stand of the Soviet government led to the disruption of the negotiations.

Since Brezhnev came to power, the Soviet revisionist renegade clique has frenziedly stepped up its disruption of the status quo of the boundary and repeatedly provoked border incidents, shooting and killing our unarmed fishermen and peasants, and encroaching upon China's sovereignty. Recently it has gone further and made successive armed intrusions into our territory of Chenpao Island. Driven beyond the limits of their forbearance, our frontier guards have fought back in self-defense, dealing the aggressors well-deserved blows and triumphantly safeguarding our sacred territory. In an effort to extricate the Soviets from their predicament, Kosygin asked on 21 March to communicate with our leaders by telephone. Immediately on 22 March our government replied with a memorandum, in which it was made clear that, "In view of the present relations between China and the Soviet Union, it is unsuitable to communicate by telephone. If the Soviet government has anything to say, it is asked to put it forward officially to the Chinese government through diplomatic channels." On 29 March the Soviet government issued a statement still clinging to its obstinate aggressor stand, while expressing willingness to resume "consultations." Our government is considering its reply to this.

The foreign policy of our party and government is consistent. It is: to develop relations of friendship, mutual assistance, and cooperation with socialist countries on the principle of proletarian internationalism; to support and assist the revolutionary struggles of all the oppressed people and nations; to strive for peaceful coexistence with countries having different social systems on the basis of the Five Principles of mutual respect for territorial integrity and sovereignty, mutual nonaggression, noninterference in each other's internal affairs, equality and mutual benefit, and peaceful coexistence; and to oppose the imperialist policies of aggression and war. Our proletarian foreign policy is not based on expediency; it is a policy in which we have long persisted. This is what we did in the past, and we will persist in doing the same in the future.

We have always held that the internal affairs of each country should be settled by its own people. The relations between all countries and between all parties, big or small, must be built on the principles of equality and noninterference in each other's internal affairs. To safeguard these Marxist-Leninist principles, the Communist Party of China has waged a long struggle against the sinister great-power chauvinism of the Soviet revisionist renegade clique. This is a fact known to all. The Soviet revisionist renegade clique glibly talks of "fraternal parties" and "fraternal countries," but in fact it regards itself as the patriarchal party, and as the new tsar who is free to invade and occupy the territory of other countries. They conduct sabotage and subversion against the Chinese Communist party, the Albanian Workers' party, and other genuine Marxist-Leninist parties. Moreover, when any party or any country in their so-called socialist community holds a slightly different view, they act ferociously and stop at nothing in suppressing, sabotaging, subverting, and even sending troops to invade and occupy their so-called fraternal countries and kidnapping members of their so-called fraternal parties. These fascist piratical acts have sealed their doom.

U.S. imperialism and Soviet revisionism are always trying to "isolate" China; this is China's honor. Their rabid opposition to China cannot do us the slightest harm. On the contrary, it serves to further arouse our people's determination to maintain independence and keep the initiative in our own hands, rely on our own efforts, and work hard to make our country prosperous and powerful; it serves to prove to the whole world that China has drawn a clear line between herself on the one hand, and U.S. imperialism and Soviet revisionism on the other. Today, it is not imperialism, revisionism, and reaction; but the proletariat and the revolutionary people of all countries that determine the destiny of the world. The genuine Marxist-Leninist parties and organizations of various countries, which are composed of the advanced elements of the proletariat, are a new rising force that has infinitely broad prospects. The Communist Party of China is determined to unite and fight together with them. We firmly support the Vietnamese people in carrying their war of resistance against U.S. aggression—and for national salvation—through to the end. We firmly support the revolutionary struggles of the people of Laos, Thailand, Burma, Malaya, Indonesia, India, Palestine, and other countries and regions in Asia, Africa, and Latin America. We firmly support the proletariat, the students and youth, and the masses of the black people of the United States in their just struggle against the U.S. ruling clique. We firmly support the proletariat and the laboring people of the Soviet Union in their just struggle to overthrow the Soviet revisionist renegade clique; we firmly support the people of Czechoslovakia and other countries in their just struggle against Soviet revisionist social-imperialism. We firmly support the revolutionary struggles of the people of Japan and the West European and Oceanian countries. We firmly support the revolutionary struggles of the people of all countries; and we firmly support all the just struggles of resistance against aggression and oppression by U.S. imperialism and Soviet revisionism. All countries and people subjected to aggression, control, intervention, or bullying by U.S. imperialism and Soviet revisionism, unite and form the broadest possible united front and overthrow our common enemies!

On no account must we relax our revolutionary vigilance because of victory, or ignore the danger of U.S. imperialism and Soviet revisionism launching a large-scale war of aggression. We must make full preparations against their launching a big war, and against their launching a war at an early date. We must make preparations against their launching a conventional war and against their launching a large-scale nuclear war. *In short, we must be prepared.* Chairman Mao said long ago: *"We will not attack unless we are attacked; if we are attacked, we will certainly counterattack."* If they insist on fighting, we will keep them company and fight to the finish. The Chinese revolution won out on the battlefield. Armed with Mao Tse-tung Thought, tempered in the Great Proletarian Cultural Revolution, and with full confidence in victory, the Chinese people in their hundreds of millions and the Chinese People's Liberation Army, are determined to liberate their sacred territory of Taiwan and *resolutely, thoroughly, wholly, and completely wipe out* all aggressors who dare to come!

Our great leader Chairman Mao points out:

> *Working hand in glove, Soviet revisionism and U.S. imperialism have done so many foul and evil things that the revolutionary people the world over will not let them go unpunished. The people of all countries are rising. A new historical period of opposing U.S. imperialism and Soviet revisionism has begun.*

Whether the war gives rise to revolution or revolution prevents the war, U.S. imperialism and Soviet revisionsm will not last long! Workers of all countries, unite! Proletarians and oppressed people and nations of the world, unite! Bury U.S. imperialism, Soviet revisionism, and their lackeys!

Document 17: Excerpts from the Report of the CC CCP to the Tenth Party Congress, Delivered 24 August 1973 by Chou En-lai*

ON THE LINE OF THE NINTH NATIONAL CONGRESS

*   *   *

In accordance with the theory of Marxism-Leninism-Mao Tse-tung Thought on continuing the revolution under the dictatorship of the proletariat, the Ninth Congress summed up the experience of history as well as the new experience of the Great Proletarian Cultural Revolution, criticized Liu Shao-chi's revisionist line, and reaffirmed the basic line and policies of the party for the entire historical period of socialism. . . .

As we all know, the political report to the Ninth Congress was drawn up under Chairman Mao's personal guidance. Prior to that congress, Lin Piao had produced a draft of a political report in collaboration with Chen Po-ta. They were opposed to continuing the revolution under the dictatorship of the proletariat, contending that the main task after the Ninth Congress was to develop production.

This was a refurbished version, under new conditions, of the same revisionist trash that Liu Shao-chi and Chen Po-ta had smuggled into the resolution of the Eighth Congress, which alleged that the major contradiction in our country was not the contradiction between the proletariat and the bourgeoisie, but that "between the advanced socialist system and the backward productive forces of society." Naturally, this draft by Lin Piao and Chen Po-ta was rejected by the Central Committee. Lin Piao secretly supported Chen Po-ta in the latter's open opposition to the political report drawn up under Chairman Mao's guidance, and it was only after his attempts were frustrated that Lin Piao grudgingly accepted the political line of the Central Committee and read its political report to the congress. However, during and after the Ninth Congress, Lin Piao continued with his conspiracy and sabotage in spite of the admonishments, rebuffs, and efforts to save him by Chairman Mao and the party's Central Committee. He went further to start a counterrevolutionary coup d'etat—which was aborted—at the second plenary session of the Ninth Central Committee in August 1970; then in March 1971 he drew up the plan for an armed counterrevolutionary coup d'etat entitled "Outline of Project '571'," and on 8 September he launched

*Source: *Foreign Broadcast Information Service, China Supplement*, no. 175, supp. 31 (10 September 1973), pp. 7-19.

the coup in a wild attempt to assassinate our great leader Chairman Mao and set up a rival central committee. On 13 September, after his conspiracy had collapsed, Lin Piao surreptitiously boarded a plane and fled as a defector to the Soviet revisionists in betrayal of the party and country, and died in a crash at Undur Khan in the People's Republic of Mongolia.

The shattering of the Lin Piao antiparty clique is our party's greatest victory since the Ninth Congress and [represents] a heavy blow dealt to enemies at home and abroad. After the 13 September incident, the whole party, the whole army, and the hundreds of millions of people of all nationalities in our country seriously discussed the matter and expressed their intense proletarian indignation at the bourgeois careerist, conspirator, double-dealer, renegade, and traitor Lin Piao and his sworn followers, and pledged resolute support for our great leader Chairman Mao and the party's Central Committee which he headed. . . .

*   *   *

In the international sphere, our party and government have firmly implemented the foreign policy laid down by the Ninth Congress. Our revolutionary friendship with fraternal socialist countries and with the genuine Marxist-Leninist parties and organizations of various countries, and our cooperation with friendly countries has been further strengthened. Our country has established diplomatic relations with an increasing number of countries on the basis of the five principles of peaceful coexistence. The legitimate status of our country in the United Nations has been restored. The policy of isolating China has gone bankrupt; Sino-U.S. relations have been improved to some extent. China and Japan have normalized their relations. Friendly contacts between our people and the people of other countries are more extensive than ever; we assist and support each other, impelling the world situation to continue to develop in the direction favorable to the people of all countries.

*   *   *

On the Victory of Smashing the Lin Piao Antiparty Clique

*   *   *

Marxism-Leninism holds that inner-party struggle is the reflection within the party of class struggle in society. The Liu Shao-chi renegade clique collapsed and the Lin Piao antiparty clique sprang out to continue the trial of strength with the proletariat. This was an acute expression of the intense domestic and international class struggles.

As early as 13 January 1967, when the Great Proletarian Cultural Revolution was at high tide, Brezhnev, the chief of the Soviet revisionist renegade clique, frantically attacked China's Great Proletarian Cultural Revolution in his speech at a mass rally in Gorky region and openly declared that he and his followers stood on the side of the Liu Shao-chi renegade clique, saying that the downfall of this clique was "a big tragedy for all real Communists in China, and we express our deep sympathy to them."

At the same time, Brezhnev publicly announced continuation of the policy of subverting the leadership of the Chinese Communist party, and ranted about "struggling . . . for bringing it back to the road of internationalism" (*Pravda*, 14 January 1967). In March 1967 another chief of the Soviet revisionists said even more brazenly at mass rallies in Moscow that "sooner or later the healthy forces expressing the true interests of China will have their decisive say, . . . and achieve the victory of Marxist-Leninist ideas in their great country" (*Pravda*, 4 and 10 March 1967). What they called "healthy forces" are nothing but the decadent forces representing the interests of social-imperialism and all the exploiting classes; what they meant by "their decisive say" is the usurpation of the supreme power of the party and the state; what they meant by "victory of ideas" is the reign of sham Marxism-Leninism and real revisionism over China; and what they meant by the "road of internationalism" is the road of reducing China to a colony of Soviet revisionist social-imperialism. The Brezhnev renegade clique has impetuously voiced the common wish of the reactionaries and blurted out the ultra rightist nature of the Lin Piao antiparty clique.

Lin Piao and his handful of sworn followers were a counterrevolutionary conspiratorial clique who never showed up without a copy of "Quotations" in hand, and never opened their mouths without shouting "long live," and "who spoke nice things to your face but stabbed you in the back." The essence of the counterrevolutionary revisionist line they pursued and the criminal aim of the counterrevolutionary armed coup d'etat they launched was to usurp the supreme power of the party and the state, thoroughly betray the line of the Ninth Congress, radically change the party's basic line and policies for the entire historical period of socialism, turn the Marxist-Leninist Chinese Communist party into a revisionist fascist party, subvert the dictatorship of the proletariat, and restore capitalism. Inside China, they wanted to reinstate the landlord and bourgeois classes, which our party, army, and people had overthrown with their own hands under the leadership of Chairman Mao, and to institute a feudal-comprador-fascist dictatorship. Internationally, they wanted to capitulate to Soviet revisionist social-imperialism and ally themselves with imperialism, revisionism, and reaction; in order to oppose China, communism, and revolution.

* * *

Comrades, in the last fifty years our party has gone through ten major struggles between the two lines. The collapse of the Lin Piao antiparty clique does not mean the end of the two-line struggle within the party. Enemies at home and abroad all understand that the easiest way to capture a fortress is from within. It is much more convenient to have the capitalist-roaders in power, who have sneaked into the party, do the job of subverting the dictatorship of the proletariat, than for the landlords and capitalists to come to the fore themselves. This is especially true when the landlords and capitalists are already quite odious in society. In the future, even after classes have disappeared, there will still be contradictions between the superstructure and the economic base, and between the relations of production and the productive forces. And there will still be two-line struggles reflecting these contradictions, that is, struggles between the advanced and the backward, and between the correct and the erroneous. Moreover, socialist society now covers a long historical period. Throughout this historical period, there have been classes, class contradictions, and class struggle; there is the struggle between the socialist road and the capitalist road, there is the danger of capitalist restoration, and there is the threat of subversion and aggression by imperialism and social-imperialism.

For a long time to come, there will still be two-line struggles within the party, reflecting these contradictions; and such struggles will occur ten, twenty, or thirty times. Lin Piao will appear again and so will persons like Wang Ming, Liu Shao-chi, Peng Te-huai and Kao Kang. This is something independent of man's will. Therefore, all comrades in our party must be fully prepared mentally for the struggles in the long years to come and be able to make the best use of the situation and guide the struggle to victory for the proletariat, no matter how the class enemy may change his tactics.

Chairman Mao teaches us that: "THE CORRECTNESS OR INCORRECTNESS OF THE IDEOLOGICAL AND POLITICAL LINE DECIDES EVERYTHING." If one's line is incorrect, one's downfall is inevitable, even with the control of the central, local, and army leadership. If one's line is correct, even if one has not a single soldier at first, there will be soldiers; and even if there is no political power, political power will be gained. This is borne out by the historical experience of our party, and by that of the international Communist movement since the time of Marx. Lin Piao wanted to "have everything under his command and everything at his disposal," but he ended up having nothing under his command and nothing at his disposal. The crux of the matter is line. This is an irrefutable truth.

* * *

On the Situation and Our Tasks

* * *

Chairman Mao has often taught us: We are still in the era of imperialism and proletarian revolution. On the basis of fundamental Marxist principle, Lenin made a scientific analysis of imperialism and defined: "IMPERIALISM AS THE HIGHEST STAGE OF CAPI- TALISM." Lenin pointed out that imperialism is monopolistic capitalism, parasitic or decaying capitalism, and moribund capitalism. He also said that imperialism intensified all the contradictions of capitalism to the extreme. He therefore concluded that: "IMPERIALISM IS THE EVE OF THE SOCIAL REVOLUTION OF THE PROLE- TARIAT," and put forward the theories and tactics of the proletarian revolution in the era of imperialism. Stalin said, "LENINISM IS MARXISM OF THE ERA OF IMPERIALISM AND THE PROLE- TARIAN REVOLUTION." This is entirely correct. Since Lenin's death, the world situation has undergone great changes. But the era has not changed. The fundamental principles of Leninism are not outdated; they remain the theoretical basis guiding our thinking today.

The present international situation is one characterized by great disorder on the earth. "The wind sweeping through the tower heralds a rising storm in the mountains." This aptly depicts how the basic world contradictions as analyzed by Lenin show themselves today. Relaxation is a temporary and superficial phenomenon, and great disorder will continue. Such great disorder is a good thing for the people, not a bad thing. It throws the enemies into confusion and causes division among them, while it arouses and tempers the people, thus helping the international situation develop further in the direction favorable to the people and unfavorable to imperialism, modern revisionism, and all reaction.

The awakening and growth of the third world is a major event in contemporary international relations. The third world has strengthened its unity in the struggle against hegemonism and power politics

271

of the superpowers, and is playing an ever more significant role in international affairs. The great victories won by the people of Vietnam, Laos, and Cambodia in their war against U.S. aggression and for national salvation have strongly encouraged the people of the world in their revolutionary struggles against imperialism and colonialism. A new situation has emerged in the Korean people's struggle for the independent and peaceful reunification of their fatherland. The struggles of the Palestinian and other Arab peoples against aggression by Israeli Zionism, the African peoples' struggle against colonialism and racial discrimination, and the Latin American peoples' struggles for maintaining 200-nautical-mile territorial waters or economic zones all continue to forge ahead. The struggles of the Asian, African, and Latin American peoples to win and defend national independence and safeguard state sovereignty and national resources have further deepened and broadened. The just struggles of the third world, as well as of the people of Europe, North America, and Oceania support and encourage each other. Countries want independence, nations want liberation, and the people want revolution—this has become an irresistible historical trend.

Lenin said that "AN ESSENTIAL FEATURE OF IMPERIALISM IS THE RIVALRY BETWEEN SEVERAL GREAT POWERS IN THE STRIVING FOR HEGEMONY." Today, it is mainly the two nuclear superpowers—the U.S. and the U.S.S.R.—that are contending for hegemony. While hawking disarmament, they are actually expanding their armaments every day. Their purpose is to contend for world hegemony. They contend, as well as collude, with each other. Their collusion serves the purpose of more intensified contention. Contention is absolute and protracted, whereas collusion is relative and temporary. The declaration of this year as the "year of Europe" and the convocation of the European security conference indicate that strategically the key point of their contention is Europe. The West always wants to urge the Soviet revisionists eastward to divert the peril towards China, and this would be fine with them so long as all is quiet in the West. China is an attractive piece of meat coveted by all. But this piece of meat is very tough, and for years no one has been able to bite into it. It is even more difficult now that Lin Piao, the "super-spy," has fallen. At present, the Soviet revisionists are "making a feint to the east while attacking in the west," and stepping up their contention in Europe, and their expansion in the Mediterranean, the Indian Ocean, and every place their hands can reach. The U.S.-Soviet contention for hegemony is the cause of world intranquility. It cannot be covered up by any false appearances they create, and is already perceived by an increasing number of people and countries. It has met with strong resistance from the third world and has caused resentment on the part of Japan and West European countries. Beset with troubles internally and externally, the two hegemonic powers—the U.S. and the U.S.S.R.—find the going tougher and tougher. As the verse goes, "flowers fall off, do what one may"; they are in a sorry plight indeed. This has been further proved by the U.S.-Soviet talks last June and the subsequent course of events.

"THE PEOPLE, AND THE PEOPLE ALONE, ARE THE MOTIVE FORCE IN THE MAKING OF WORLD HISTORY." The ambitions of the two hegemonic powers—the U.S. and the U.S.S.R.—are one thing, but whether they can achieve them is quite another. They want to devour China, but find it too tough even to bite. Europe and Japan are also hard to bite, not to speak of the vast third world. U.S. imperialism started to go downhill after its defeat in the war of aggression against Korea. It has openly admitted that it is increasingly on the decline; it could not but pull out of Vietnam. Over the last two decades, the Soviet revisionist ruling clique, from Khrushchev to Brezhnev, has made a socialist country degenerate into a social-imperialist country. Internally, it has restored capitalism, enforced a fascist dictatorship, and enslaved the people of all nationalities, thus deepening the political and economic contradictions, as well as the contradictions among nationalities. Externally, it has invaded and occupied Czechoslovakia, massed its troops along the Chinese border, sent troops into the People's Republic of Mongolia, supported the traitorous Lon Nol clique, suppressed the Polish writers' rebellion, intervened in Egypt—causing the expulsion of the Soviet experts—dismembered Pakistan, and carried out subversive activities in many Asian and African countries. This series of facts has profoundly exposed its ugly features as the new tsar, and its reactionary nature, namely, "SOCIALISM IN WORDS, IMPERIALISM IN DEED." The more evil and foul things it does, the sooner the time when Soviet revisionism will be relegated to the historical museum by the people of the Soviet Union and the rest of the world.

Recently, the Brezhnev renegade clique has talked a lot of nonsense on Sino-Soviet relations. It alleges that China is against relaxation of world tension and unwilling to improve Sino-Soviet relations. These words are directed to the Soviet people and the people of other countries in a vain attempt to alienate their friendly feelings for the Chinese people and disguise the true features of the new tsar. These words are above all meant for the monopoly capitalists in the hope of getting more money in reward for services in opposing China and communism. This was an old trick of Hitler's, only Brezhnev is playing it more clumsily. If you are so anxious to relax world tension, why don't you show your good faith by doing a thing or two? For instance, withdraw your armed forces from Czechoslovakia or the People's Republic of Mongolia and return the four northern islands to Japan. China has not occupied any foreign country's territory. Must China give away all the territory north of the Great Wall to the Soviet revisionists in order to show that we favor relaxation of world tension and are willing to improve Sino-Soviet relations? The Chinese people are not to be deceived or cowed. The Sino-Soviet controversy on matters of principle should not hinder the normalization of relations between the two states on the basis of the five principles of peaceful coexistence. The Sino-Soviet boundary question should be settled peacefully through negotiations free from any threat. "WE WILL NOT ATTACK UNLESS WE ARE ATTACKED; IF WE ARE ATTACKED, WE WILL CERTAINLY COUNTERATTACK"— this is our consistent principle. And we mean what we say.

We should point out here that necessary compromises between revolutionary countries and imperialist countries must be distinguished from collusion and compromise between Soviet revisionism and U.S. imperialism. Lenin put it well:

> THERE ARE COMPROMISES AND COMPROMISES. ONE MUST BE ABLE TO ANALYZE THE SITUATION AND THE CONCRETE CONDITIONS OF EACH COMPROMISE, OR OF EACH VARIETY OF COMPROMISE. ONE MUST LEARN TO DISTINGUISH BETWEEN A MAN WHO GAVE THE BANDITS MONEY AND FIREARMS IN ORDER TO LESSEN THE DAMAGE THEY CAN DO AND FACILITATE THEIR CAPTURE AND EXECUTION, AND A MAN WHO GIVES BANDITS MONEY AND FIREARMS IN ORDER TO SHARE IN THE LOOT ("Left-Wing Communism, an Infantile Disorder").

The Brest-Litovsk Treaty concluded by Lenin with German imperialism comes under the former category; and the doings of Khrushchev and Brezhnev, both betrayers of Lenin, fall under the latter.

Lenin pointed out repeatedly that imperialism means aggression and war. Chairman Mao pointed out in his statement of 20 May 1970: "THE DANGER OF A NEW WORLD WAR STILL EXISTS, AND THE PEOPLE OF ALL COUNTRIES MUST GET PREPARED. BUT REVOLUTION IS THE MAIN TREND IN THE WORLD TODAY." It will be possible to prevent such a war, so long as the peoples, who are becoming more and more awakened, keep the orientation clearly in sight, heighten their vigilance, strengthen unity, and persevere in struggle. Should the imperialists be bent on unleashing such a war, it will inevitably give rise to greater revolutions on a worldwide scale and hasten their doom.

In the excellent situation now prevailing at home and abroad, it is most important for us to run China's affairs well. Therefore, on the international front, our party must uphold proletarian internationalism, uphold the party's consistent policies, strengthen our unity with the proletariat and the oppressed people and nations of the whole world, and with all countries subjected to imperialist aggression, subversion, interference, control, or bullying, and form the broadest united front against imperialism, colonialism and neocolonialism, and in particular, against the hegemonism of the two superpowers—the U.S. and the U.S.S.R. We must unite with all genuine Marxist-Leninist parties and organizations the world over, and carry the struggle against modern revisionism through to the end. On the domestic front, we must pursue our party's basic line and policies for the entire historical period of socialism, persevere in continuing the revolution under the dictatorship of the proletariat, unite with all the forces that can be united, and work hard to build our country into a powerful socialist state, so as to make a great contribution to mankind.

We must uphold Chairman Mao's teachings that we should "BE PREPARED AGAINST WAR, BE PREPARED AGAINST NATURAL DISASTERS, AND DO EVERYTHING FOR THE PEOPLE" and "DIG TUNNELS DEEP, STORE GRAIN EVERYWHERE, AND NEVER SEEK HEGEMONY," maintain high vigilance and be fully prepared against any war of aggression that imperialism may launch, and particularly against surprise attack on our country by Soviet revisionist social-imperialism. Our heroic People's Liberation Army and our vast militia must be prepared at all times to wipe out any enemy that may invade.

Taiwan province is our motherland's sacred territory, and the people in Taiwan are our kith and kin. We have infinite concern for our compatriots in Taiwan, who love and long for the motherland. Our compatriots in Taiwan can have a bright future only by returning to the embrace of the motherland. Taiwan must be liberated. Our great motherland must be unified. This is the common aspiration and sacred duty of the people of all nationalities of the country, including our compatriots in Taiwan. Let us strive together to attain this goal.

Comrades, we must be aware that although we have achieved great successes in socialist revolution and socialist construction, we are lagging. . . . We still face very heavy tasks in our socialist revolution. The tasks of struggle-criticism-transformation in the Great Proletarian Cultural Revolution need to be carried on in a thoroughgoing way on all fronts. More efforts are required to overcome shortcomings, mistakes, and certain unhealthy tendencies in our work. Our whole party must make good use of the present opportune time to consolidate and carry forward the achievements of the Great Proletarian Cultural Revolution and work well in all fields.

First of all, we should continue to do a good job of criticizing Lin Piao and rectifying our style of work. We should make full use of that teacher by negative example, the Lin Piao antiparty clique, to educate the whole party, army, and the people of all nationalities of our country in class struggle and two-line struggle, and criticize revisionism and the bourgeois world outlook, so that the masses will be able to draw on the historical experience of the ten struggles between the two lines in our party, acquire a deeper understanding of the characteristics and laws of class struggle and two-line struggle in the period of socialist revolution in our country, and raise their ability to distinguish genuine from sham Marxism.

All party members should conscientiously study works by Marx, Engels, Lenin, and Stalin, and by Chairman Mao. They should adhere to dialectical materialism and historical materialism, combat idealism and metaphysics and remold their world outlook. Senior cadres, in particular, should make greater efforts to "READ AND STUDY CONSCIENTIOUSLY AND HAVE A GOOD GRASP OF MARXISM," try their best to master the basic theories of Marxism, learn the history of the struggles of Marxism against old and new revisionism and opportunism of all descriptions, and understand how Chairman Mao has inherited, defended, and developed Marxism-Leninism in the course of integrating the universal truth of Marxism-Leninism with the concrete practice of revolution. We hope that through sustained efforts "THE VAST NUMBERS OF OUR CADRES AND THE PEOPLE WILL BE ABLE TO ARM THEMSELVES WITH THE BASIC THEORIES OF MARXISM."

We should attach importance to the class struggle in the superstructure—including all spheres of culture—and transform all parts of the superstructure which do not conform to the economic base. We should handle correctly the two types of contradictions of different nature. We should continue to carry out in earnest all of Chairman Mao's proletarian policies.

We should continue to carry out well the revolution in literature and art, the revolution in education, and the revolution in public health. We should also continue the work with regard to the educated youth who go to mountairous and other rural areas, run the 7 May cadre schools well, and support all the newly emerging aspects of socialism.

Economically, ours is still a poor and developing country. We should thoroughly carry out the general line of "GOING ALL OUT, AIMING HIGH AND ACHIEVING GREATER, FASTER, BETTER, AND MORE ECONOMICAL RESULTS IN BUILDING SOCIAL-ISM." We should grasp revolution and promote production. We should continue to implement the principle of "TAKING AGRI-CULTURE AS THE FOUNDATION AND INDUSTRY AS THE LEADING FACTOR," we should walk on our own two legs, and build our own country independently, with the initiative in our own hands, through self-reliance, hard struggle, diligence, and frugal-ity. Marx pointed out that "THE GREATEST PRODUCTIVE POWER IS THE REVOLUTIONARY CLASS ITSELF." One basic experience from our socialist construction over more than two decades is to rely on the masses. In order to learn from Taching in industry and to learn from Tachai in agriculture, we must persist in putting proletarian politics in command, vigorously launching mass move-ments, and giving full scope to the enthusiasm, wisdom, and creative-ness of the masses. On this basis, planning and coordination must be strengthened, rational rules and regulations improved, and both central and local initiative further brought into full play. Party organizations should pay close attention to questions of economic policy, concern themselves with the well-being of the masses, do a good job of investigation and study, and strive effectively to fulfill or overfulfill the state plans for developing the national economy so that our socialist economy will make still greater progress.

We should further strengthen the centralized leadership of the party. OF THE SEVEN SECTORS—INDUSTRY, AGRICULTURE, COMMERCE, CULTURE AND EDUCATION, THE ARMY, THE GOVERNMENT, AND THE PARTY—IT IS THE PARTY THAT EXERCISES OVERALL LEADERSHIP. Party committees at all levels should study "On Strengthening the Party Committee System," "Methods of Work of Party Committees" and other writings by Chairman Mao, sum up their experience, and further strengthen the centralized leadership of the party ideologically and organizationally, as well as through rules and regulations. At the same time the role of revolutionary committees and mass organizations should be brought into full play. We should strengthen the leadership given to primary organizations in order to ensure that the leadership there is truly in the hands of Marxists and in the hands of workers, poor, and lower-middle peasants, and other working people, and that the task of consolidating the dictatorship of the proletariat is fulfilled in every primary organization. Party committees at all levels should apply democratic centralism better and improve their art of leadership. It should be emphatically pointed out that quite a few party committees are engrossed in daily routines and minor matters, paying no attention to major issues. This is very dangerous. If they do not change, they will inevitably step onto the road of revisionism. It is hoped that comrades throughout the party, leading comrades in particular, will guard against such a tendency and earnestly change such a style of work.

The experience with regard to combining the old, the middle-aged, and the young in the leadership which the masses created during the Great Proletarian Cultural Revolution, has provided us favorable conditions for training millions of successors to the revolutionary cause of the proletariat in accordance with the five requirements put forward by Chairman Mao. Party organizations at all levels should keep on the agenda this fundamental task which is crucial for generations to come. Chairman Mao says: "REVOLUTIONARY SUCCESSORS OF THE PROLETARIAT ARE INVARIABLY BROUGHT UP IN GREAT STORMS." They must be tempered in class struggle and two-line struggle, and educated by both positive and negative experience. Therefore, a genuine Communist must be ready to accept a higher or lower post, and be able to stand the test of going up or stepping down many times. All cadres, veteran and new alike, must maintain close ties with the masses, be modest and prudent, guard against arrogance and impetuosity, go to any post as required by the party and the people, and firmly carry out Chairman Mao's revolutionary line and policies under every circumstance.

Comrades, the Tenth National Congress of the party will have a far-reaching influence on the course of our party's development. We will soon convene the Fourth National People's Congress. Our people and the revolutionary people of all countries place great hopes on our party and our country. We are confident that our party, under the leadership of Chairman Mao, will uphold his proletarian revolutionary line, do our work well, and live up to the expectations of our people and the people throughout the world!

THE FUTURE IS BRIGHT; THE ROAD IS TORTUOUS. Let our whole party unite, let our people of all nationalities unite, BE RESOLUTE, FEAR NO SACRIFICE AND SURMOUNT EVERY DIFFICULTY TO WIN VICTORY!

Long live the great, glorious, and correct Communist party of China!

Long live Marxism-Leninism-Mao Tse-tung thought!

Long live Chairman Mao! A long, long life to Chairman Mao!

ALBANIA

Document 18: Excerpts from the Report of the CC AWP to the Sixth Party Congress, Delivered 1 November 1971 by Enver Hoxha, General Secretary of the CC AWP*

THE INTERNATIONAL SITUATION AND THE FOREIGN POLICY OF THE ALBANIAN PEOPLE'S REPUBLIC

Our Sixth Congress is being held at a time marked by great contradictions and confrontations on a world scale; at a time when very important social, political, economic, and military forces covering the whole world are grouping together and opposing one another on an unprecedented scale.

On one side of the barricade are the forces of imperialism, revisionism, and reaction; and on the other, the forces of socialism, the people's front, led by the international working class. The demarcation line separating them becomes more clearly defined in every sphere.

*   *   *

The trend of development in the world today is toward revolution and the victory of socialism. . . . Analyzing the present world situation, we can assert that not only is it in favor of revolution, but that revolution is becoming the people's general aspiration.

*   *   *

Today we are witnessing great class confrontations between workers on the one hand, and capital and its power on the other. The proletariat's class struggle, and that of the other exploited social strata, has reached such a vast extent, because of the number of those involved and its bitter nature, that the present time can be compared—as far as the capitalist bourgeoisie is concerned—to the most critical times it has ever experienced. The brilliant battles of French, Italian, Spanish, British, Belgian, and other workers; the positive and negative experience which they have acquired, will leave indelible imprints on their consciences. Even in countries which bourgeois propaganda used to hold up as zones of eternal "social peace," violent battles are being waged between workers and capital. In this

---

*Source: Foreign Broadcast Information Service, Daily Report, Supplement, no. 222, supp. 54 (17 November 1971), pp. 3-21.

279

way the myth which the social-democrats perpetuate, concerning the creation of general well-being under the capitalist system, has been destroyed.

Even in the United States social contradictions have grown considerably worse. Failures in foreign and domestic policy have resulted in a further deepening of the political, economic, and social crises of Yankee imperialism; the revolutionary struggle of the American people has been further extended. Imperialism's fortress is being shaken by the wide revolt of American Negroes who are fighting to obtain equality and civil rights, as well as by the entire population's revolt against the Vietnam War.

* * *

Another characteristic of the class struggle against the exploiting capitalist system and imperialist policy is the eruption everywhere of the youth and student movement, which is being turned into a powerful revolutionary force of our time. . . .

International imperialism is being dealt increasingly harder blows by the liberation struggle of the peoples in Asia, Africa, and Latin America, a struggle which is developing rapidly everywhere. A brilliant example of its impulse, and a powerful stimulus to this struggle, is represented by the determined anti-imperialist struggle of the Vietnamese people and of the other peoples of Indochina who have broken once and for all time the myth of the invincibility of the U.S. superpower, its military machine, and modern weapons.

In Asia, the armed anti-imperialist struggle of the peoples of Thailand, Burma, Malaysia, and Indonesia is assuming ever-wider dimensions. The revolutionary struggle has also developed broadly among the peoples of Brazil, Colombia, Chile, Peru, Bolivia, Argentina, and other Latin American countries, who struggle against American imperialism and the domestic oligarchies, and for the defense of national sovereignty and independence, independent democratic development, and social progress. A new revolutionary situation has begun to be created in Africa also. . . .

Imperialism and revisionism attract to them the hatred of people, who see in American and Soviet revisionist policy a danger to their freedom and independence. People want freedom; they are against the brutal intervention of imperialists and revisionists; they condemn their policy of hegemony and blackmail. Everywhere one can see anti-American feelings growing and getting stronger, just as opposition to Soviet social-imperialism is growing and strengthening.

Great People's China and Albania, which consistently follow the Marxist-Leninist line and build socialism, constitute an important factor in the revolutionary movement, a source of inspiration and encouragement for its expansion, and an unshakable basis of support for the people's revolutionary and liberation struggles. Their successes in the socialist revolution; their economic, political, and ideological strength; their determined struggle without compromise, and victory on two fronts—both against imperialism, headed by American imperialism, and against modern revisionism, led by Soviet revisionism —the brilliance of their revolutionary policy, and their firm support for the liberation struggle, are all facts which have given, and are giving, courage everywhere to peoples and revolutionaries, and are strengthening their confidence in the victory of their just cause; consolidating their faith in socialism to which the future belongs.

The role of the People's Republic of China, powerful citadel of revolution and socialism, is particularly important for the growth and strengthening of the revolutionary movement throughout the world.

The triumph of the Great Proletarian Cultural Revolution, begun and guided by the great Marxist-Leninist, Comrade Mao Tse-tung, constitutes a victory and a source of inspiration for the entire world revolutionary movement. Imperialists and revisionists, who through their agents tried to stifle the Chinese revolution, were badly disappointed. Mao Tse-tung's China has remained Red; it has emerged from the Cultural Revolution a hundred times more powerful, the determined enemy of imperialism and revisionism, the great friend of peoples in powerful support of their struggle.

*   *   *

The betrayal of the Khrushchevite modern revisionists, who caused great harm to the revolutionary movement, represented only a temporary advantage for the capitalist system as a whole. But this betrayal was not able to save capitalism from the general crisis into which it plunged, nor was it able to change the course of history— the course of its development toward revolution and the victory of socialism.

In the very framework of its system of exploitation, the aim of imperialism was to eliminate the economic crisis and smooth out the deep contradictions existing between the various capitalist countries. In this, as in other things, it failed. The big capitalist countries, not to speak of the small ones, find themselves going through a period in which the phenomena of crisis have become chronic and even created new difficulties for the whole of their economy. . . .

*   *   *

The economic and political struggle between capitalist countries acquires increasingly greater proportions. The economic integrations and the creation of military blocs have further intensified the ruthless competition existing between them. The European Common Market is now trying to defy American supremacy in the world markets, while the action of the new economic power of Japan appreciably hinders the expansion of American monopolies in Asia. Serious differences have occurred within NATO and the other imperialist alliances. These rivalries and contradictions between imperialist countries tend to become even deeper.

*   *   *

A situation just as serious also prevails today in the revisionist camp. Enlightened by Marxist-Leninist theory, our party foresaw where the course of betrayal would lead the revisionists; it foresaw their general decline and fall. The crisis through which revisionism is living is ideological, political, and economic. The ringleaders of Moscow not only failed in their efforts to establish their domination over the Communist movement and control the national liberation movement, but also today they are not even able to control their closest allies, the revisionist cliques of the satellite countries.

Among the various detachments of revisionism there is neither ideological unity nor unity of action. . . . The revisionist countries and their ringleader, the Soviet Union itself, have started to suffer from the chronic afflictions of the bourgeois society. The dissatisfaction created by the revisionist line in the masses turns into open revolt. Last year's events in Poland show that the working class has risen openly against the revisionist power. . . .

At the present stage, and despite their apparent power, imperialism and revisionism are weak. They are decaying and declining more and more every day. In actual fact they are not in a position to solve any major internal problem or to achieve any of their external aims. . . . However, our revolutionary optimism does not prevent us from simultaneously seeing the dangers and threats to our country, and to all the peoples, which arise from American imperialism and its aggressive policy, as well as from the new Soviet social imperialism, which, together, claim world hegemony and domination.

. . . American imperialism cannot live without trying to subjugate other countries economically. It cannot live without political interventions and military aggressions; without oppressing and exploiting other peoples. . . . The American imperialists continue their savage war in Vietnam. They have also extended their aggression to Cambodia and Laos, thus inflicting serious afflictions, devastation, and massacres on all the heroic people of Indochina. Instigated by, and with the active and direct support of the United States of America, Israel has launched its aggression against the Arab countries and continues to occupy their territories. The plots, subversive actions, interference, and armed violence which took place, and continue to take place, against Libya, the Congo People's Republic, Somalia, Guinea and many other countries of Asia and Latin America are the work of American imperialists. The United States is the ally and backer of all reactionary and fascist regimes; it is the chief defender of the international capitalist system of exploitation.

Overt aggression is increasingly emerging as a primary means of securing the positions of U.S. economic, political, and military domination in other countries. The U.S. imperialists are also trying to achieve the realization of this strategy by means of the policy of neocolonialism and through their attempts to preserve technological and scientific monopoly as a means of intervention, oppression, and exploitation.

*   *   *

A great, insatiable, and barbaric enemy faces the people. The struggle against imperialism has therefore become a supreme task for all revolutionary forces of our age, for all peoples. . . . But American imperialism is not the only enemy of the people, and one cannot consider the reactionary puppets which are tied directly to Washington politically, militarily, and financially as its only allies. Great Britain, West Germany, Japan, and the other imperialist countries, despite differences with the United States of America, remain its main partners. They pursue a policy of economic expansion and neocolonialism regarding other countries as well. They seek to create spheres of influence, and support world reaction at every opportunity. United Europe, created by the capital of Western Europe, aims at becoming an imperialist power having the same claims of hegemony and domination as the United States and the U.S.S.R. The struggle against American imperialism would be ineffective if it were not also directed against its friends and allies; against all imperialist powers.

*   *   *

The latest form of Soviet revisionist imperialism is, for other peoples and the revolution, an enemy which is just as dangerous, crafty, and aggressive as American imperialism. Our party, from the time when modern revisionism usurped power in the Soviet Union and other socialist countries, has correctly summed up the situation and has pointed out that a second front is beginning to oppose socialism and communism in the world.

Today we all are witnessing the transformation of the revisionist Soviet Union into a chauvinistic and neocolonialist state. The Soviet revisionists' foreign policy is none other than the great Russian policy of the old tsars; it is composed of the same expansionist ambitions, with the same objectives of achieving the submission and enslavement of peoples. . . .

. . . As contradictions within the U.S.S.R. grow worse, as quarrels and clashes within the revisionist camp increase, and finally, as competition between it and its rival and ally, American imperialism, intensifies, military adventure becomes more and more the main form of action for the Soviet revisionists.

The barbaric aggression against Czechoslovakia was not a chance action, nor was it part of an exceptional situation without any future. Rather it was the paroxysm of an aggressive and chauvinistic policy drawn up as an official line—the beginning of a great offensive directed against the freedom and independence of many countries and peoples. It is a fact that at the same time that Czechoslovakia was being openly invaded, the silent occupation of Poland, Democratic Germany, Hungary, Bulgaria, and Mongolia was increasing. These countries have been turned into military provinces of Moscow's empire, where Soviet generals not only keep "order," but also make policies and even law.

The ironic feature of the chauvinistic policy, in all the efforts which the Soviet revisionists use to dominate people, is that they are seeking to "theoretically legitimize" this policy, and that they call it "proletarian," and even "Leninist." Brezhnev brought out the infamous theory of "limited sovereignty" and his zealous propagandists are trying to convince the world that the Soviet Union sent not its tanks to Prague, but "international aid," that it is not oppressing satellite countries but is "strengthening the socialist community," that it is not exploiting them, but is accelerating their "socialist integration."

The theory of "limited sovereignty" is the theory of chauvinism and great power expansion; the theory by whose help the new Soviet imperialists are trying to stifle all sovereignty of other peoples and arrogate the "sovereign right" to intervene where and when they think they should. . . . By "limited sovereignty" they try to legitimize the right of the strongest to stifle the weakest, of the largest to swallow up the smallest. This is a theory trying to justify imperialist aggression.

The Soviet revisionists' "proletarian internationalism" also has the same reactionary content—that every struggle and revolutionary action should be subordinate to the U.S.S.R.'s interests and its policy. . . . The transition of Soviet revisionism to social imperialism, the intensification of its expansionist policy and activity gave new tasks to the revolutionary and anti-imperialist forces.

The Soviet-American alliance is the biggest counterrevolutionary force opposed to the peoples' struggle for freedom and socialism. The imperialist courses of the United States of America and the Soviet Union are constantly coming closer, and tend to become one in every sphere—economic, political, and military. To achieve their aims of hegemony and domination, the two superpowers need one another; they set their watches by the same clock and constantly coordinate their plans and concrete activity.

Their strategic objective is directed at destroying socialism, stifling revolution, and establishing their domination throughout the world. The spearhead of this alliance is directed against the People's Republic of China, which represents the main obstacle to the realization of their counterrevolutionary plans. The United States and the Soviet Union do their utmost—although it is a fanciful dream—to encircle China and isolate it, so as someday to be able to strangle the revolution and destroy the People's Republic of China. . . . Although World War II ended twenty years ago the United States and the Soviet Union still keep their troops in different countries. The two superpowers have recognized and accepted as a fact their respective zones of influence.

*   *   *

. . . [Their] coordination of politics and their common attitude appear even more clearly in the activity of the United Nations which became a tool of their policy of hegemony. Practically no decision is taken at the United Nations, and no suggestion is accepted, unless it is to the liking of the two big powers. . . .

. . . The American imperialists and Soviet revisionists . . . are anxious to keep their monopoly over new weapons and their technical-scientific superiority in key branches of development, in order to keep other countries under their domination and exert on them constant political, economic, and military pressure. Nobody doubts that the very secret meetings during the SALT negotiations—from which even their closest allies are barred—have brought [the two big powers] into a body where they are not just satisfied with coordinating military problems, but where they also work to determine concrete political positions, as well as their long-term common strategy.

. . . Given their imperialist nature, the United States and the revisionist Soviet Union are also rent by conflicts, rivalries, and deep contradictions which prevent them from always acting in harmony and complete unison. The existence and deepening of the contradictions are inherent in the very foundations of this alliance, in the capitalist social system of these two countries, and in their imperialist aims. Preparing for war, the two sides are also planning to devour each other. . . .

Since American imperialism and revisionist imperialism represent the two imperialist superpowers, and since they advertise a common counterrevolutionary strategy, it is impossible for the people's struggle against them not to be channeled into a single current. It is not possible to use one imperialism in order to oppose the other.

*   *   *

True peace and the people's security can be insured only by the struggle against U.S. imperialism and Soviet social-imperialism! Our party and government have paid particular attention to certain important and acute problems of international life, which directly affect the destinies and future of the peoples to a large extent.

. . . Owing to the united struggle of the peoples of Indochina, and to their unity and determination, the strategic and tactical plans of the Nixon administration have failed completely. Indochina has now become the main battlefield of the people's liberation struggle against U.S. imperialism, and it is for this very reason that the victories of the peoples of Vietnam, Laos and Cambodia have been a great source of revolutionary inspiration for all those who oppose imperialism—who fight for freedom, national independence, democracy, and social justice. . . .

The historic lesson of Vietnam shows that the aggression of a great imperialist power can be fought victoriously by a people's war; that in present conditions even a small country can beat a superpower, when it is firmly determined to undergo any sacrifice and to proceed courageously along the path of liberty and revolution.

Nixon's new doctrine on the alleged "Vietnamization of the war" and his maneuvers to start "peace negotiations" cannot meet with success. "Vietnamization" means extension and continuation of the imperialist aggression. It means pitting Vietnamese against Vietnamese—Asians against Asians—in order that the American imperialists can dominate, oppress, exploit, and use them as cannon fodder in the interest of their own policy of aggression and hegemony. But Nixon's plan aimed at "Vietnamizing" the war has failed in the face of the heroic resistance of the peoples of Indochina, and cannot but lead its authors toward further, even greater defeats. Neither can the U.S. imperialists be rescued from the Vietnam catastrophe by their friends the Soviet revisionists, who for many years have been sabotaging the efforts of the Vietnamese people and exerting pressure on them to cease their anti-U.S. struggle.

There can be no true peace in Vietnam nor in the rest of Indochina until the U.S. forces have withdrawn totally and finally from that area, and until the U.S. military bases and installations there have been entirely destroyed. . . .

* * *

The Middle East has become another hotbed of tension. Israeli imperialist aggression, which aims at subduing and enslaving all the Arab peoples, has been going on for a long time. Likewise, the situation in this region has been aggravated by the intervention of the Soviet revisionists who, while saying that they are friends of the Arab peoples, seek to take over strategic positions and extend their hegemony there. . . . The two superpowers, which are trying to take over the destiny of the Middle East and play the role of umpire, propose dividing it into zones of influence and building on the life and death of the Arab peoples new bases from where they will sally forth to new conquests on the continents of Asia and Africa.

* * *

The Albanian People's Republic is interested in the establishment of true peace and security in Europe, in a realistic and just settlement of problems pending since the end of World War II, and above all a solution to the German problem.

But the situation in Europe is not as the Soviet revisionists try to show it—as if there were now détente and peace because the Moscow-Bonn treaty has been signed, or because the U.S.S.R. and the Federal Republic of Germany have allegedly guaranteed the inviolability of the frontiers of European states.

On the contrary, the conclusion of the Soviet-German treaty has created fresh tension in Europe—provoked by the serious threats of the Soviet revisionists and the German revanchists made against the interests, sovereignty, and rights of European countries, and by their wish to insure hegemony and domination over our continent. The F.R.G. has now become the most powerful capitalist state in Western Europe. It defies American influence and is trying to diminish the powers of France and Britain, not to mention the other NATO partners. Instead of contributing to some kind of solution, the Soviet-

German treaty is causing contradictions, rivalries, and new complications of an imperialist nature which could have dangerous consequences for all European countries.

*   *   *

In Europe there is the NATO bloc, which is an aggressive alliance dominated by the American imperialists, and in which the West German revanchists play a leading role. NATO has always had as its aim to fight communism, stifle revolution in Europe, and guarantee U.S. imperialist interests. In Europe there is also the Warsaw Pact, which has been turned into an instrument for maintaining Soviet revisionists' domination in the member countries and a force of aggression and intimidation against the independence of other countries. How can one talk about European security when these two blocs keep under their thumb the peoples of both sides of Europe; when they are the main pillars of the domination exerted by the two superpowers and the supports of their diktats? It is obvious that, while these two blocs exist in Europe—while American and Soviet bases and troops are kept in European countries—there will never be true European security.

Our country left the Warsaw Pact and has publicly denounced its policy and aggressive activity. . . .

*   *   *

As a Mediterranean country, the Albanian People's Republic is interested in the Mediterranean basin remaining an area of peace and fruitful cooperation, and it is striving in this direction. It resolutely condemns the aggressive policy of the imperialist powers—in the first place the United States and the Soviet Union—which seriously threaten the freedom and independence of Mediterranean countries with their war fleets. . . .

For a long time throughout the whole world, much noisy attention has been given to the problem of disarmament. This problem was purposely raised by the American imperialists and the Soviet social-imperialists to lull the vigilance of the peoples and intensify plans for their schemes of aggression. The facts prove that while they endlessly talk about disarmament, organize hundreds and thousands of meetings, and set up innumerable committees and commissions, the two superpowers continue their unbridled armaments race. . . . The permanent stockpiling of weapons is a condition for the existence of imperialism, inherent in the very nature of its economic system and its policy of aggression. . . .

The arms race which the two superpowers are trying to carry out in a balanced way is pregnant with considerably dangerous consequences. They are preparing for aggressive wars which they may unleash separately against other countries, or even against each other. . . . As long as the imperialist and social-imperialists are arming themselves and preparing for wars of aggression, the socialist states cannot remain idle. . . .

The peoples cannot fail to see that the aggressive military groupings of NATO and the Warsaw Pact, where the U.S. imperialists and Soviet social-imperialists rule respectively, constitute today the primary threat against peace and international security. . . .

The responsibility for the aggressive actions of the two superpowers falls not only on their governments but on their peoples, and on the governments and peoples of the countries taking part in the military alliances in question. As for the aggression against Czechoslovakia, for instance, responsibility for it falls not only on the Soviet social-imperialists who organized it, but also on the members of the Warsaw Pact which took part in it. Responsibility also falls on the peoples of the Soviet Union, Poland, the G.D.R., Bulgaria, and Hungary who remained passive and tolerated this barbaric act. The same goes for the help, direct or indirect, which the partners of the United States give the U.S. aggressors in Vietnam. The members of NATO and the Warsaw Pact justify their presence in these organizations—their alliance and friendship with the United States or the Soviet Union—by invoking the need to defend themselves. By doing so they strengthen the superpowers, and help them to keep their zones of influence, and maintain their policy of hegemony, diktats, and aggression.

* * *

The Soviet Union, Hungary, Bulgaria, and Czechoslovakia often hold military maneuvers on the borders of Yugoslavia and Romania. Obviously, what we have here are pressure, blackmail, and threats which may at any moment result in open aggression against sovereign countries. Do the peoples of the countries participating in these exercises not realize and feel that dangerous plans and plots are being hatched? History will condemn them severely if they remain passive and leave the aggressors a free hand. The foreign policy of the People's Republic of Albania is a consistent and principled policy in all its aspects.

Comrades, the Albanian People's Republic today occupies an honorable place in the international arena; it has gained the respect and admiration of the peace-loving peoples and all progressive forces.

Socialist Albania has not found itself isolated as was alleged and hoped for by its enemies, but rather it has further strengthened its international relations, authority, and position in the world.

*   *   *

Aware of the high responsibility which it assumes toward its own people and toward socialism, our party will never stop halfway; it will fight firmly on with all its might against imperialism and social-imperialism until they are totally destroyed and world revolution triumphs. Our people and our party consider this double struggle as one indivisible whole, because one cannot successfully thwart imperialism without at the same time fighting Soviet social-imperialism and vice versa.

*   *   *

We are proud to have an ally and friend in the 700-million-strong Chinese people—in the People's Republic of China and in the Chinese Communist Party [CCP], headed by their great leader Chairman Mao Tse-tung, the Albanian people's dearest friend. The great Albanian-Chinese revolutionary friendship, the unity and general brotherly cooperation between Albania and China, founded on the teachings of Marxism-Leninism, and proletarian internationalism, steeped in the common struggle against imperialism, revisionism, and all reactionaries, have allowed our two countries to face up to all tests and score great successes and victories.

Our party and our people infinitely rejoice at all the brilliant victories won by our Chinese brothers. . . . The decisive historical victory of the revolutionary and proletarian line of Chairman Mao Tse-tung over the reactionary bourgeois line of the renegade Liu Shao-chi, which was approved and ratified at the Ninth CCP Congress, has further strengthened the party's revolutionary unity, consolidated the positions of the dictatorship of the proletariat, raised to a higher level the revolutionary and fighting spirit in the country, and opened to the Chinese people brilliant prospects for their socialist future.

Our party and our government fully support the unquestionable right of the People's Republic of China to liberate Taiwan which is part of its territory.

*   *   *

The UN General Assembly's recent approval of the Albanian resolution—a resolution which invites the P.R.C. to occupy its rightful place in the United Nations and expels the Chiang Kai-shek clique, represents a great victory for the P.R.C. and its correct policy. It is confirmation on an international scale of the P.R.C.'s prestige and international role in the interest of the cause of peace and the security of peoples. It is also a great victory for the Albanian People's Republic which has for many years perseveringly and consistently defended the just cause of People's China. . . .

*   *   *

Our party and our people are linked to the Vietnamese people and the D.R.V. by powerful bonds of socialist friendship and solidarity. . . . Today, as in the past, the Albanian People's Republic favors the further development and strengthening of friendly relations with the Democratic People's Republic of Korea [D.P.R.K.] on the basis of the principles of Marxism-Leninism and proletarian internationalism, in the interest of building socialism in our two countries. The Albanian people firmly support the just struggle of the Korean people against imperialism and its lackeys, for the defense of the D.P.R.K., and for the reunification of the homeland. We condemn the aggressive policy of the Japanese imperialists against the D.P.R.K. as well as the schemes of Soviet revisionists who encourage this expansionist policy.

Our party and our government have supported and will always unreservedly support the struggle of the peoples of Asia, Africa, and Latin America for their national and social liberation against imperialism, racial discrimination, oppression, and colonial exploitation. [We also support] the just and heroic struggle of the Cuban people against the threats, blockade, and provocations of the Yankee imperialists for the defense of their national independence and sovereignty. [In particular,] friendly relations exist between Albania and the Arab Republic of Egypt, Algeria, Syria, Libya and other Arab countries. . . .

Our country has always shown proof of good will and has begun to take constructive steps to initiate and develop normal relations with all countries having different social systems, on the basis of the principles of peaceful coexistence, equality, respect for state sovereignty, and territorial integrity, mutual nonintervention in internal affairs, and reciprocal advantage.

While fighting against imperialism and revisionism, we scrupulously stick to the principle according to which the domestic affairs of every country are within its exclusive competence without anyone imposing a solution on it or anyone interfering from outside. . . . The ties and diplomatic relations which Albania has established with several countries this year are a noteworthy success of our foreign policy and witness to the strengthening of the international standing of the Albanian People's Republic. They harmonize with common interests and serve the strengthening of understanding and cooperation among peoples.

Our party and government have devoted particular care to our country's relations with neighboring states. Friendly relations between Albania and Romania are developing normally and to the mutual benefit of both countries, and they meet with the interests of our peoples and of socialism. The Albanian people will always support the just struggle which the Romanian people are waging to defend the independence and sovereignty of their homeland in the face of any external threat.

It is in a spirit of good neighborliness that our relations with Yugoslavia are also developing. . . . Despite known ideological differences, we are in favor of the continued improvement of state relations in every field where there exist common interests. . . .

Good relations exist between our country and Italy and Turkey. . . . This year diplomatic relations were also established between Albania and Greece. This is an important development which has ended an abnormal situation and serves to reinforce peace and security in the Balkans.

*   *   *

Friendship and understanding among the Balkan countries must be rooted in the people. We have no intention of putting forward or accepting proposals aimed at forming Balkan blocs and alliances. The Albanian People's Republic wishes to forge bonds of friendship with the peoples of the Balkans on the basis of the principles of peaceful coexistence, and it will strive in that direction. The regime adopted by each country is a matter that only concerns that country. We shall not interfere in the domestic affairs of anyone, nor must others interfere in our affairs. This does not preclude mutual criticisms and polemics. . . .

For us times have changed. If the new tsars of the Kremlin or the various imperialist or chauvinistic cliques of the Balkans try to violate the frontiers of the Albanian People's Republic, the Albanians united as one, will not be caught unprepared as in 1878 or 1914, or in the times of Mussolini and Hitler. Short reckonings make long friends.

The Albanian people, who suffered for centuries under cruel occupiers, and who won their freedom at the cost of heavy bloodshed, say to the fraternal peoples of the Balkans to beware of the intrigues by imperialists of all kinds so that altogether we can say to them:

Hands off our countries, we shall not allow anyone to abuse our friendship.

The Balkan peoples are fully in a position to decide by themselves and with sovereignty on everything concerning their mutual relations. The Balkans have never been a "powderkeg" on their own account. They were so in the past through the fault of foreigners— imperialists who held all the detonators. The imperialists want this to be so again today. It is the duty of the Balkan peoples to cut all detonator pins with a sword so that peace and security be restored in the Balkans.

* * *

If ever a Balkan state, pushed by the imperialist powers, undertakes aggression against another Balkan state, it is obvious that intervention by other Balkan states will be inevitable. Such a war will not remain localized, but will provoke a general conflagration.

* * *

Our country's relations with the East European states which are members of the Warsaw Pact have fallen. This is not our fault. Their leaderships, entirely subservient to Moscow's will, and blindly following Moscow's foreign policy, have conducted a hostile policy toward our country, which has been greatly damaging to Albania, as is well known. Despite the failure of their efforts at intimidating and forcing us to give in, they persist stubbornly in their anti-Albanian attitude. So much the worse for them.

Regarding the people of those countries, who bear no guilt for the situation which has been created in this way, we must say that we have been, and shall continue to be, their friends; we wished them well and will always do so. Our party and people, who condemned the aggression of August 1968, support with the same firmness the resistance of the Czechoslovak people against the Soviet revisionist occupiers and the traitors to their country's liberty and national independence. We also support the struggle of the Polish people and of the peoples in the other countries where revisionist cliques are in power—the struggle against the revisionist domination and the chauvinistic and dictatorial great power policy of the Soviet social-imperialists.

A number of times our party has approached the people and Communists of the Soviet Union, outlining to them in minute detail and with supporting documents the true motives of the break in Soviet-Albanian relations. . . . Of late the Soviet leaders have been making a show of wanting to "normalize" relations with our country.

This is nothing but demagogy and an effort to exonerate themselves. But we shall not allow ourselves to be caught in their traps. We shall not allow ourselves to be intimidated by their saber-rattling any more than by the olive branch they wave. . . .

Our people understand, defend, and implement consistently and to the end, our party's and our government's foreign policy, because it is a clear, correct, and principled policy. . . .

NORTH KOREA

Document 19: Excerpts from the Report of the CC KWP to the Fifth Party Congress, Delivered 2 November 1970 by Kim Il-sung, General Secretary of the CC KWP*

Comrades, to strengthen the defense power of the country has been a question of particular importance for us who are building socialism in frontal confrontation with the aggressors of U.S. imperialism—the chieftain of world reaction—under conditions of territorial partition. That is why our party has always been deeply concerned with the work of national defense and has rightly combined economic construction with defense upbuilding.

*   *   *

The most important achievement we have attained in strengthening our defense capabilities during the period under review is that the entire people have been armed and the whole country has been fortified. In our country, everyone knows how to fire a gun, and everyone carries a gun. [Applause.]

*   *   *

The national defense capabilities we have now were achieved at a very great cost. Frankly speaking, our national defense expenditures, as compared with the small size of the country and its population, have proven to be too great a burden. If even a single small portion of it had been allocated to economic construction, our people's economy would have developed even faster and our people's living standards would have increased to a much higher level. However, the situation did not permit us to do so. We could not afford to give up the basic interests of the revolution for the sake of brief comfort, and we did not want to become country-ruining traitors.

*   *   *

At the time of the incident of the U.S. imperialists' armed spy ship Pueblo in 1968 and the incident of the large-type spy plane EC-121, the situation in our country turned very tense. The U.S. imperialist bandits then brought large forces right to the door of our

*Source: *Foreign Broadcast Information Service, Asia and Pacific, Supplement*, no. 222, supp. 21 (16 November 1970), pp. 14-15; 34-37; 39; 44-56.

country in an open attempt at an armed invasion of the northern half of the republic. The situation was grave indeed, and the whole world kept a close watch on its development, expressing deep concern.

Thanks to the powerful nationwide defense system, with the people's army as its nucleus, our people—with no fear at all—could take a resolute position of retaliation to the "retaliation" of the enemy, thus eventually bringing the aggressors to their knees. [Applause.]

*   *   *

Comrades, the situation in our country still remains tense and strained. The U.S. imperialists continue to step up their aggressive maneuvers, and their schemes to touch off a new war are becoming more and more undisguised.

Under the wing of U.S. imperialists, the Japanese militarists are also stepping up their expansionist maneuvers against Korea. The puppet clique of South Korea, the dual stooge of U.S. and Japanese reactionaries, is running about recklessly in an endeavor to execute the war policies of its masters. In our country the threat of war is growing bigger with every passing day.

To cope with the situation thus created, we must further strengthen our national defense capabilities while simultaneously accelerating socialist construction to the maximum. . . . The most important thing in increasing the defense capabilities of the country is to arm the entire people more perfectly. All the people should learn military affairs in earnest and take a more active part in military training. The workers, peasants, and all other working people should always keep themselves fully ready to annihilate the aggressors at any place if the enemies attack us, while accelerating socialist construction with a hammer and sickle in one hand, and a rifle in the other. When all the people are armed and hate the enemy, and when all the people rise and fight against the aggressors, we can defeat any enemy. [Applause.]

*   *   *

Ours is a small and newly developed country. Frankly speaking, we are not in a position to compete with developed countries in military technical equipment, nor are we required to do so. The destiny of war is by no means decided by modern weapons or military technique. Although the imperialists have a military-technical preponderance, our people's army has, on its part, politico-ideological superiority over them. . . . We must never be captivated by a pacifist mood and in particular, we must strictly guard against the revisionist ideological trend of war phobia, in order to prevent it from infiltrating into our ranks.

*　　*　　*

Comrades, our national defense power is actually defensive in nature and is designed to defend the security of our country and our people against imperialist aggression. We have no intention to threaten or launch aggression against anybody. . . .

*　　*　　*

. . . While the U.S. imperialists are occupying half of the country's territory and incessantly perpetrating provocations against the northern half of the republic, and while the cause of unification of the fatherland is not yet achieved, we can never live in luxury and extravagance but must always lead a frugal life befitting the people in the era of revolution. . . .

*　　*　　*

. . . The U.S. imperialists have converted South Korea more thoroughly into their military base of aggression—into their military appendage—and furthered their policies of aggression and war, as never before, by dint of the military fascist dictatorship. On the other hand, in South Korea national and class contradictions have become more acute, the revolutionary advance of the workers, peasants and other sections of broad popular masses has been stepped up, and consequently, there has been created a more serious crisis for the colonial rule of U.S. imperialism. . . .

The South Korean revolution is a national liberation revolution against the U.S. imperialist aggressors, and at the same time, a people's democratic revolution against the stooges of U.S. imperialism— the landlords, comprador capitalists, and reactionary bureaucrats—and their fascist rule. The basic task of this revolution is to drive the U.S. imperialist forces of aggression out of South Korea, to eliminate their colonial domination, to overthrow the military fascist dictatorship, and to establish a progressive social system—thereby attaining the democratic development of South Korean society.

The U.S. imperialists are the real rulers who have seized all the power in South Korea, and [they] are the first target of struggle in the South Korean revolution. . . . The tiny handful of landlords, comprador capitalists, and reactionary bureaucrats in South Korea faithfully execute the aggressive policy of the U.S. imperialists, and under their patronage, oppress and cruelly exploit the South Korean people.

The motive power of the South Korean revolution is the working class and its reliable ally, the peasantry; and the progressive student youths, intellectuals, patriotic-minded armymen, some patriotic-minded national capitalists, and people of small-propertied classes who are opposed to U.S. imperialism and its lackeys.

*   *   *

What is of paramount importance in preparing the revolutionary forces is to strengthen the Marxist-Leninist party, the general staff in the revolution, and to rally the workers and peasants closely around it to firmly build up the main force of the revolution. The South Korean revolutionaries should strive to expand and strengthen the party forces in all places where there are workers, peasants, and other revolutionary masses [in order to] root themselves deeply among the masses. . . . The revolutionary organizations of South Korea should do their utmost to form an anti-U.S. united front for national salvation, embracing all the patriotic political parties, public organizations, the masses of various strata, and individual personages under the banner of anti-imperialism, antifascism, and democratization. . . .

*   *   *

The people in the southern half are not alone in their struggle! They have the powerful revolutionary base in the northern half. Of course, the South Korean revolution is a revolution of the South Korean people who must liberate themselves from the racial and class oppressions, and exploitations of the U.S. imperialist aggressors and their lackeys.

The oppressed and exploited popular masses can win freedom and emancipation only through their own revolutionary struggle. Therefore, the South Korean revolution must be fulfilled primarily by the South Korean people themselves. However, the people in the northern half, as members of the same nation, have the duty and obligation to actively support the revolutionary struggle of the South Korean people.

At present, the general international situation is making a turn in favor of revolution, with all the progressive people of the world denouncing the U.S. policy of aggression and supporting the liberation struggle of the South Korean people. [Applause.]

*   *   *

Comrades, to reunite the divided fatherland is a great national duty of all the Korean people at the present stage. It is our most urgent task, and we cannot forget it even for a moment. The policy of our party for the unification of our fatherland is already known widely throughout the world.

We have made it clear time and again that if democratic personages with a national conscience come to power in South Korea, and demand the withdrawal of U.S. troops, release political prisoners, and guarantee democratic freedom, then we are ready to hold negotiations with them on the question of the peaceful unification of the fatherland at any time and at any place.

Even after the present South Korean rulers staged the fascist military coup and usurped power, we advanced most fair and reasonable proposals for the unification of the fatherland and made persevering efforts for their materialization, hoping that the southern rulers would desist from the treacheries against the country and the nation, and take a truly national stand. We proposed more than once to the South Korean authorities that after the U.S. imperialist army has been driven out from South Korea, the North and the South each reduce their armies to 100,000 men, conclude an agreement on refraining from use of armed force against each other, take a number of measures encouraging economic and cultural intercourse and allowing mutual visits of individual personages between the North and the South, and establish a unified democratic government through a free North-South general election to be held when these basic conditions are reached. . . . We proposed that if the general election throughout North and South Korea is not immediately acceptable to them for some reason or another, a system of confederation of North and South Korea be established as a transitional step for solving urgent matters of common concern for the nation and hastening the unification of the fatherland.

The South Korean rulers, however, have ignored our just proposals which reflect the unanimous aspirations of the whole nation, and they have doggedly opposed the independent peaceful unification of the fatherland. The South Korean puppets, under the aegis of the U.S. imperialists and the Japanese militarists, clamor that the unification of Korea must always be a "unification by prevailing over communism." . . . The "unification by prevailing over communism" vociferously advocated by the South Korean rulers means attaining "unification" after wiping out communism. This is nothing more than a wild daydream and the jargon of a stupid person. . . .

As for the "peaceful unification formulas" currently being publicized by the South Korean puppets, they are nothing more than political conspiratorial propaganda, containing no measures, whatsoever, to carry out the unification of the fatherland, and they are filled with falsehood and deception from beginning to end.

* * *

How can we discuss the question of the unification of the country with those traitors to the nation who hamper the independent peaceful unification of the country with bayonets, repress the struggle of the South Korean people for national unification, call for the continued occupation of South Korea by U.S. troops, usher into South Korea even the aggressor forces of Japanese militarism, sell out their fellow countrymen to foreign countries as slaves, and who send young and middle-aged South Koreans into the war of aggression in Vietnam as bullet shields for the U.S. imperialists? The peaceful unification of the country is utterly unthinkable so long as the U.S. imperialist aggressive army and the present puppets are left alone in South Korea.

* * *

During the period under review our party has made a timely and correct appraisal of the changing complex international situation and followed a just foreign policy, and it has shown progress in the domain of international relations. The independent and principled foreign policy of the party has won support of many fraternal parties and countries, numerous revolutionary organizations and people of the world, and further consolidated the international position of our country. We have come to have a large number of revolutionary comrades and friends internationally, and the international solidarity of our revolution is being cemented steadily. This is a result of the serious efforts made by our party for solidarity with the international revolutionary forces, and conclusive proof of the correctness of our party's foreign policy. [Applause.]

. . . The main feature of the present international situation is that whereas the anti-imperialist revolutionary struggle of the people is surging up with each passing day, the imperialists headed by U.S. imperialism are further stepping up their policies of aggression and war.

All the events that have taken place in the international arena in recent years reveal more glaringly the aggressive and predatory nature of imperialism—above all of U.S. imperialism. The aggressive ambition of U.S. imperialism knows no bounds. With the invariable aim of dominating the whole world, U.S. imperialism is stretching out its crooked hands of aggression to every continent . . . be it Asia or the Near and Middle East, Africa or Latin America, Europe or

Oceania. . . . While overtly pursuing the "policy of strength," the U.S. imperialists are putting up ostentatious signboards of "peace," "negotiation," "intercourse" and what not, and ballyhooing about what they call "peace strategy." But this is no more than their stereotyped deceptive artifice to hide their true colors as aggressors, and divert the world's attention elsewhere. . . .

U.S. imperialism is the most ferocious and shameless aggressor and plunderer of modern times, and the principal common enemy of all progressive peoples of the world. There is no more pressing task than fighting against the U.S. imperialist policies of aggression and war in the international arena today. . . .

Today the struggle of peoples against the U.S. imperialist policies of aggression and war has become a trend of the times that cannot be held in check. The flames of the anti-imperialist, national liberation struggle of the Asian, African and Latin American peoples are flaring up furiously. The working-class movement is growing in intensity in capitalist countries, and more peace loving people are coming out in the struggle against the aggressive war policies of imperialism headed by the U.S. The antiwar movement has assumed a mass character in the United States itself. U.S. imperialism is being battered in all parts of the world and driven into dead ends internally and externally. A powerful antiwar movement should be waged on a worldwide scale, first of all against U.S. imperialism's criminal aggression in Vietnam, and all the anti-imperialist forces should render more positive support to the peoples of Indochina and other peoples of fighting countries. [Applause.]

Comrades, Asia has become the fiercest battlefront against imperialism, the main arena of the anti-imperialist revolutionary struggle today. . . . The U.S. imperialists are making desperate efforts to check rapid growth of the revolutionary forces, and to prop up their colonial rule in Asia. . . .

The U.S. imperialists, openly revealing their thieving nature, not only continue their criminal war of aggression against the Vietnamese people, but also further intensify their armed intervention in Laos, and of late, have thrown their armed forces of aggression and the mercenaries of their satellite countries into action to launch a naked armed invasion of Cambodia. As a result, war has spread all over Indochina. The U.S. imperialists perpetrate provocative acts every day to ignite another aggressive war in Korea, and continue to occupy Taiwan—an inalienable territory of the People's Republic of China. . . .

In an endeavor to cover up their policy of Asian aggression, the present U.S. rulers are clamoring about a sort of change in their policy. But there has not been, nor can there be, any change in the aggressive policy pursued by the U.S. imperialists in Asia. The only change is that their aggressiveness and craftiness have further increased. While stepping up aggression, by mobilizing their armed forces directly, the U.S. imperialists are seeking a more sinister means to realize their aggressive designs on Asia—mainly by "making Asians fight Asians"—raking up Japanese militarism and other satellite countries and puppets in Asia in accordance with the notorious "new Asia policy." Owing to such aggressive maneuverings of the U.S. imperialists, the situation has become extremely tense everywhere in Asia, and world peace as a whole is exposed to grave danger.

* * *

. . . In order to thwart the U.S. imperialist aggression in Asia, it is of particular importance to cement the fighting solidarity of the peoples of the revolutionary Asian countries. . . . The people of Korea, China, Vietnam, Laos, and Cambodia, suffering directly from U.S. imperialist aggression—and all other revolutionary countries in Asia—should further consolidate the anti-U.S. united front and wage a forceful anti-U.S. joint struggle to deal a more powerful collective counterblow at the U.S. imperialist aggression on Asia. [Applause.] The U.S. imperialist aggressors should thus be driven out from South Korea and Taiwan, from South Vietnam and Laos, from Cambodia and all other parts of Asia where they have set foot; their stratagem of making Asians fight Asians should be foiled. [Applause.]

* * *

Under the active patronage of U.S. imperialism, Japanese militarism has now raised its head again in Asia. It represents an ever-growing menace to world peace and to the independence and security of Asian countries. This cannot but arouse deep anxiety and apprehension among all those who treasure peace in Asia and the world. . . . In the past, the Japanese militarists, in collusion with and under the patronage of the U.S. and British imperialists, occupied Korea, stretched out their talons of aggression to the Asian continent, and brought immeasurable sufferings and calamities to the Asian peoples. In conspiracy and collaboration with fascist Germany and Italy, they also ignited the Pacific war and ran wild to become the "leader" in Asia. Japanese militarism became fat on aggression and war, and ended in ruin. The history of crimes committed by the Japanese militarists against the Asian peoples and all humanity is still fresh in the memory of our peoples. This crime-woven history of the Japanese militarists is repeating itself today. The aggressive nature of Japanese militarism remains unchanged and will never change.

With the backing of U.S. imperialism, revived Japanese militarism is now overtly stretching out its tentacles of aggression again to Korea and other Asian countries, and recklessly running about to realize its old dream of the so-called Greater East Asia Coprosperity Sphere. . . . The conspiracy and collaboration between the U.S. imperialists and the Japanese militarists is presenting a greater threat because U.S. imperialism is directing the spearhead of aggression to Asia, using Japan as a base. . . .

Japan has again become the hotbed of fresh aggression and war in Asia, against which the Asian peoples have to heighten their vigilance. Our country is the first target of attack of Japanese militarism in its foreign aggression. . . .

With a foul ambition for overseas expansion, the Japanese reactionaries are now bustling about as they please in all parts of the world, with impunity, and under the cloak of "peace" and "helper," intensifying their economic and cultural infiltration into countries in Southeast Asia, the Near and Middle East, Africa, and Latin America. . . .

* * *

One must not harbor any illusions regarding the Japanese reactionary ruling circles or pin any hope on them. It is an immutable law of imperialism that when monopoly capital inflates at home, it takes the course of foreign aggression. Japanese monopoly capital has already swelled to the fullest extent and reestablished its supremacy. The Japanese militarist policy of rearmament and overseas expansion is carried out precisely on the basis of the revival of Japanese monopoly capital and the establishment of its ruling system.

* * *

Asia today is not the backward Asia of yesterday. The days are gone when the imperialists could lord it over Asia. Hundreds upon millions of Asian people, who were long oppressed and plundered by imperialism, have risen vigorously and appeared on the scene of history. The political, economic, and military might of the Democratic People's Republic of Korea and the People's Republic of China has been strengthened incomparably. The furious flames of the liberation struggle of the heroic Vietnamese people and other peoples of Indochina are raging with an irresistible force, and the revolutionary awakening of the Japanese people is being heightened still further.

No imperialist force can conquer the Asian people and break their united strength. [Applause.] The Asian people have now grown into a great revolutionary force, that carries imperialism and colonialism to their graves. [Applause.]

* * *

The peoples of revolutionary countries in Asia, the Palestinian people and other fighting Arab peoples, the African and Latin American peoples fighting for freedom and liberation, and all the revolutionary peoples of the world should firmly band together to deal blows at U.S. imperialism and dismember it. The peoples in revolutionary and fighting countries should tear the arms and legs off U.S. imperialism and behead it in all parts of the world. . . .

. . . Cemented solidarity with the international revolutionary forces is, at present, one of the important factors forcing the U.S. imperialist aggressors out of South Korea, accomplishing the national liberation revolution, dispelling the tension in Korea, and achieving the peaceful unification of our country. Therefore our party and people must make every effort to develop the international revolutionary movements and to achieve close ties with them, while strengthening and developing their own *chuche*-oriented revolutionary might in every possible way.

The Workers' Party of Korea and the Korean people, holding aloft the banner of Marxism-Leninism and proletarian internationalism and the revolutionary banner of the anti-imperialist, anti-U.S. struggle, will in the future, as in the past, continue to fight staunchly against U.S. imperialism and Japanese militarism, for the triumph of the cause of peace, democracy, national independence, socialism, and communism, in unity with the peoples of socialist countries, in unity with the Communist and workers' parties, in unity with the international working class, in unity with the fighting peoples in Asia, Africa, and Latin America, and in unity with all the peace-loving peoples of the world.

* * *

Today the unitary ideological system has been solidly established within our party. The whole party has attained monolithic unity and cohesion based on Marxist-Leninist ideas—the *chuche* idea of our party. [Applause.] This is the most important result achieved in party work during the period under review, and the basic factor that has increased the fighting capacity of our party still further.

In the past, the internal and external conditions of our party's activities were very difficult and complicated. The imperialists stepped up their aggression and war provocation maneuvers in all parts of the world as never before, and revisionism appeared in the international Communist movement and obstructed its unity and cohesion, causing ideological confusion.

*　*　*

As the aggressive machinations of the imperialists were intensified and as revisionist ideological trends penetrated from without, revisionist elements lurking within the party did not sincerely implement the party's policies. They resorted to double-dealing, and schemed overtly and covertly to resurrect bourgeois and feudalistic Confucian ideas.

*　*　*

While waging a resolute struggle against bourgeois and revisionist elements and their noxious ideological aftereffects, our party tirelessly strove to equip party members and the working people with the revolutionary ideas of the party and to build up in the tone of defending and implementing the party's lines and policies to the end.

*　*　*

Today, the unity and cohesion of our party have been lifted to a new, higher plane, and have become most vitalized and most solid. We can say it was not until today that the unity and cohesion of the party, which we Communists wanted to see so much, have been fully realized on the basis of the unitary ideological system of *chuche*. This is a splendid fruit of our protracted striving, and a great victory of historic significance in our party building. [Applause.]

*　*　*

Establishing *chuche* means, in a nutshell, having the attitude of master toward revolution and construction in one's own country. This means holding fast to an independent position, refraining from dependence on others, and using your own brains; believing in your own strength and displaying the revolutionary spirit of self-reliance. Thus, under all circumstances, you solve your own problems for yourself on your own responsibility. It means adhering to the creative position of opposing dogmatism and applying the universal principles of Marxism-Leninism and the experiences of other countries to suit the historical conditions and national peculiarities of your own country.

The *chuche* idea is in full accord with the fundamental principles of Marxism-Leninism; it came into being as a reflection of the new stage of development of the international Communist movement and its essential requirements.

The question of establishing *chuche* was a particularly important question for us because of the peculiarities of the historical development of our country, its geographical environment and conditions, and the complex and arduous nature of our revolution.

In our country, capitalism has long historical roots. The servile spirit—formed long ago—of refusing to depend on one's own ability and blindly worshiping and admiring others, still lurks in the minds of some of our people today. Even after liberation, flunkeyism constituted an enormous obstacle to revolution and the development of the party.

To make matters worse, dogmatism existed along with flunkeyism, causing double harm. Even at the time when our people became masters of their country and came into possession of their own sovereignty and party, flunkeyism and dogmatism still made people refuse to rely on their own abilities. It made them look to others for help. They mechanically imitated others, and failed to study their own conditions. . . .

Unless flunkeyism and dogmatism can be rooted out of the minds of our people and *chuche* thoroughly established, it will be impossible to conduct the revolutionary struggle and constructive work successfully in strict adherence to the revolutionary principles of Marxism-Leninism. . . .

. . . The struggle to establish *chuche* brought about a fundamental change in the ideological life of the party membership and the working people and in their way of thinking, and it resulted in a great leap forward in the revolutionary struggle and constructive work. [Applause.]

The practice of blindly despising our own things, and swallowing foreign things whole, has disappeared from among cadres and party members, whose national pride and consciousness of independence have increased further. The revolutionary trait of relying on their own efforts has been thoroughly instilled in them. [Applause.]

Now we can say that flunkeyism, national nihilism, and dogmatism as ideological trends have been eliminated in the main from among our party members and people. The establishment of *chuche* in ideology is a great victory in the realm of the ideological revolution that has freed our people from the shackles of obsolete ideas detrimental to their consciousness of national independence. [Applause.]

. . . Our party's consistent principles of independence in politics, self-sustenance in economy, and self-defense in national defense are the embodiment of the *chuche* idea in all realms. Under the revolutionary banner of the *chuche* idea, our country has become a socialist state with complete political sovereignty; a solid independent national economy, a strong self-defense power, and a brilliant national culture. [Applause.]

CUBA

Document 20: Excerpts from a Speech to the Fourth Conference of Nonaligned Nations (Algiers), Delivered 7 September 1973 by Fidel Castro Ruz, First Secretary of the Cuban Communist Party*

INVENTING A FALSE ENEMY CAN HAVE ONLY ONE AIM, TO EVADE THE REAL ENEMY

*   *   *

In expressing to you, Comrade Boumediene, to your compatriots, and to the distinguished representatives of the peoples meeting at this conference, the greetings of the Cuban delegation, we would like to emphasize the meaning we assign to the fact that this Fourth Conference of Nonaligned Nations is taking place in Algeria, whose people, with their heroic and sustained struggle, awakened the admiration and served as encouragement for countries that have fought for national independence against the oppressors.

I want to remind you that Cuba is a socialist country: a Marxist-Leninist country whose final objective is communism. [Applause.] We are proud of this! On the basis of that concept of human society, we determine our domestic and foreign policies. We are, above all, loyal to the principles of proletarian internationalism, and my words will be consistent with those ideas. All revolutionaries are duty-bound to defend their views in valiant fashion, and that is what I propose to do here. . . .

*   *   *

There has been talk at this conference of the different ways of dividing the world. To our way of thinking, the world is divided into capitalist and socialist countries, imperialist and neocolonialized countries, colonialist and colonized countries, reactionary and progressive countries—governments, in a word, that back imperialism, colonialism, neocolonialism, and racism, and governments that oppose imperialism, colonialism, neocolonialism, and racism.

This seems to us to be basic in the issue of alignment and nonalignment, because there is nothing exempting us in any way from

---

* Source: *Granma* (Havana), 16 September 1973, p. 12. Note: Although Cuba has not developed any clear commitment to the policies of any one ruling CP group recently it has begun to articulate the policy positions of Group I. This document is included in this chapter merely for convenience.

our central obligation to steadfastly fight the crimes committed against humanity.

The movement has grown without any question, and that is a source of satisfaction to us, as is the case of Latin America, when the presence at this conference of three new states—Peru, Chile, and Argentina—is due to progressive political changes in those countries. But the quality, not the number, is what should take primacy for the purposes of this movement if we really mean to wield moral and political force before the peoples of the world. Otherwise, we run the risk that the reactionary forces could succeed in penetrating its ranks to thwart its aims, and that the unity and prestige of the nonaligned countries could be irremediably lost. [Applause.]

Although the economic issues connected with the interests of the countries we represent take on justified and necessary importance, the political criteria we uphold will continue to be a basic factor in our activity.

In this political terrain there has been an observable tendency during the months of preparation leading up to this conference that unquestionably militates against our cause and serves only imperialist interests: to seek to pit the nonaligned countries against the socialist camp.

*   *   *

The theory of "two imperialisms," one headed by the United States and the other allegedly by the Soviet Union, encouraged by the theoreticians of capitalism, has been echoed at times deliberately and at others through ignorance of history and the realities of the present-day world, by leaders and spokesmen of nonaligned countries. This is fostered, of course, by those who regrettably betray the cause of internationalism from supposedly revolutionary positions.

In certain political and economic documents drafted for this conference, we have seen that current come to the fore in one way or another, with different shadings. The revolutionary government of Cuba will always oppose that current in all circumstances. That is why we find ourselves obliged to deal with this delicate matter as an essential issue.

There are some who with patent historic injustice and ingratitude, forgetting the real facts and disregarding the profound, unbridgeable abyss between the imperialist regime and socialism, try to ignore the glorious, heroic, and extraordinary services rendered to the human race by the Soviet people. [Applause.] As if the collapse of the colossal system of colonial rule implanted in the world up to World War II and the conditions that made possible the liberation of scores

of peoples heretofore under direct colonial subjugation, the disap-
pearance of capitalism in large parts of the world and the holding at
bay of the aggressiveness and insatiable veracity of imperialism—as
if all that had nothing to do with the glorious October Revolution!
[Applause.]

How can the Soviet Union be labeled imperialist? Where are its
monopoly corporations? Where is its participation in the multinational companies? What factories, what mines, what oilfields does
it own in the underdeveloped world? What worker is exploited in
any country of Asia, Africa, or Latin America by Soviet capital?

The economic cooperation that the Soviet Union provides to
Cuba and many other countries comes not from the sweat and the
sacrifice of the exploited workers of other peoples, but from the
sweat and efforts of the Soviet workers.

Others regret the fact that the first socialist state in history has
become a military and economic power. We underdeveloped and
plundered countries must not regret this. Cuba rejoices that this is
so. Without the October Revolution and without the immortal feat
of the Soviet people, who first withstood imperialist intervention and
blockade and later defeated the fascist aggression at the cost of
20 million dead, who have developed their technology and economy
at an unbelievable price in efforts and herosim without exploiting the
labor of a single worker of any country on the face of the earth—
without them, the end of colonialism and the balance of power in
the world that favors the heroic struggles of so many peoples for
their liberation would not have been possible. Not for a moment
can we forget that the guns with which Cuba crushed the Playa Girón
mercenaries and defended itself from the United States; the arms in
the hands of the Arab peoples, with which they withstand imperialist
aggression; those used by the African patriots against Portuguese
colonialism; and those taken up by the Vietnamese in their heroic,
extraordinary, and victorious struggle, came from the socialist countries, especially from the Soviet Union. [Applause.]

The very resolutions of the nonaligned countries aid us in understanding where the dividing line in international politics comes today.
What state have those resolutions condemned from Belgrade [1961]
to Lusaka [1970] for its aggression in Vietnam and all Indochina?
The imperialist United States. Whom do we accuse of arming,
supporting, and continuing to maintain the Israeli aggressor state
in its rapacious war against the Arab countries and in its cruel
occupation of the territories where the Palestinians have the right
to live? We accuse U.S. imperialism. Against whom did the nonaligned countries protest over the intervention in, and blockade of,

Cuba, the intervention in the Dominican Republic, and for maintaining bases at Guantanamo, in Panama, and in Puerto Rico, against the will of their peoples? Who was behind the murder of Lumumba? Who supports the killers of Amilcar Cabral? Who helps to maintain in Zimbabwe a white racist state and turn South Africa into a reserve of black men and women in conditions of semislavery? In all these cases the culprit is the same: U.S. imperialism, which also backs Portuguese colonialism against the peoples of Guinea-Bissau and Cape Verde, Angola, and Mozambique.

When our resolutions list the millions of dollars, pounds, francs, or marks that leave the developing neocolonialized or colonialized countries as a consequence of plundering investments and onerous loans, they condemn imperialism and not any other social system. It is not possible to change reality with equivocal expressions.

Any attempt to pit the nonaligned countries against the socialist camp is profoundly counterrevolutionary and benefits only imperialist interests. Inventing a false enemy can have only one aim—to evade the real enemy. [Applause.]

* * *

The success and the future of the nonaligned movement will depend on its refusal to allow itself to be penetrated, confused, or deceived by imperialist ideology. Only the closest alliance among all the progressive forces of the world will provide us with the strength needed to overcome the still-powerful forces of imperialism, colonialism, neocolonialism, and racism, and to wage a successful fight for the aspirations to peace and justice of all the peoples of the world. Because of the increasing needs for energy resources and raw materials required by the developed capitalist countries in order to maintain the absurd consumer societies they have created, new wars would plague the human race. Were it not for the extraordinary containing power of the socialist camp, imperialism would carve up the world all over again. Right now there are leading circles in the United States that are pushing for military intervention in the Middle East should fuel requirements warrant it.

Any estrangement from the socialist camp means weakening and exposing ourselves to the mercy of the still-powerful forces of imperialism. It would be a stupid strategy, a case of severe political short-sightedness.

* * *

Mr. Chairman, Latin America notes with concern the way that Brazil, under U.S. sponsorship, is building up a military might that goes way beyond the needs of its rulers to employ armed brutality, murder, torture, and imprisonment against its people. Brazil is visibly growing into a military enclave in the heart of Latin America, at the service of imperialism. The government of Brazil—which, along with that of the United States, took part in the invasion of the Dominican Republic and then with the same partner worked to overthrow the progressive government of Bolivia and recently helped to implant a reactionary dictatorship in Uruguay—is not only a tool of the United States but is gradually becoming an imperialist state. Today it has an observer status at this conference, as has Bolivia. We hope that such governments, under which some peoples of our hemisphere still suffer, are never admitted to the nonaligned movement. [Applause.]

There has been considerable talk here of the situation prevailing in Southeast Asia and in the Near East; of the peoples oppressed and bled by Portuguese colonialism; of the brutal racist repression in South Africa, Zimbabwe, and Namibia.

*   *   *

U.S. imperialism continues to back the neocolonial regime in South Vietnam, which refuses to comply with the Paris agreements, and the puppet government of Lon Nol in Cambodia; Israel mocks the United Nations resolutions and refuses to return the territories it occupied by force; Portugal, with the backing of the United States and NATO, scorns world opinion and the resolutions against it adopted by international bodies. The racist governments not only step up repression but also threaten other African states.

These are bitter, outrageous truths that put the strength, unity, and will to struggle of the nonaligned countries to the test. We who are meeting here are the leaders and representatives of more than seventy states. Let us enact concrete measures and agreements to isolate and defeat the aggressors. Let us support in a determined, steadfast manner, the Arab peoples under attack and the heroic people of Palestine; the fighters for the independence of Guinea-Bissau and Cape Verde, Angola, and Mozambique; [applause] the oppressed peoples of South Africa, Zimbabwe, and Namibia! Let us fight consistently against the imperialist countries that aid and abet these crimes! Let all of us nonaligned countries recognize the Provisional Revolutionary government of South Vietnam, [applause] and let us give our full support to it in the struggle for compliance with the Paris agreements! Let us back the patriots of Laos and Cambodia, and no force in the world will be able to prevent the solution of these problems that affect our peoples in the Near East, Africa, and Southeast Asia!

The true strength and profundity of the movement of nonaligned nations will be measured by the firmness of our actions regarding these problems. Cuba will back with the greatest determination the agreements adopted to that effect, even if to do so calls for contribution of our blood. [Applause.]

*   *   *

We cannot ignore the Democratic Republic of Vietnam. That people, a thousand times heroic, has undergone the most devastating war of aggression. Millions of tons of bombs were dropped on their economic facilities, cities, towns, schools, and hospitals. Their self-sacrificing and victorious struggle against imperialist aggression has served the interests of the entire human race. We must not settle for expressions of sympathy. Right now that admirable country is confronting the difficult work of reconstruction. We propose to the nonaligned countries that we take part in the rebuilding of North Vietnam, with each of us making a contribution to the extent of our possibilities. This would provide a new and revolutionary dimension to the nonaligned nations in the field of international solidarity.

The nonaligned countries must express their solidarity with Zambia and Tanzania against South African and Rhodesian aggression. We must also support the Democratic People's Republic of Korea in its efforts to attain the peaceful reunification of the Korean people. We must offer the Panamanian people full support in their just struggle for sovereignty in the Canal Zone. We must provide solidarity with the people of Chile in the face of imperialist plotting. [Applause.] We must join with Argentina in its just demand for the return of the usurped Malvina [Falkland] Islands. [Applause.] And we must defend the right of the people of Puerto Rico to their full sovereignty. [Applause.]

*   *   *

Our country must put up with the humiliating presence of a U.S. base on a part of our territory, maintained by force completely against the will of our people, who confront a rigorous and criminal economic blockade by the United States. Despite that, the Cuban people stand firm and are successfully building socialism right at the gateway to the United States. Our country has been able to resist because it has carried out a genuine revolution that radically wiped out all forms of exploitation of man by man, building upon that base a lofty fighting morale and a solid, indestructible unity.

When there is a real desire to free the country from imperialist exploitation, then the people must also be freed from the plunder of the fruits of their labor by the feudal lords, the landholders, the oligarchs, and the social parasites of all kinds. [Applause.]

We also ask for your solidarity with the Cuban people. If an understanding with the socialist countries is a vital factor for our victory, unity among the nations fighting for independence and development is its indispensable condition. We support all pronouncements in favor of greater unity of the nonaligned in regard to the principal problems of international life that are included in the different motions presented to the conference. But we are concerned— more than concerned, we become indignant—when we see that a leader of the stature of Sekou Toure must defend himself not only against the Portuguese colonialists but also against conspiracies promoted right inside his own underdeveloped Africa. [Applause.]

Our faith in certain unity declarations and postulates wanes when we see that the People's Republic of the Congo and the Republic of Somalia are not free from threats by other African forces and we note the difficulties of the Revolutionary Government of the Democratic and People's Republic of Yemen in overcoming hostilities that may well stem from Washington but which are carried out from other areas closer at hand.

All of this shows that our true unity depends not on circumstantial nonalignment, but on a deeper, more lasting identity—an identity stemming from revolutionary principles, a common anti-imperialist program, and an aspiration to substantial, conclusive social transformations.

This is Cuba's position. The point of view that I have just outlined will surely not be shared by all the leaders meeting here, but I have complied with my duty to express them with respect and with loyalty toward all of you.

Thank you very much.

Cover and book design: Pat Taylor